IMAGES
of America
CHOCTAW COUNTY

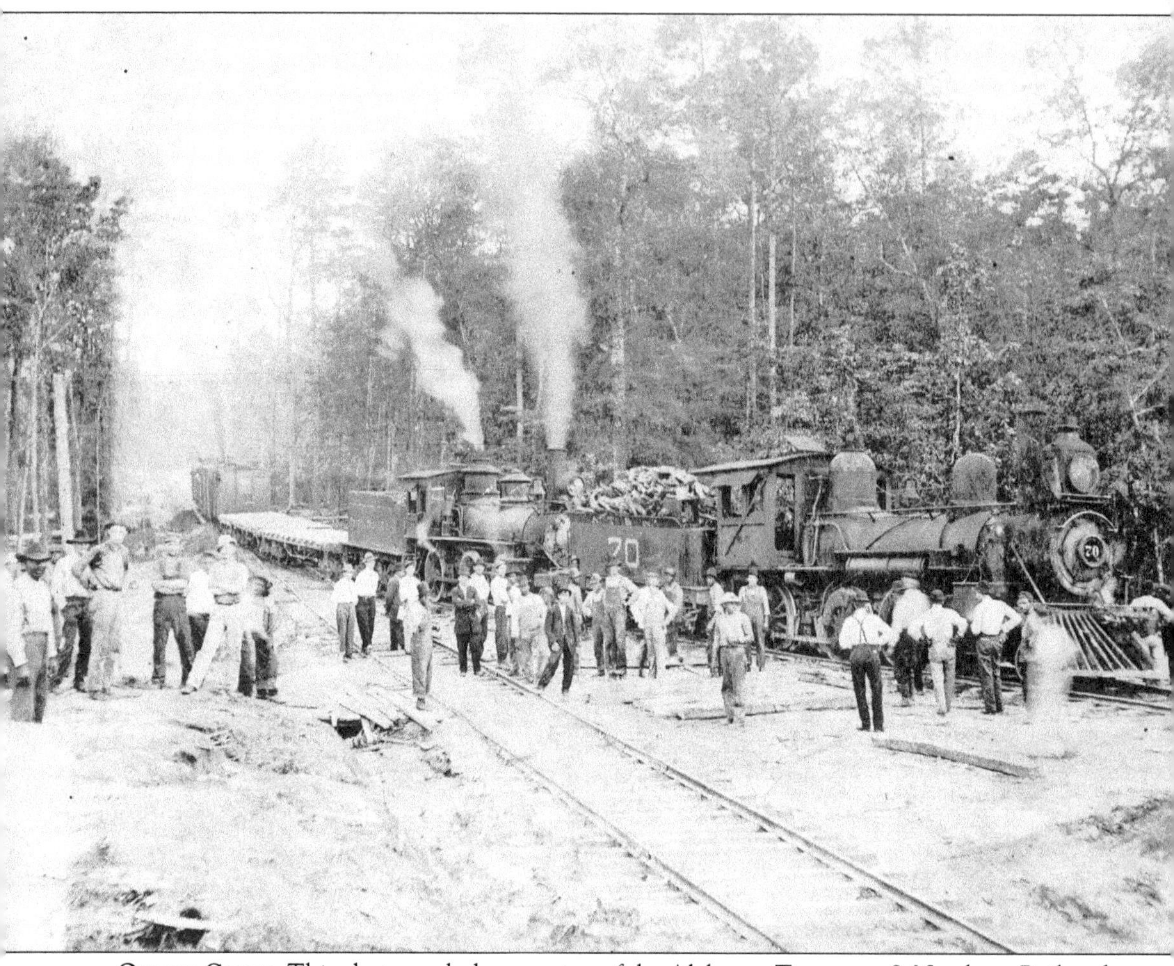

On the Cover: This photograph shows a view of the Alabama, Tennessee & Northern Railroad (AT&N) around 1910–1911 in Gilbertown, Alabama. The AT&N ran from Mobile to York and was owned and operated by John T. Cochrane. It operated until 1987, when it merged with the Burlington Northern. The last Burlington Northern train passed through Choctaw County in June 1992. (Courtesy of Choctaw County Historical Museum.)

IMAGES
of America

CHOCTAW COUNTY

Sandra Jenkins Little

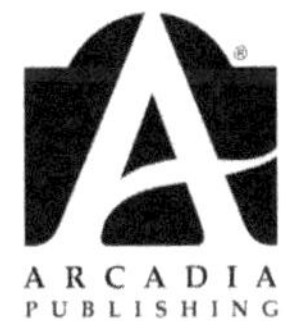

ISBN 978-1-5402-2671-6

Published by Arcadia Publishing
Charleston, South Carolina

Library of Congress Control Number: 2017933815

For all general information, please contact Arcadia Publishing:
Telephone 843-853-2070
Fax 843-853-0044
E-mail sales@arcadiapublishing.com
For customer service and orders:
Toll-Free 1-888-313-2665

Visit us on the Internet at www.arcadiapublishing.com

This book is dedicated to Ann Harwell Gay, a true Choctaw County historian and writer. She has dedicated many years to researching and preserving the history of Choctaw County, which she has shared with us through her books.

Contents

ACKNOWLEDGMENTS

In 1987, a group of volunteers was seeking a way to help preserve the artifacts related to Choctaw County's history. Articles of incorporation for the Choctaw County Historical Museum were submitted on September 4, 1987. The volunteers searched for either an existing building to purchase or a location to construct a new building. In February 1990, the old Alabama Farmer's Co-Op building in Gilbertown became available and was purchased. Over the years, hundreds of volunteers have contributed tens of thousands of hours to preserve the history of Choctaw County. The museum archives offer a treasure trove of information about the county's history.

It is with the utmost gratitude that I extend my thanks to the nine-member board of directors that governs the operations of the Choctaw County Historical Museum for allowing my use of the museum's extensive photograph collection and granting permission for the use of photographs in this book. Any photograph not provided by the museum is noted with a separate courtesy.

Introduction

Choctaw County was formed by the Alabama legislature on December 29, 1847, by taking land from both Sumter and Washington Counties. The courthouse was built in Butler. The first census, taken in 1850, listed many occupations: carpenter, farmer, attorney, blacksmith, school teacher, physician, merchant, shoemaker, miller, brick mason, architect, undertaker, clergyman, planter, and wagon maker. These individuals came from England, France, Ireland, Scotland, Tennessee, Mississippi, Georgia, Pennsylvania, and Canada. The most represented states were North and South Carolina. Choctaw County is wholly contained within the old Choctaw Indian lands ceded to the United States by the Treaty of Mount Dexter in 1805 and by the Treaty of Dancing Rabbit Creek in 1830.

Many places in Choctaw County still carry their Indian names. Pushmataha was once thriving but today is just a small community. It was named for the famed Chief Pushmataha, one of the "medal Mingos" of the Choctaw Indians. The easternmost part of his village was at Tuscahoma Landing on the Tombigbee River, and the westernmost part ended at Pushmataha. Choctaw also has creeks that bear Indian names: Bogueloosa, Puss Cuss, Souwilpa, Okatuppa, Tallawampa, and Wahalak.

In 1848, Choctaw County erected its first courthouse. It was a frame, two-story building. The courthouse burned in 1859, was rebuilt, and burned again in April 1871, destroying many of the early records. After the fire, another courthouse was built that lasted until the new brick one was built around 1905. The old building was purchased by O.C. Ulmer and moved across the street from the front of the new courthouse. This "old courthouse" burned down in September 1932.

The Bladon Springs Hotel, which was built around 1848, survived the Civil War and became a world-famous health resort. The famed hotel was known as the "Saratoga of the South." It burned down in 1927. The Cullom Hotel, with its four alum springs, is also no longer standing.

The citizens of Choctaw County have always believed in education for their children. This can be attested to by the building of many early schools. Probably the most famous was located in Mount Sterling. The Mount Sterling High School was under the leadership of Prof. Seth Smith Mellen and became known as "Mellen Academy." He led the school from 1869 to 1880 and also served as the county superintendent of education from 1872 to 1880.

Choctaw County is also known for the Jack Turner lynching in 1882. Turner was an ex-slave and was hanged on the courthouse square in Butler by a mob who had him arrested and accused him of planning to lead his private army of blacks in a general slaughter of white people. The mob declared his guilt by a vote that was reported as 998 to 2. His only real offense had been that he had dared to engage in politics and encouraged blacks to vote.

The most infamous period of Choctaw's history can be traced to what is known as the Sims War, which came to a climax in 1891. It was named after its leader, 52-year-old Robert Sims. Moonshine, politics, and religion were some of the factors that led to the Sims War. During a six-month period, 18 people were killed and eight were wounded. Sims had some deeply religious ideas that were first thought of as harmless. He made whiskey and wine to be sold, and he also drank. He acquired a reputation for being mean and vindictive. He was arrested and fined more than 20 times in the 20 years prior to the event. The deaths resulting from the turmoil were Robert Sims and his brothers Jim and John, his son Bailey, and four of his followers in the Savage family (Constantine, his two sons William and Tyree, and his brother Thomas), James Mosley, Harry Hinton, and another unidentified follower of Sims. The law-abiding persons killed were the Rev. Richard Carroll, Dr. A.B. Pugh, and Sam Isaacs. Others killed were John Kennedy, children Josephine and Charles McMillan, and schoolteacher Belle McKenzie.

The Alabama, Tennessee & Northern Railway was built through the county starting in 1910. For many years, it was the only motor-driven train operating in Alabama. The AT&N ran from Mobile to York. It merged with Burlington Northern in 1987 and continued running through Choctaw County until June 1992. The tracks belonging to the railroad have all been removed.

During the early 1920s, the E.E. Jackson Lumber Company began operations at Riderwood. The company had its own company store, hotel, motion-picture theater, and other buildings. At its peak, the E.E. Jackson Lumber Company employed 1,500 people and had its own baseball team. The company suffered after the Great Depression and closed down. It has been claimed that lumber from E.E. Jackson was used in the floor of the White House dining room. Today, nothing remains of this once-booming business, and Riderwood is just a small community.

Logging has always been a large industry in Choctaw County. From Choctaw's early days into the 1940s, there were over 50 small sawmills operating in the county. The largest impact to the county in this field was when Marathon Southern Corporation announced in August 1955 that the company was building a paper mill on the Tombigbee River at Naheola. The mill expanded over the years and changed ownership several times. At this writing, the mill is owned by Georgia Pacific.

In the early 1960s, Choctaw Mills/Vanity Fair built a plant in east Butler, across from Bumpers Funeral Home. This provided employment for many women as well as men in the undergarment industry. The plant closed and operations moved to Mexico in 1996.

Due to Choctaw County's vast land area, many landowners have set aside acres devoted to hunting. The landowners have also built large hunting cabins and lodges. The Tombigbee River, on the eastern border of the county, offers citizens many choices of recreation. Many of the residents have built houses or weekend getaways along its banks.

Today, many of the larger towns in Choctaw County have suffered and are no longer thriving as in the past. Silas, Toxey, Lisman, Gilbertown, and Butler are just shells of what they once were. Over the years, many smaller businesses have closed. After graduation from high school or college, the majority of local children never return to Choctaw County due to lack of jobs. While Choctaw County gained notoriety for incidents of violence and murder such as the Sims War and the Jack Turner lynching, locals take pride in its many accomplishments.

One

Butler, the County Seat

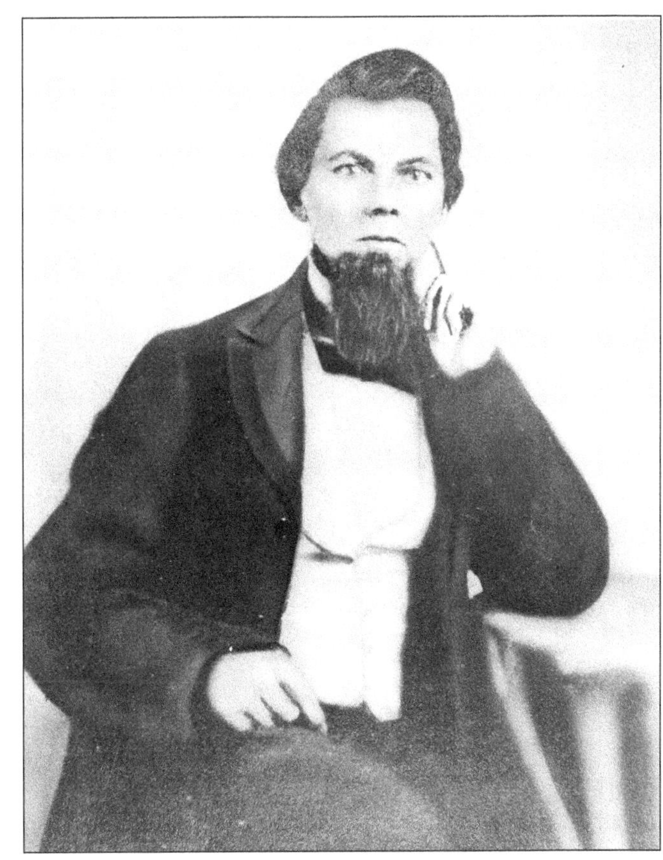

Curtis Nash Wilcox (1816–1874) was Choctaw County's first circuit court clerk in 1848 and the first elected probate judge (1850–1856). He was the son of Henry and Jeanette Bushnell Wilcox. He later moved to Meridian, Mississippi, and was mayor of Meridian when he died. He is buried at Pushmataha, Alabama. This photograph is not dated.

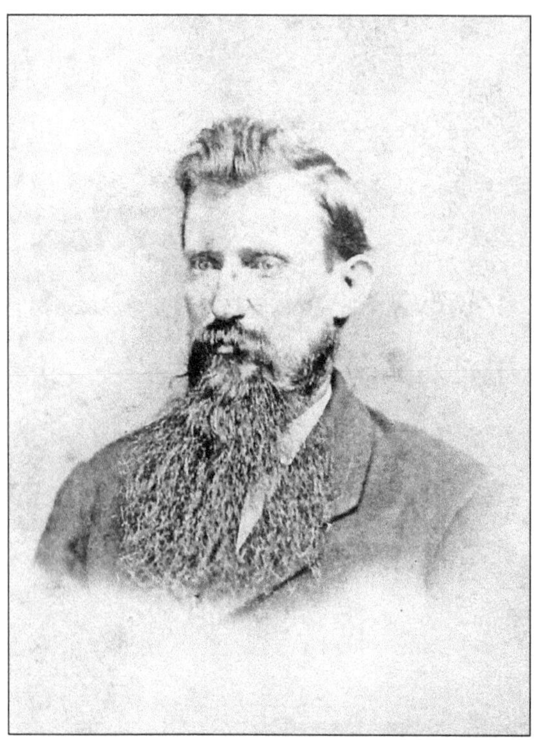

Benjamin Hartwell Warren was one of Choctaw County's early probate judges. He served from 1878 through 1887. This photograph of him is from April 1870. After the courthouse burned in 1871, he was the only person to reregister his two marriages in the probate office. No other early marriage or land records were rerecorded.

Pictured on the porch of the Taylor Hotel in Butler are, from left to right, (seated) Lula (Trice) Johnson, Mrs. Oscar L. Gray, Cora (Spinks) Taylor, and cooks Cora and Lisa; (standing) Judge Wallace H. Lindsey Sr., George W. Taylor, Marshall Smith, Hayward T. Taylor III, Hayward Taylor Jr., and Scott Spinks Turner. The child in front is Natalie Johnson.

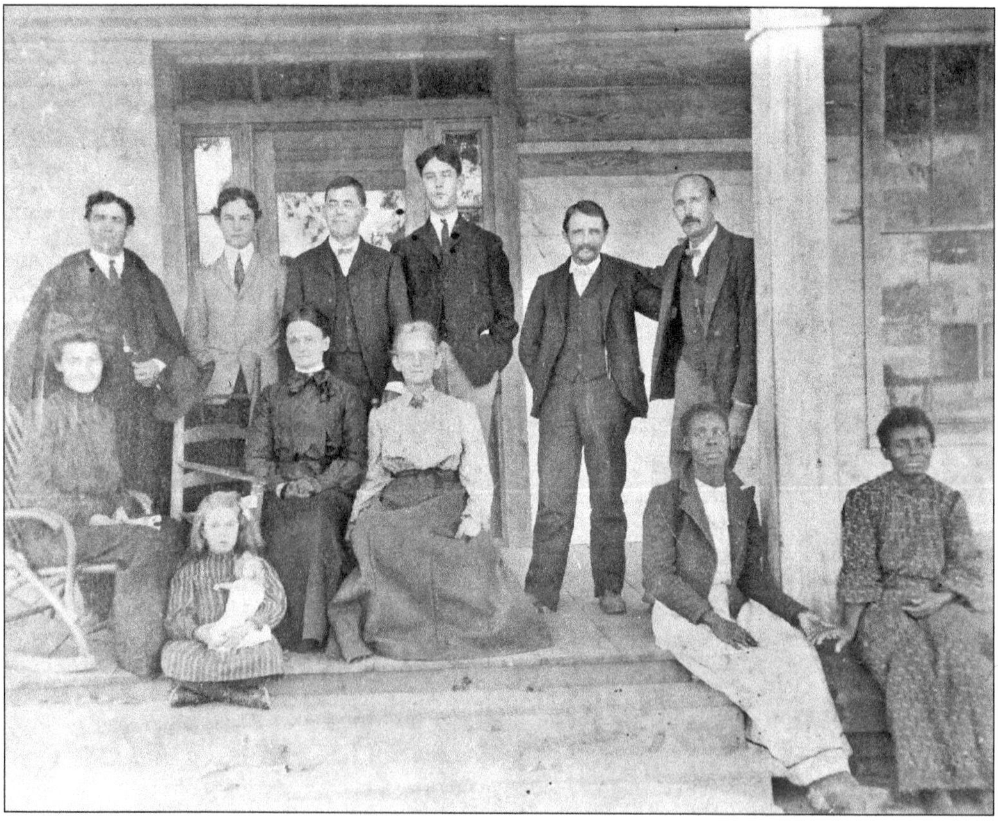

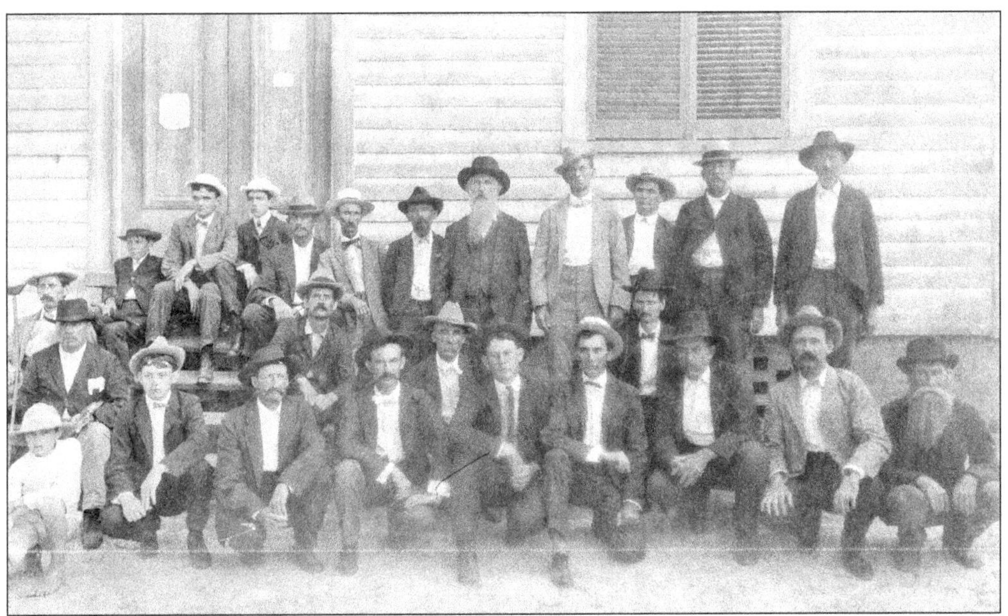

A group of unidentified men gathers in front of the old Choctaw County Courthouse prior to the construction of the new courthouse around 1905–1906. During the early years, many men would come to town and gather for business as well as pleasure. (Courtesy of Lanelle Turner.)

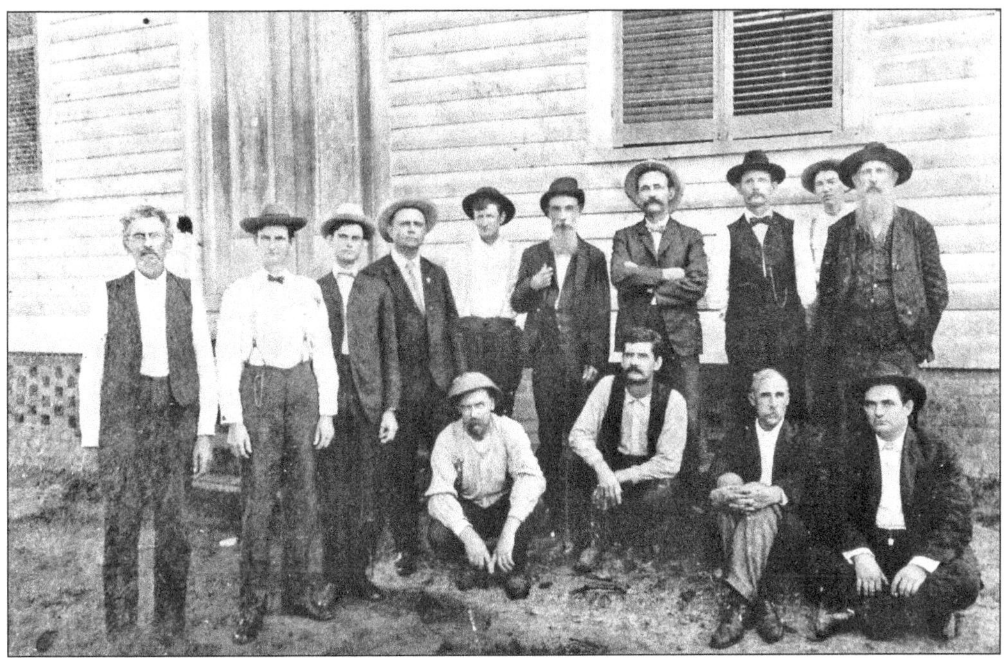

Another group of men is gathered in front of the Choctaw County Courthouse around 1902. The men could have been gathering for a jury session. None of the individuals in this photograph have been identified.

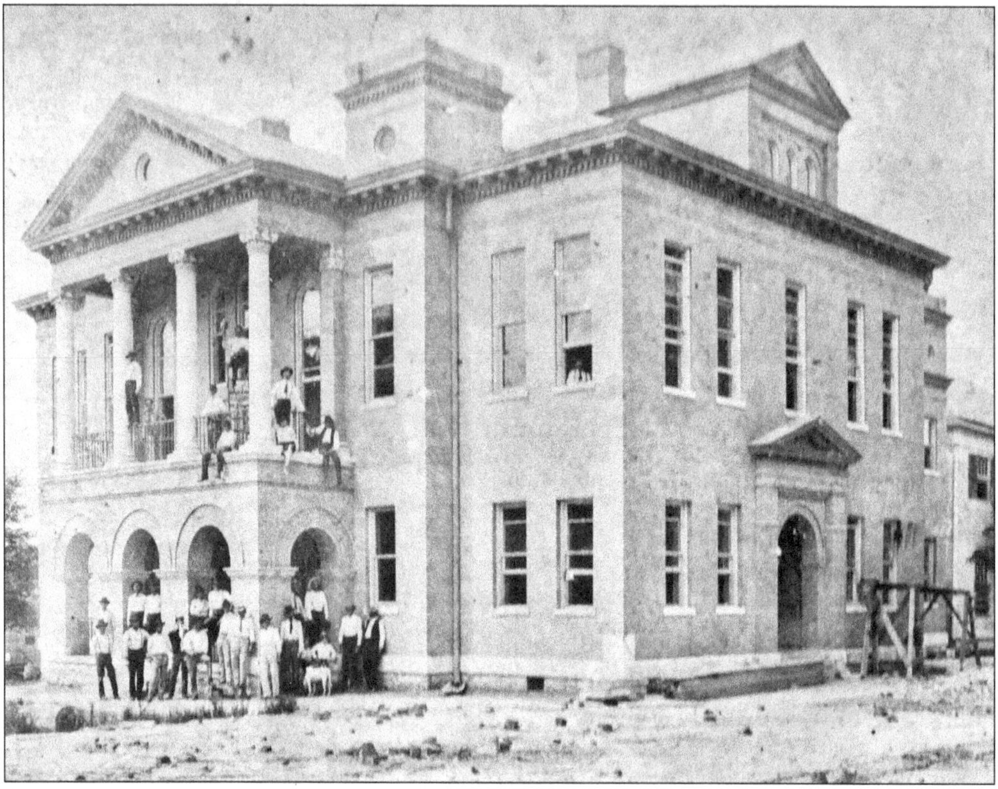

The Choctaw County Courthouse is shown during construction around 1905–1907. The courthouse still sits on the original site from 1847. A north and side wing were added in 1954–1955. In 1965, a three-story addition was built on the west side. The courthouse was placed in the Alabama Register of Landmarks and Heritage in 1997.

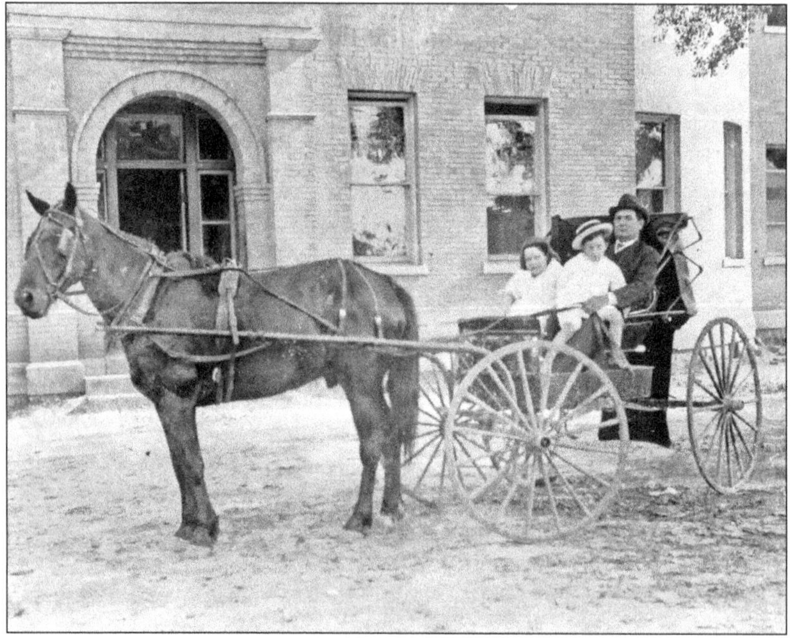

Pictured in front of the "new" Choctaw County Courthouse are Probate Judge Wallace Lindsey and his children Wallace Lindsey Jr. and Mary. The photograph is not dated but was most likely taken before 1910.

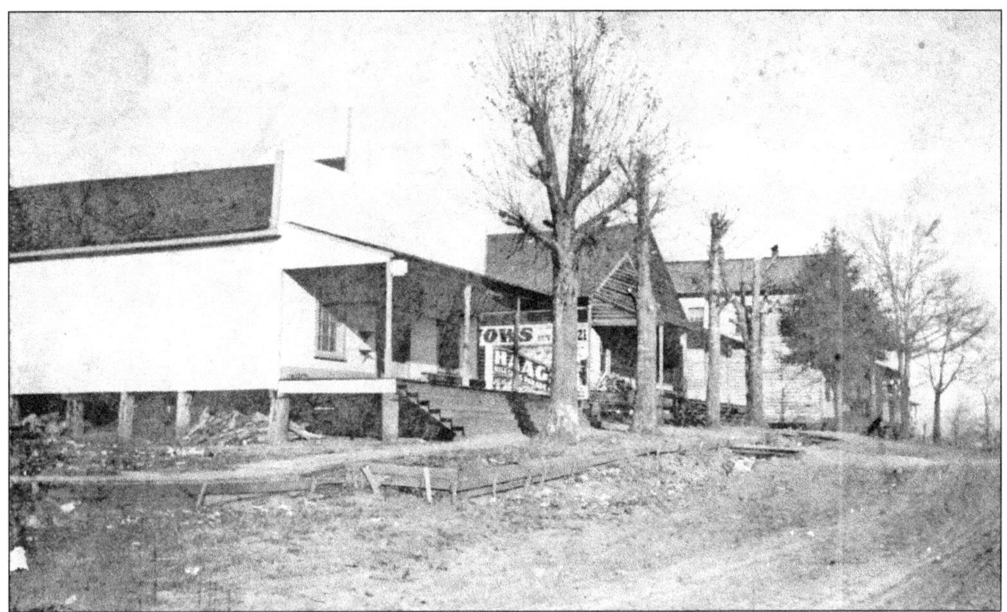

This photograph shows what the current Highway 10 West just north of the courthouse looked like in 1914. The streets were still unpaved. Shown are the stores of Jeff Bruister, Gulliam Scott, and Green Berry Bush. Today, the West Alabama Bank, an empty business, and Jackson's on the Square are located in this area.

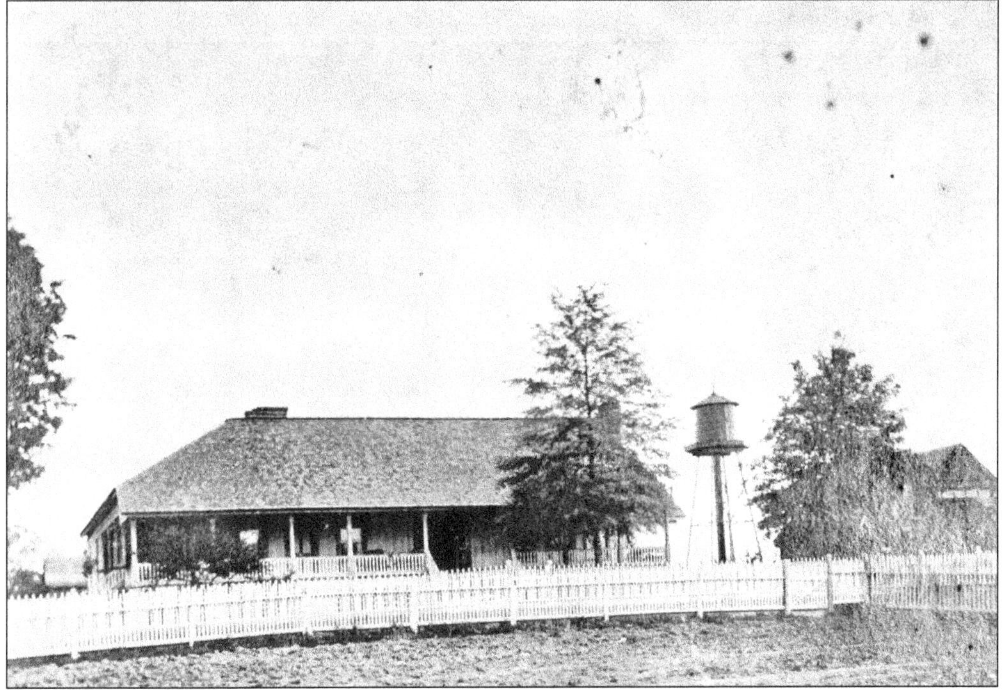

The F.A. Miller home in Butler was once used as a hotel. It had extensive picket fences and covered the width of the south end of the block where South Alabama Gas, Village Jewelry and Sports, and Alabama Power are now located. F.A. Miller's wife, Ledonia "Donie" Miller, lived here until her death in 1955.

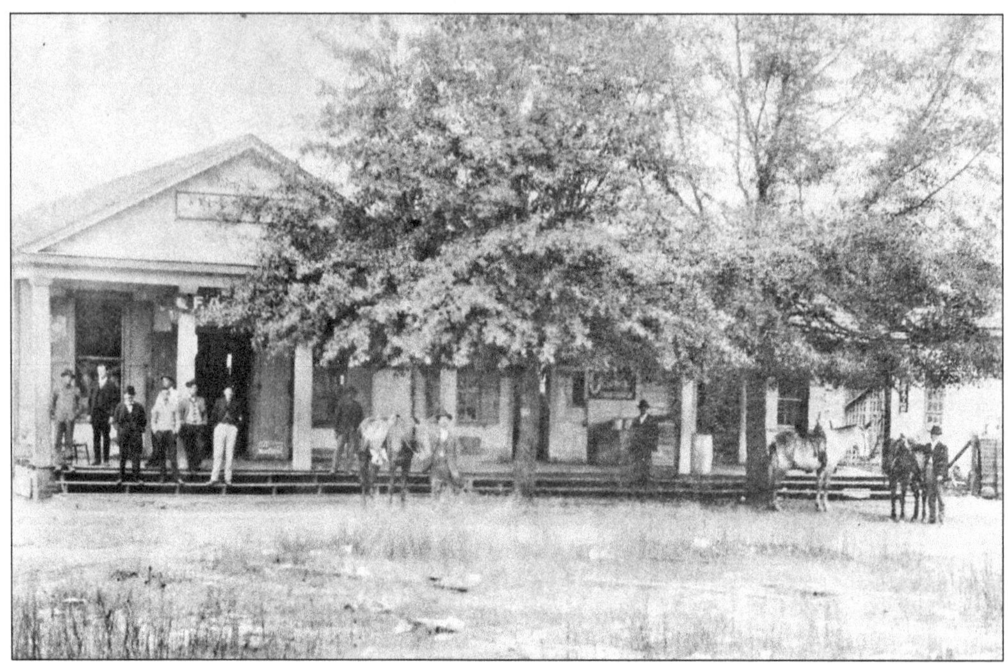

The F.A. Miller Store was established in 1890 by Frederick August Miller. It was located south of the courthouse square on Church Street. Baber's Leasing now sits on this property. The pastime for many men coming to town was to play checkers in front of the stores. The store is best remembered for being the primary source of goods for citizens for three quarters of a century.

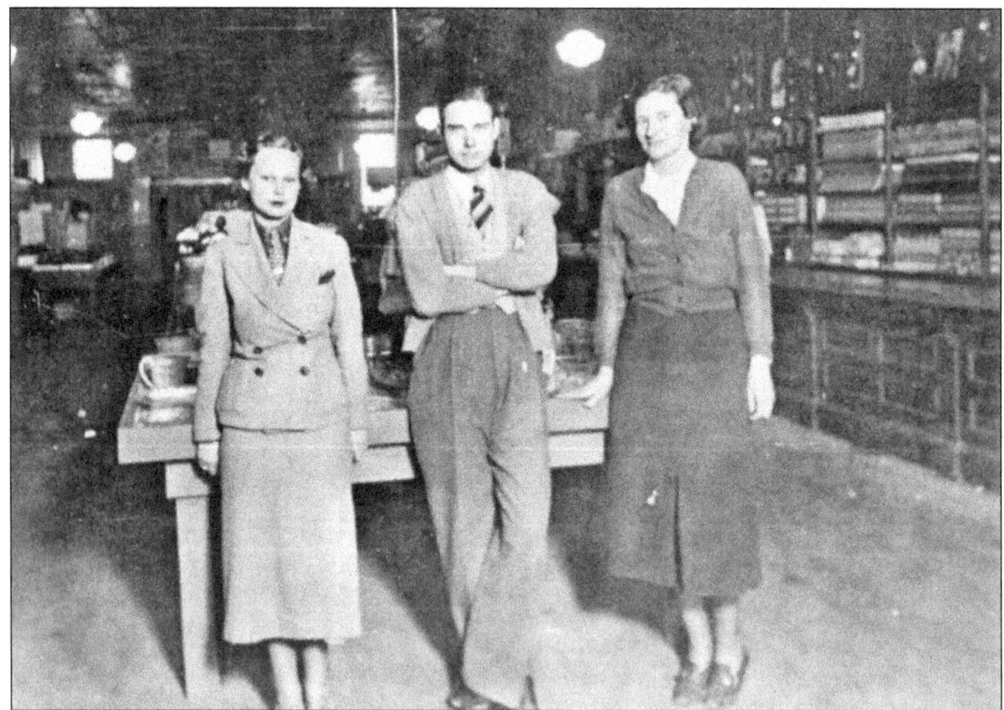

This photograph shows the interior of the F.A. Miller Store during the late 1930s. From left to right are Virginia Dubose, Paul O. Miller Jr., and Lida Bush Mosley.

Dr. Henry Howard Mason and his wife, Margaret Bruister Mason, are pictured here. Dr. Mason was born to B.F. Mason and Mattie Brewster on January 10, 1873, in Mississippi, and died on October 29, 1931, at the age of 58. He was a practicing family physician. He was 45 years of age when he registered for the World War I draft.

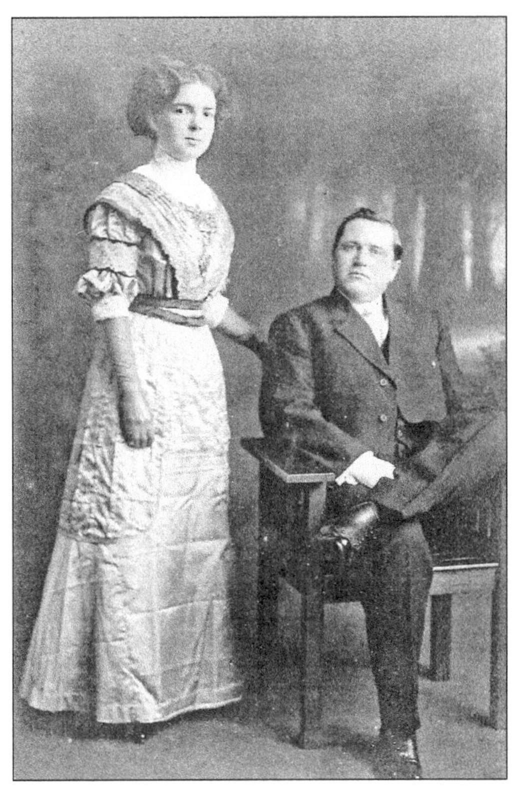

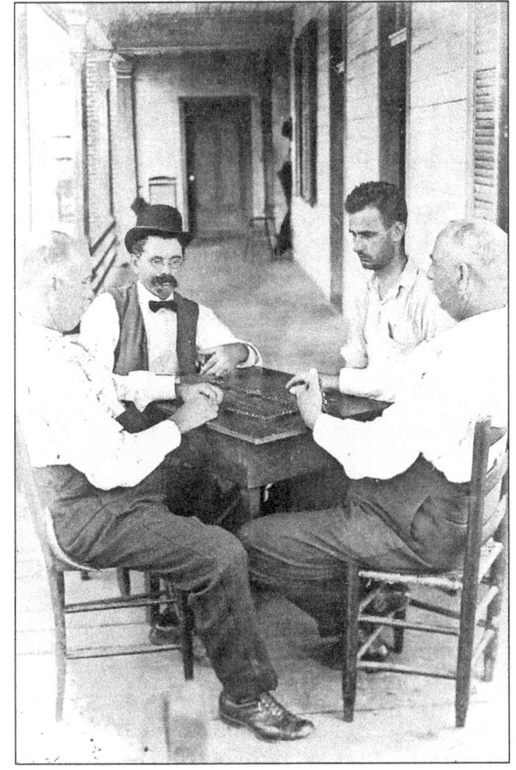

A group of friends gathers to play dominoes on the porch of the old Benjamin Lafayette Bruister home on Young Street, behind the First United Methodist Church in Butler. From left to right are unidentified, Fred Miller, Hayward Taylor, and Ben Bruister. They were local businessmen in Butler.

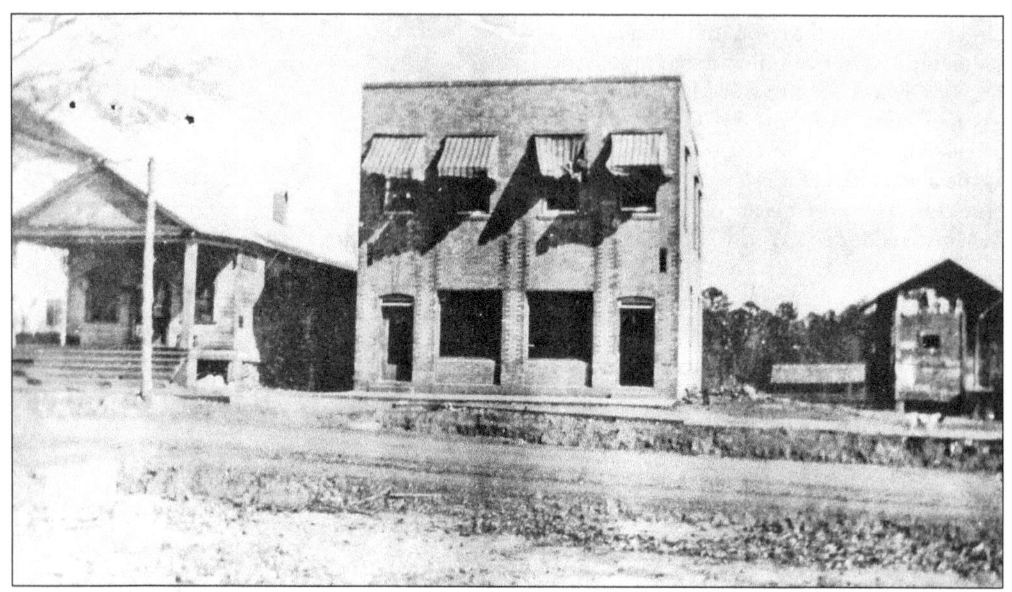

The center building is the "new" Choctaw Bank of Butler around 1920. It was replaced with a new building in the 1950s. At far left is the original Choctaw Bank. Virginia's Dress Shop occupied the building in the center for many years. It was located on Alabama Highway 17 South. Today, the building houses the law offices of D'Wayne May.

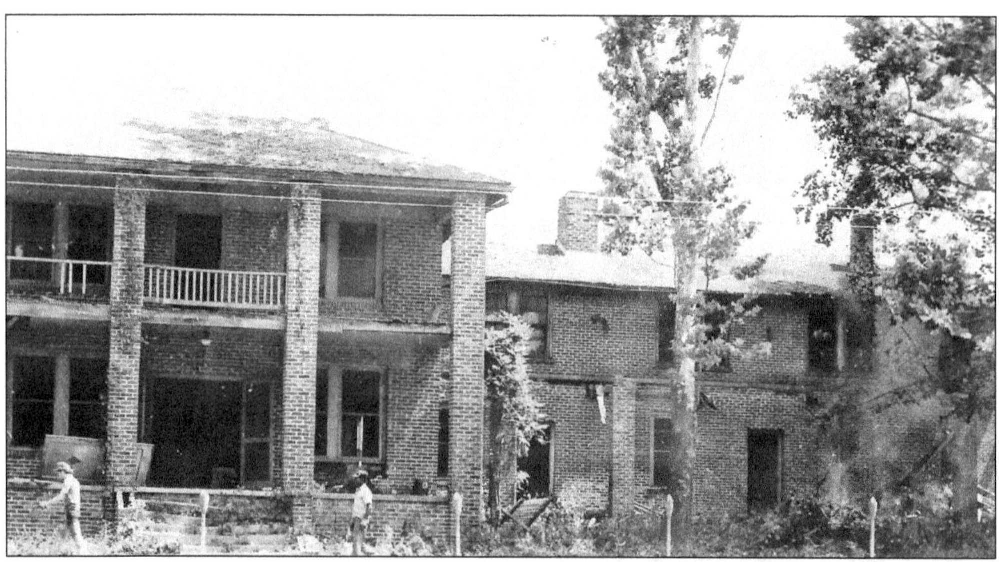

Pictured are the remains of the old Adams Hotel in Butler. The hotel opened in April 1931 and was owned by Plunk Adams and operated by his son Bryant. It had 25 bedrooms with running hot and cold water. There were also six bathrooms and a large kitchen and dining room. The hotel was torn down in 1977, and the West Alabama Bank now sits on this site.

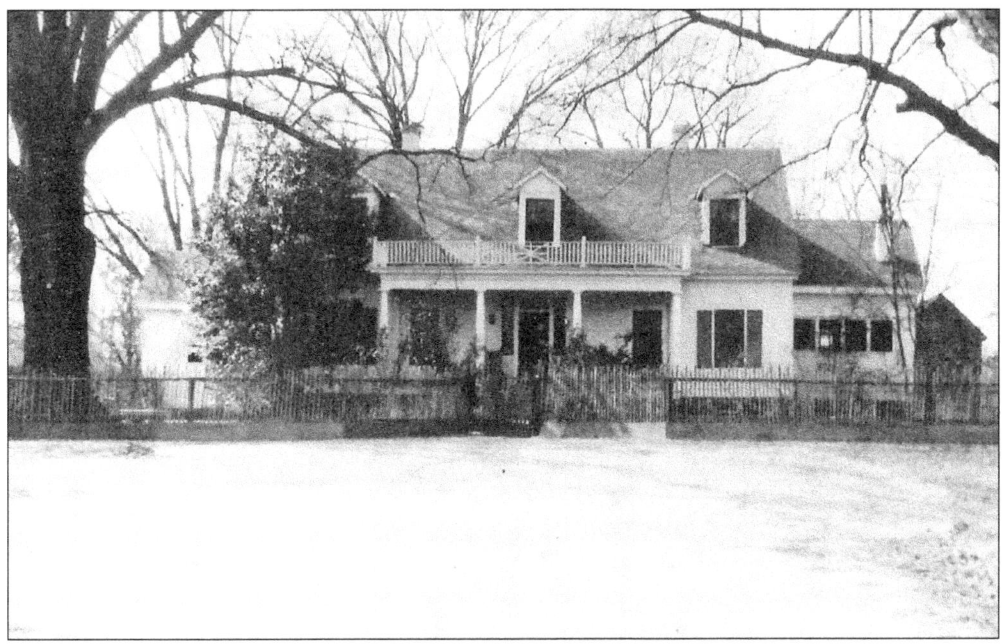

The home of Dr. Henry Howard and Margaret Mason was located at the end of Patton Street, just behind the Piggy Wiggly store on West Pushmataha Street. The house was torn down in 1949–1950.

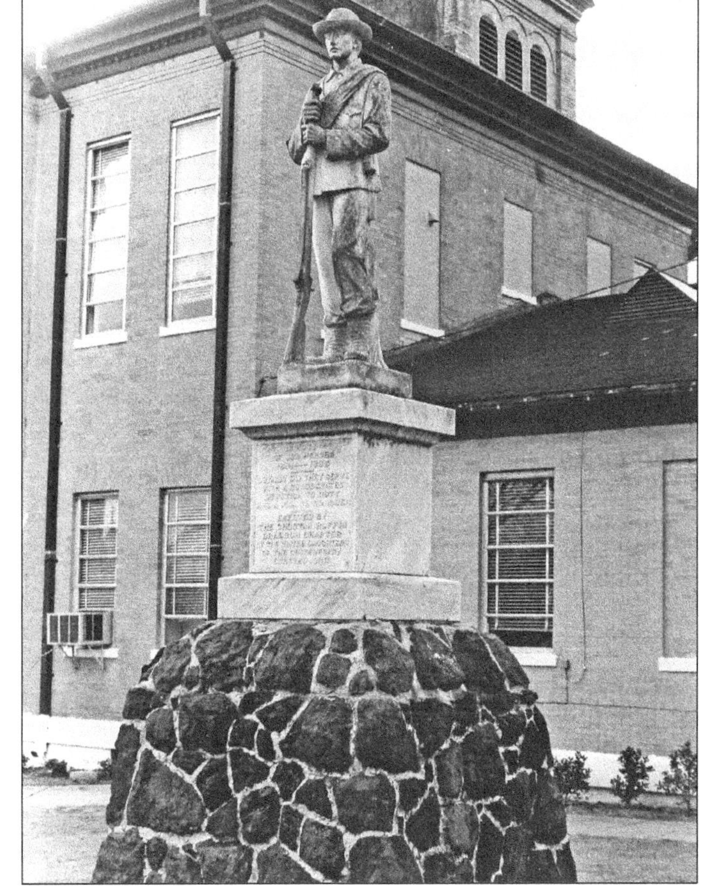

The Confederate monument sits on the grounds of the courthouse. The statue is made of Carrara marble from Italy and was sculpted at Townsend's studio in Italy. It was shipped to the Alabama state docks in Mobile and sent via rail from Mobile to Riderwood. It was then trucked the last six miles to Butler, where it was erected in 1936.

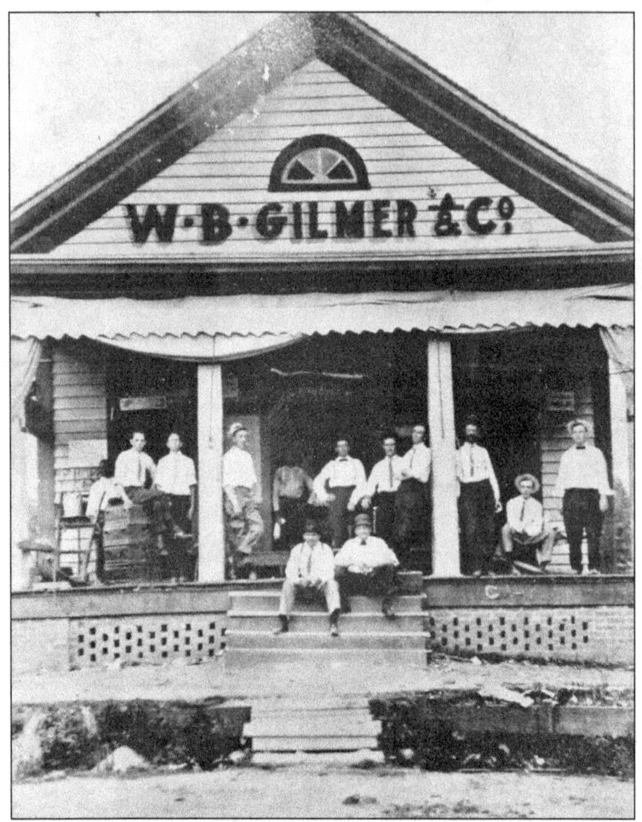

A group of men gather at the W.B. Gilmer & Company store, on the site of the former Choctaw Bank of Butler and current Regions Bank. The store was started by three brothers. The building was demolished in 1956 and a new Choctaw Bank was built on the site. The old W.B. Gilmer Sr. home used to sit on the site of the current First US Bank.

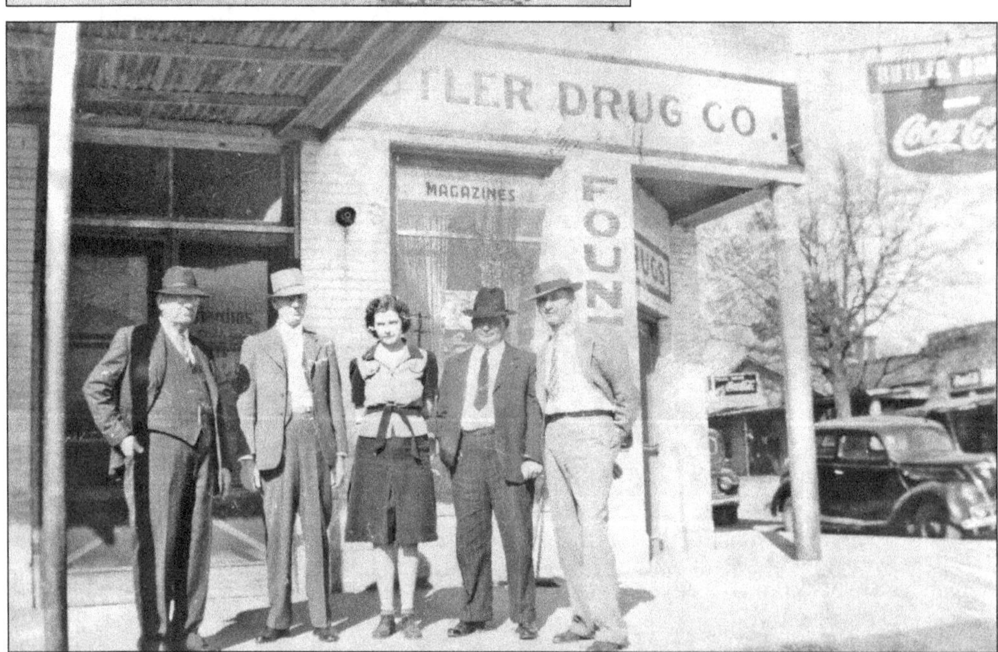

A few people gather outside the Butler Drug Company in the 1940s or 1950s. The Butler Drug Company was housed in the Elliott building, which was constructed in 1924. At that time, it was one story. A second story was added later with the name Elliott displayed in the bricks.

Dr. William Jefferson Barber was born in Butler in 1906 to Dr. H.W. and Mattie Bruister Barber. He attended medical school at Tulane University. After internship at the City Hospital of Mobile, he returned to Butler and opened his first office on November 7, 1931. He saw a need for a hospital, so he built the first unit of the Barber Hospital in 1936.

This photograph shows the remains of the old Barber Hospital. The first unit of the hospital was built in 1936 by Dr. William Barber. The unit held 32 beds. In addition to Dr. Barber, Dr. C.H. Gully and his son Dr. Virgil S. Gully practiced at this hospital. Other staff consisted of 12 nurses and support staff, for a total of 24 people.

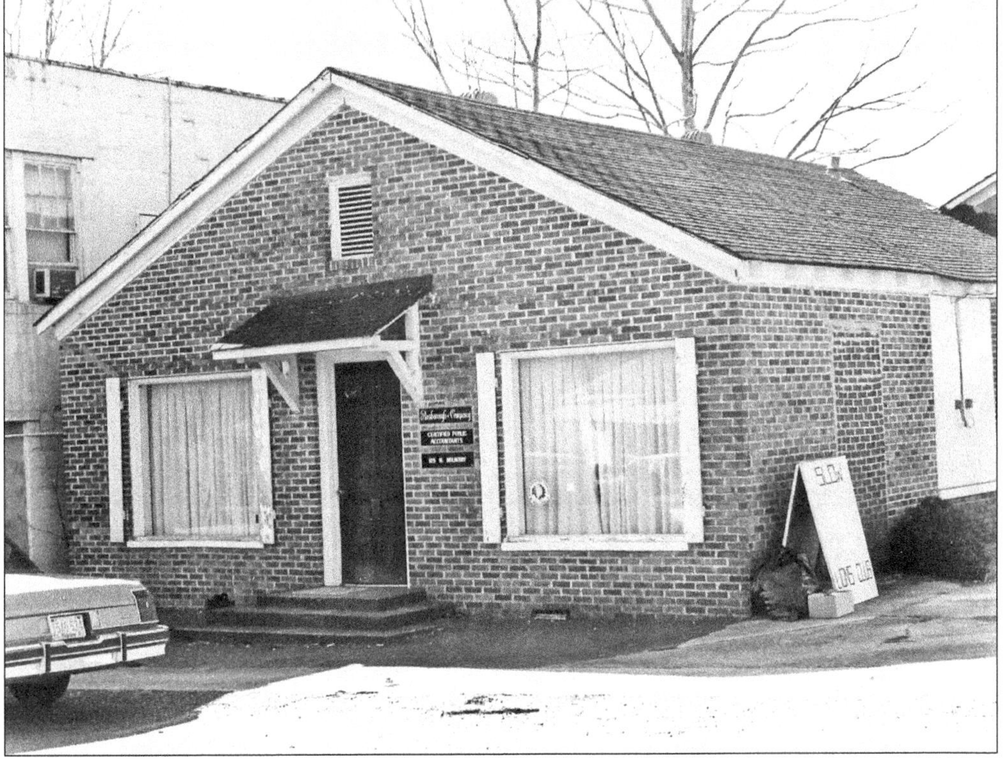

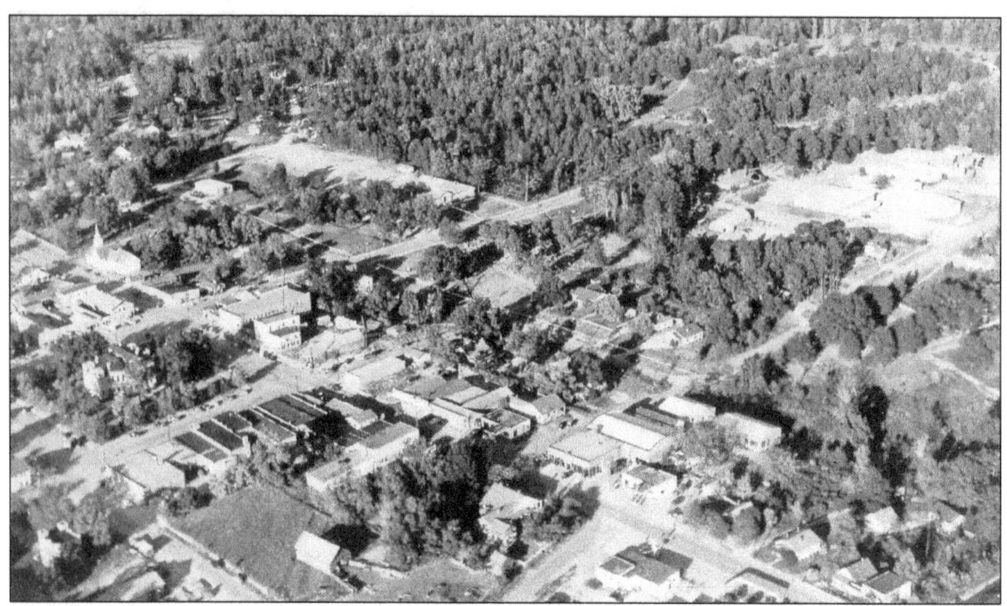

This aerial view of Butler was taken in 1950. At upper right is Choctaw County High School. The middle lower left shows the courthouse square when it was completely surrounded by trees.

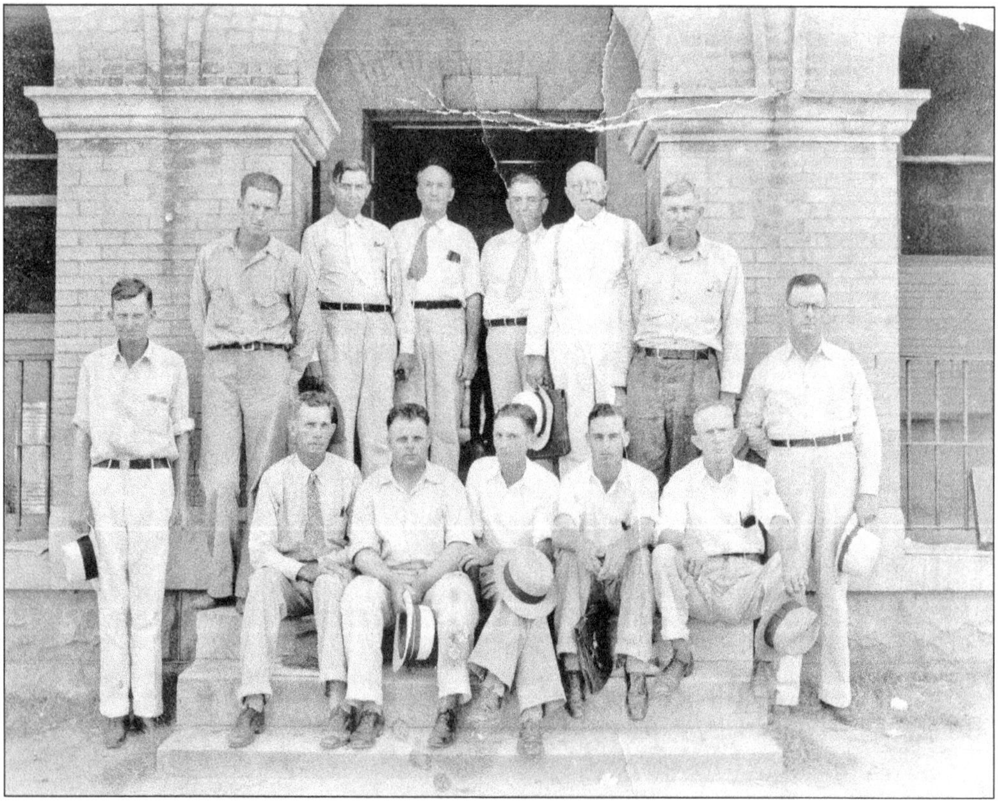

A group of unidentified men stands on the steps of the Choctaw County Courthouse for a photograph in the 1950s or early 1960s. They may have gathered for a grand jury.

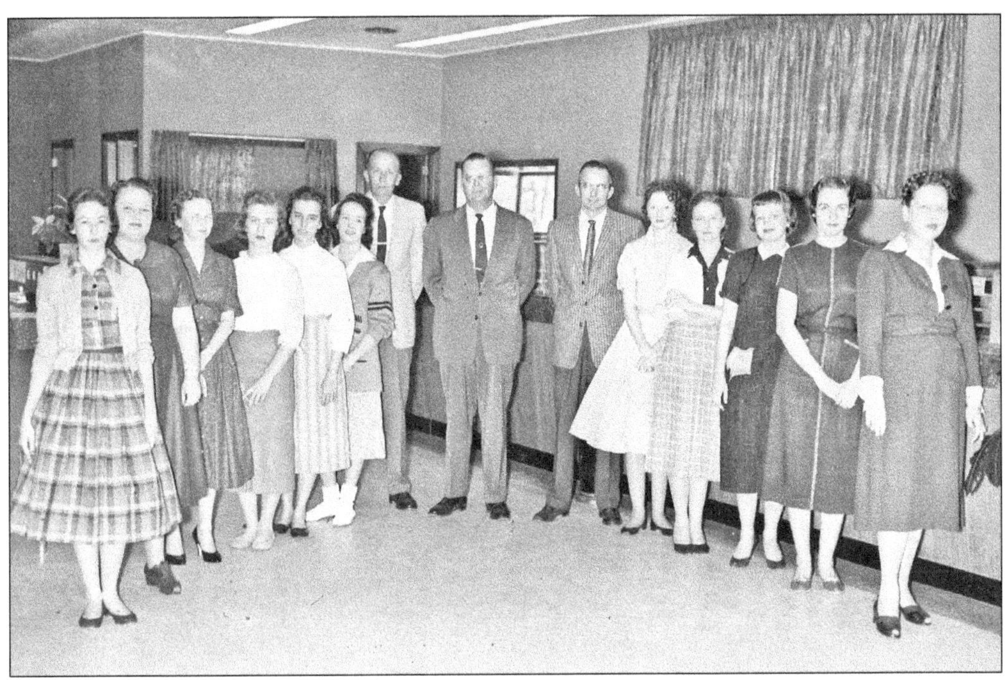

Employees of the old Choctaw Bank of Butler are shown inside the bank in the late 1950s or early 1960s. From left to right are Thelma Daugherty, Beatrice Sparrow, Mary Ruth Sample, Patricia Roberts Mosley, Dottie Jo Whittington, Jackie Harris, Allen Abston, Albert Evans, O.D. Mason, Patty Boney, Marie Mosley, Anita Ezell, Robye Jean Parten, and Lois Sexton.

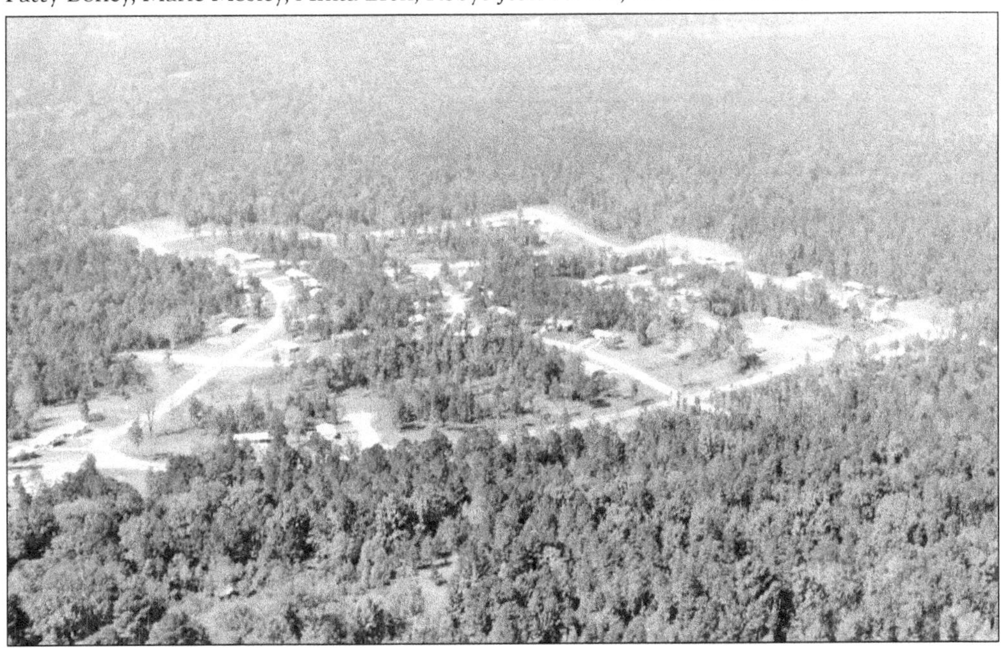

This aerial view shows the newly developed Green Acres subdivision in Butler around 1959. This development grew rapidly throughout the 1960s as the paper mill expanded. Housing was built for many of the employees coming to Choctaw County from northern states. Today, it is the largest subdivision in Butler. (Courtesy of Choctaw County Historical Society.)

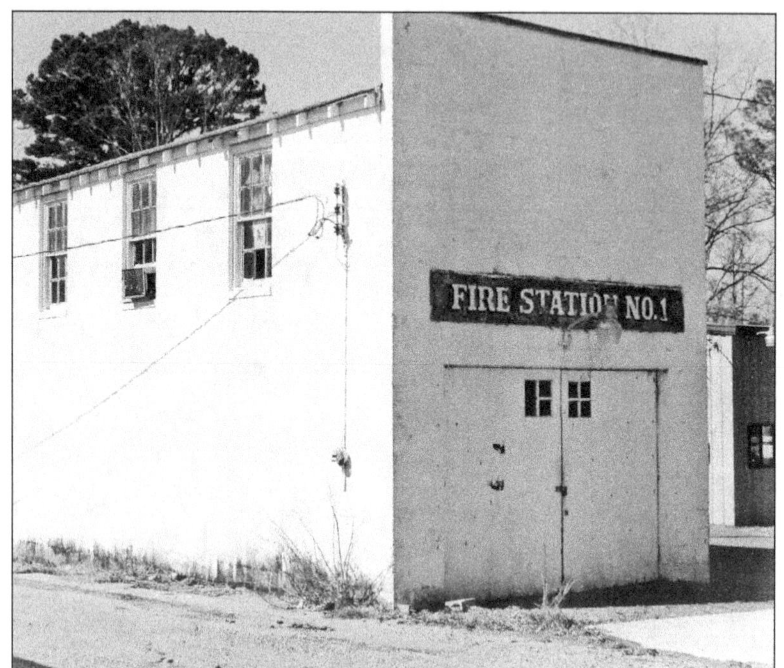

Butler's first fire station was built around 1950, when the town got its first fire truck. It was a combination building, as city offices were upstairs. This building was torn down in the 1980s after the town built a new fire station next to the old one.

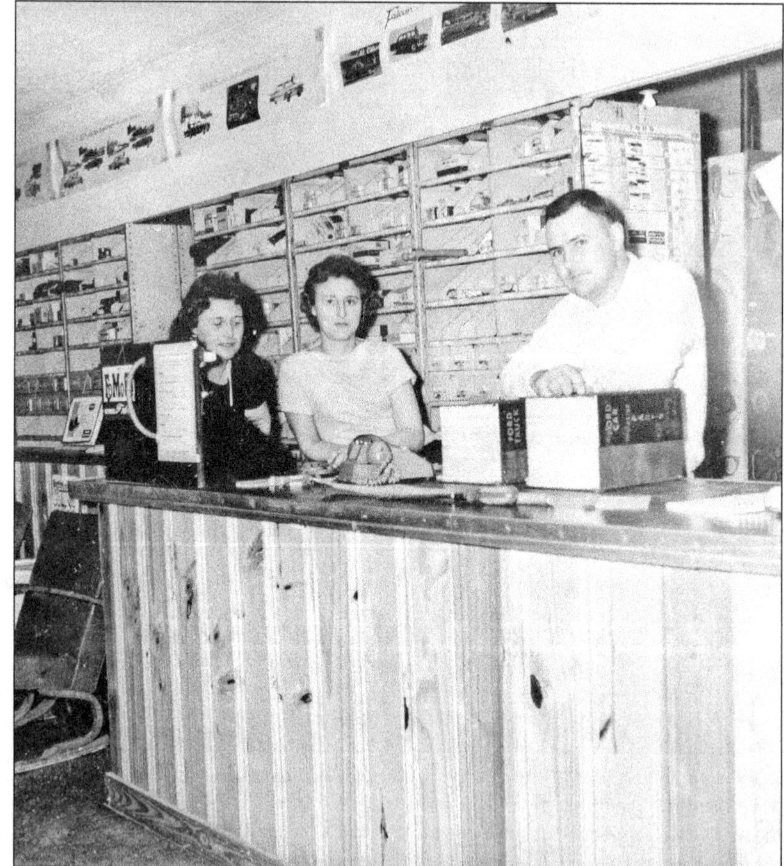

Paul "Peachie" Turner (far right) is shown inside McBride Motor Company on Highway 10 West in Butler in the 1960s. The two women on the left have not been identified. (Courtesy of Peggy Turner Tyson.)

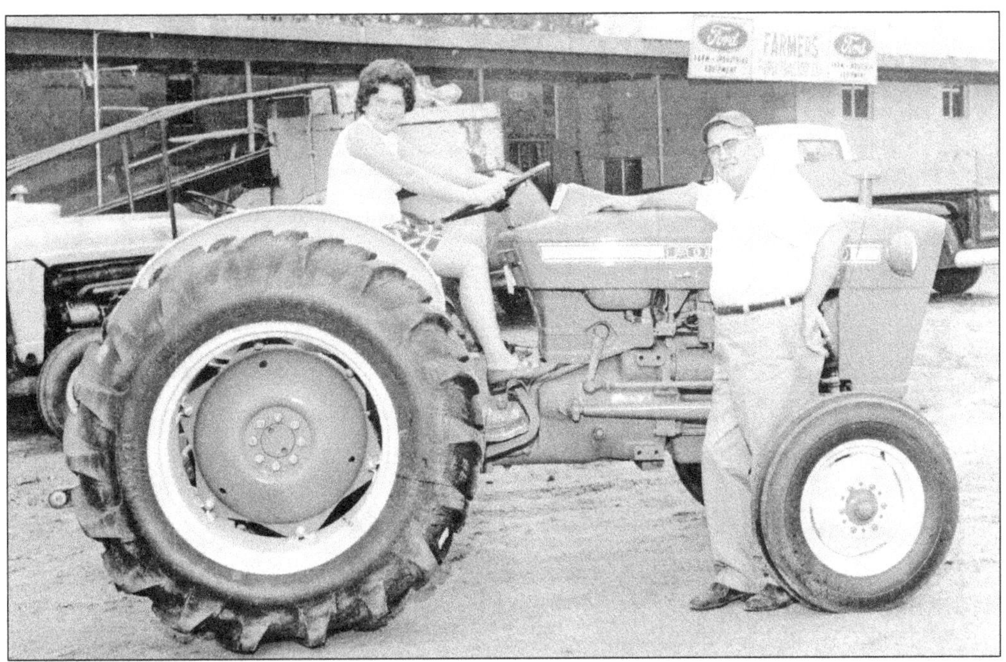

Peggy Turner (age 10) and her grandfather Luther Turner are pictured at the Ford tractor dealership on Highway 10 West in Butler in 1968. Her grandfather worked there, and he would let her play on the tractors when she came to visit. (Courtesy of Peggy Turner Tyson.)

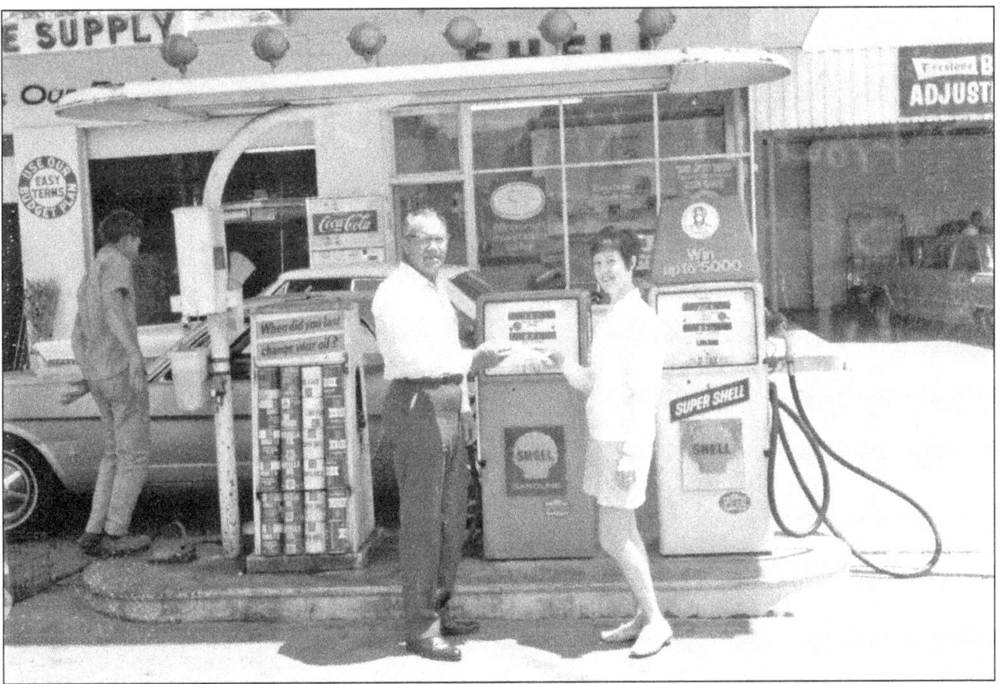

Ramsey's Shell station was located at the current site of South Alabama Gas on the corner of Highway 17 and Alabama Street. The station was owned and operated by Elton Ramsey. In this 1968 photograph, Elton Ramsey is handing Gayle Harmon a prize she had won from the Shell Oil Company.

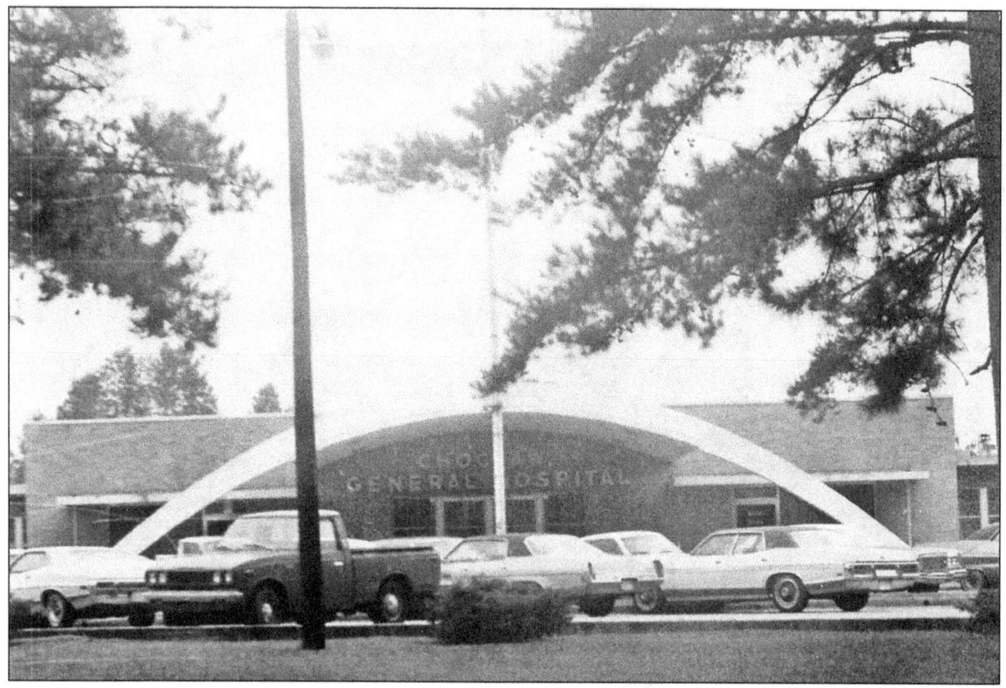

The old Choctaw General Hospital was on Highway 10 East in Butler. It opened in 1961 and closed in 1981. The hospital had several practicing doctors who performed surgery in the 1960s. A doctor's office and Willow Trace Nursing Home now occupy the facility. A new Choctaw General Hospital was built on the former Vanity Fair Mills site and opened in March 2012. It is operated by Rush Health Systems.

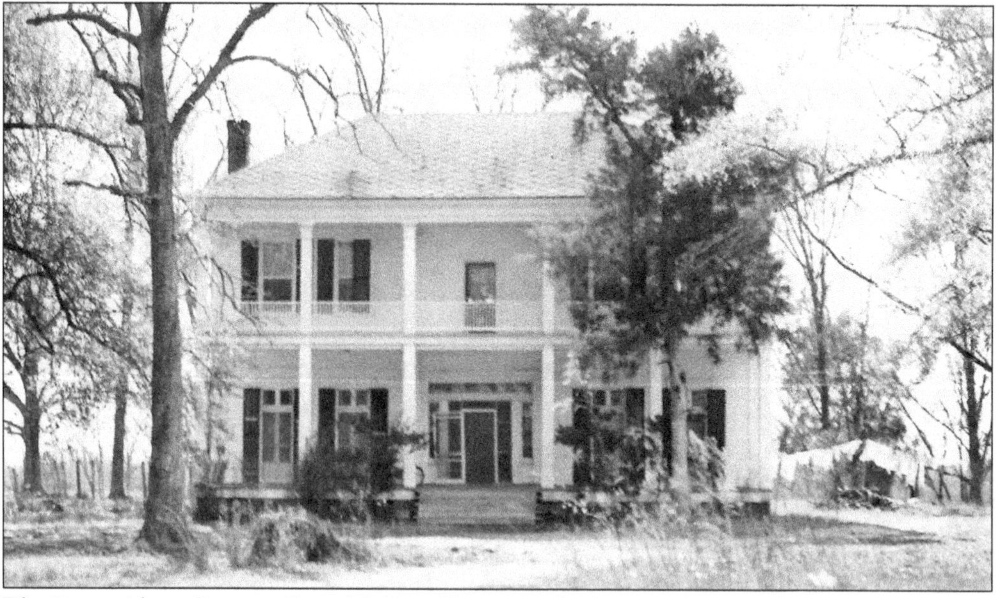

The Foster-Abney-Bruister-Swan-McCary Home was built around 1850. The home was owned by Dr. John T. Foster, who practiced medicine in Mount Sterling. In 1950, the home was owned by Florence Bruister Swann. It was also the longtime home of Benjamin Lafayette Bruister. The home is directly behind the First United Methodist Church of Butler on Young Street.

Two

OTHER PLACES

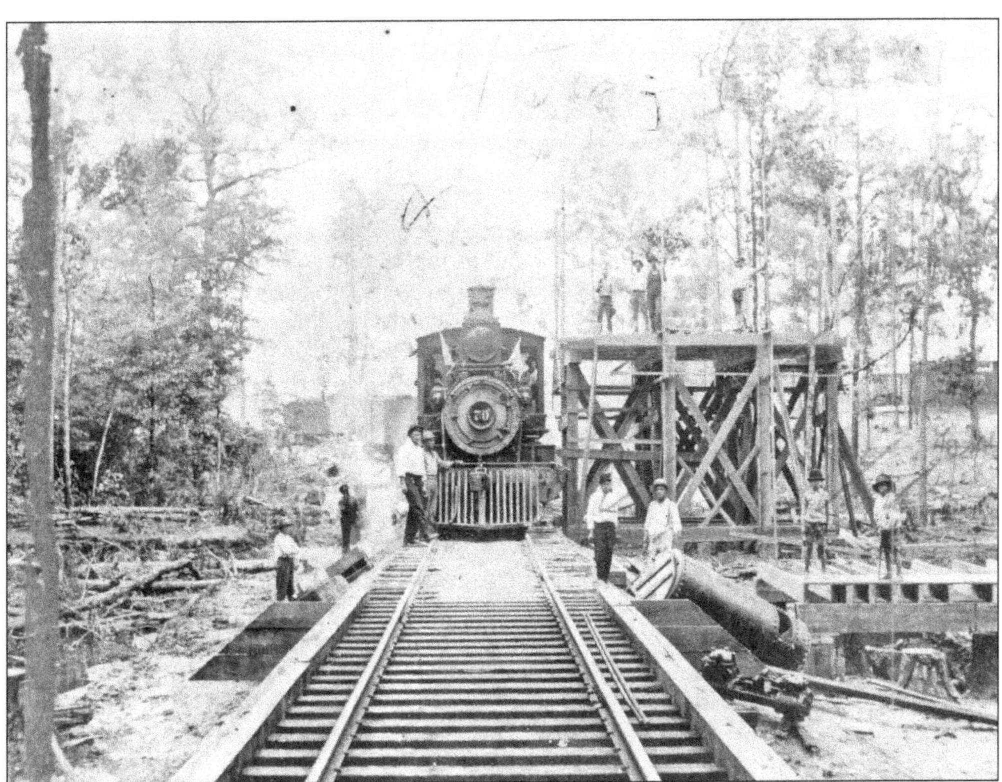

The AT&N railroad tracks were laid around 1910, and the train came through Gilbertown in 1912. The water tank on the right is being built near the south side of Gilbertown and Mill Creek. The two small boys are Thomas and Ruddell Gibson. Their job was to pump the water into the steam engine. The man with the derby hat is Albert Pruitt.

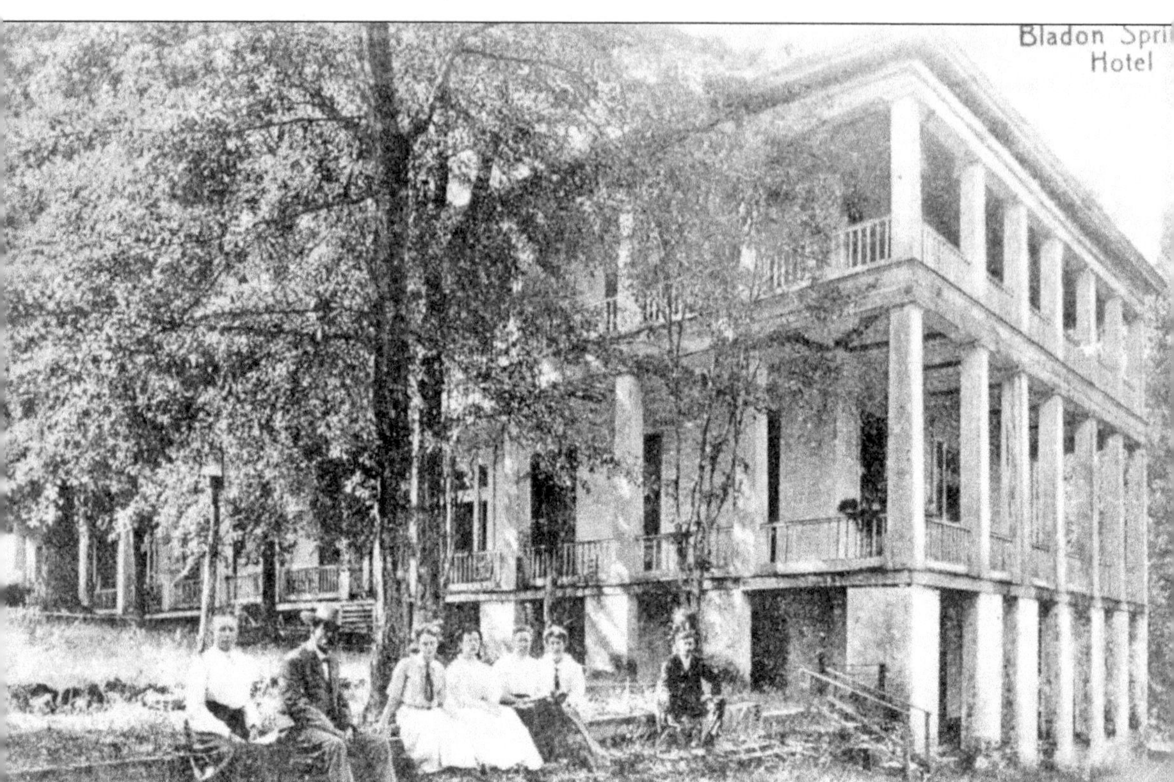

Bladon Springs was named for John Bladon, the original patentee of the land. The waters of the property were found in 1838 and opened to the public by owner James Conner. In 1845, the water was analyzed by the state geologist, Richard T. Brumby. He reported that it contained "sulphuretted hydrogen, carbonic acid, crenic and nypocrenic acids, muriate of soda, carbonate of soda, carbonate of lime, carbonate of magnesia and carbonate of protoxide of iron." The famed Bladon Springs Hotel was built around 1846 by Peter Flint, a master carpenter who lived in the area. It was a beautiful two-story hotel that included a bowling alley, skating rink, billiard rooms, croquet, swings, and a bar in the basement. The hotel accommodated 200 guests. The cottages were built before the hotel could house 100 guests. It was surrounded by six fountains. The Bladon Springs Hotel resort was often referred to as the "Saratoga of the South." It was destroyed by fire in 1927.

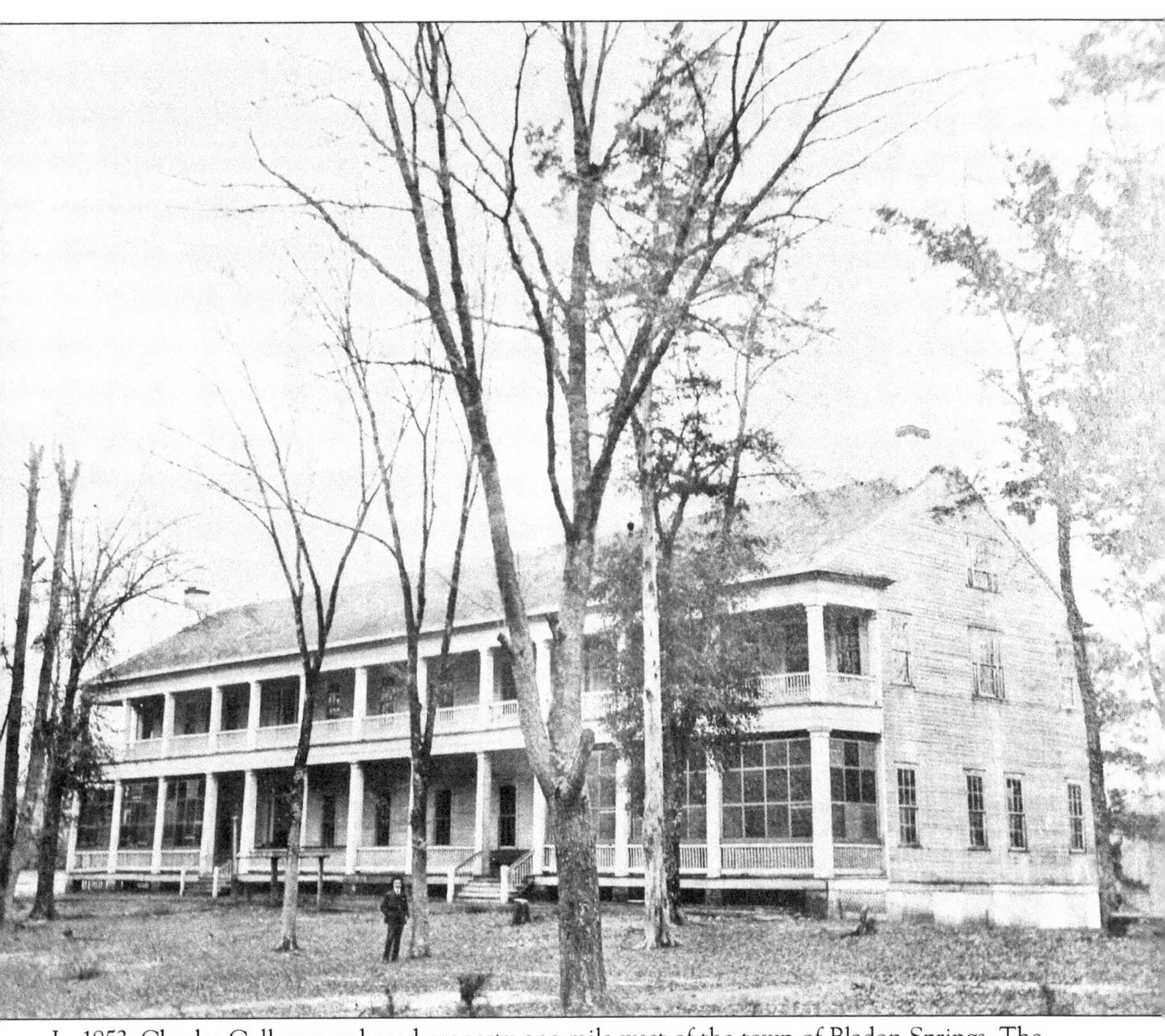

In 1853, Charles Cullum purchased property one mile west of the town of Bladon Springs. The property had four springs: Healing Spring, Vichy Spring, Vichy Spring No. 2 (Soda Spring), and Ferruginous Spring. Two sulphur springs, Point Spring and Bridge Spring, were about 10 feet apart near Vichy Spring. The water in those two springs consisted of 50 percent more bicarbonate of soda and one-third more sulphur hydrogen than in any other mineral spring in Alabama, Mississippi, or Louisiana. Cullum built the two-story Cullum Hotel (later called the Cullom Hotel). It reportedly had 24 rooms, two parlors, a 100-foot-by-150-foot dining room, a kitchen, and swimming pool. Cullum also had 30 double and single cabins built surrounding the hotel. The hotel was about five miles from the Tombigbee River. In 1884, a Captain Trowbridge purchased the property. He bored for petroleum but instead found more mineral water. The water was salty and had a temperature of 83 degrees. The hotel was reconditioned in 1908. The grounds covered about 560 acres.

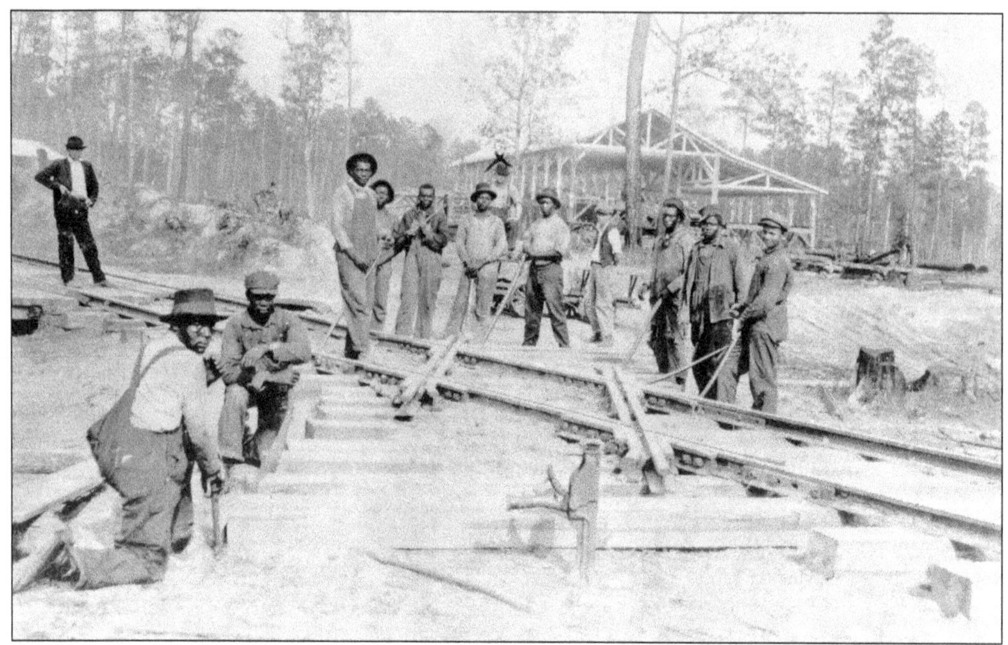

These workers are laying tracks near the Blake Sawmill in Gilbertown for the AT&N around 1910 or 1911.

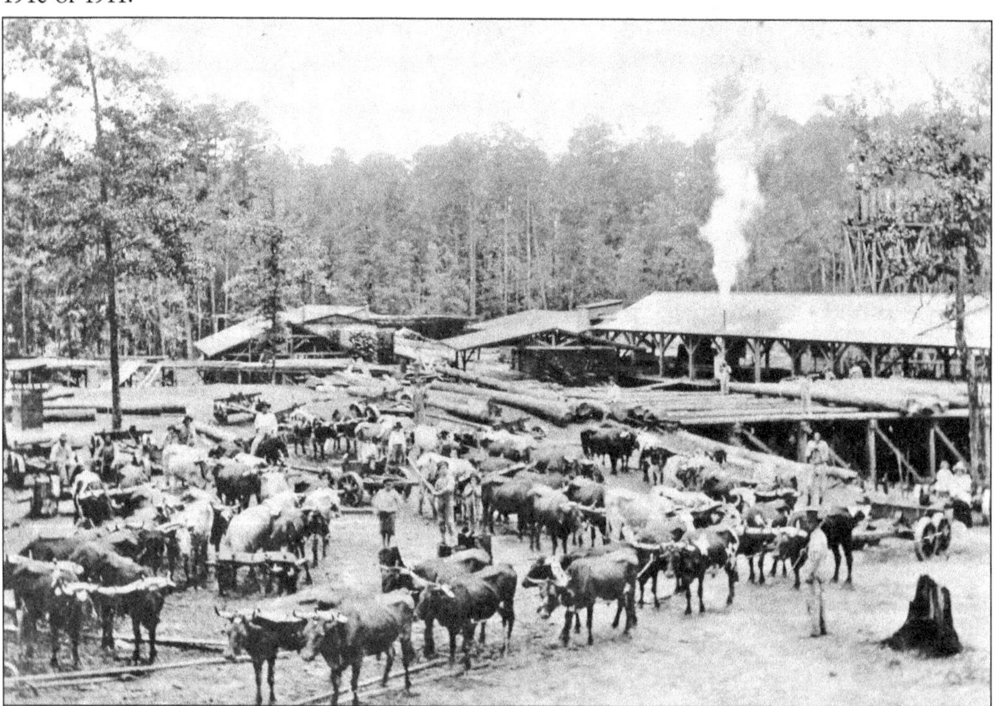

The Blake Sawmill was built around 1910 by Sam O. Rogers and J.E. Gibson in the southern end of Gilbertown, east of Mill Creek. The co-owners operated the business about a year before Rogers bought Gibson's part due to Gibson's health. Rogers operated the mill for about another year before selling to Thomas Blake around 1912. The sawmill was only in operation for about six years.

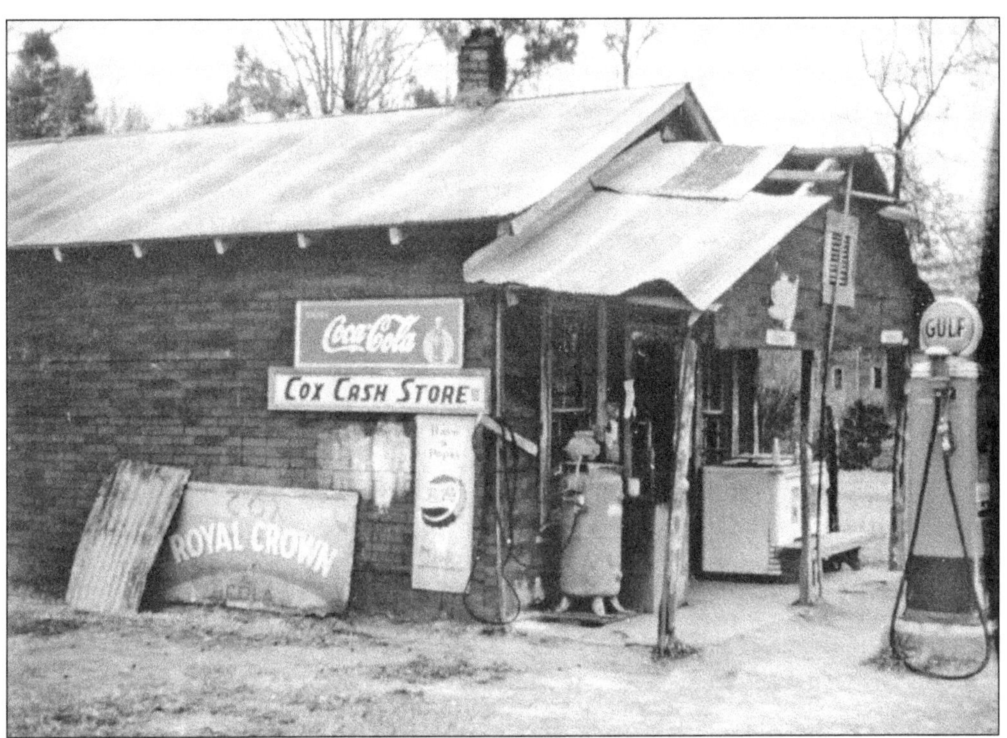

The Cox Cash Store, in the Womack Hill community, was operated by Milton "Bud" Cox. This photograph was taken in 1955. It has not been determined how long this business was in operation nor when it ceased operation.

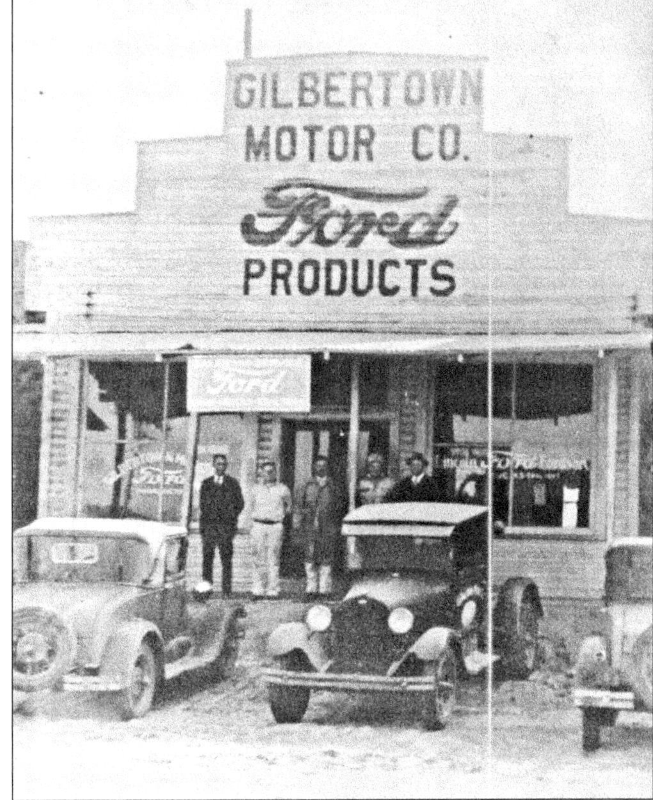

The Gilbertown Motor Company is shown as it appeared in 1929. The business was founded in 1921 by G.A. Rentz and S.L. Bonner, a couple of the leading businessmen in Gilbertown at the time.

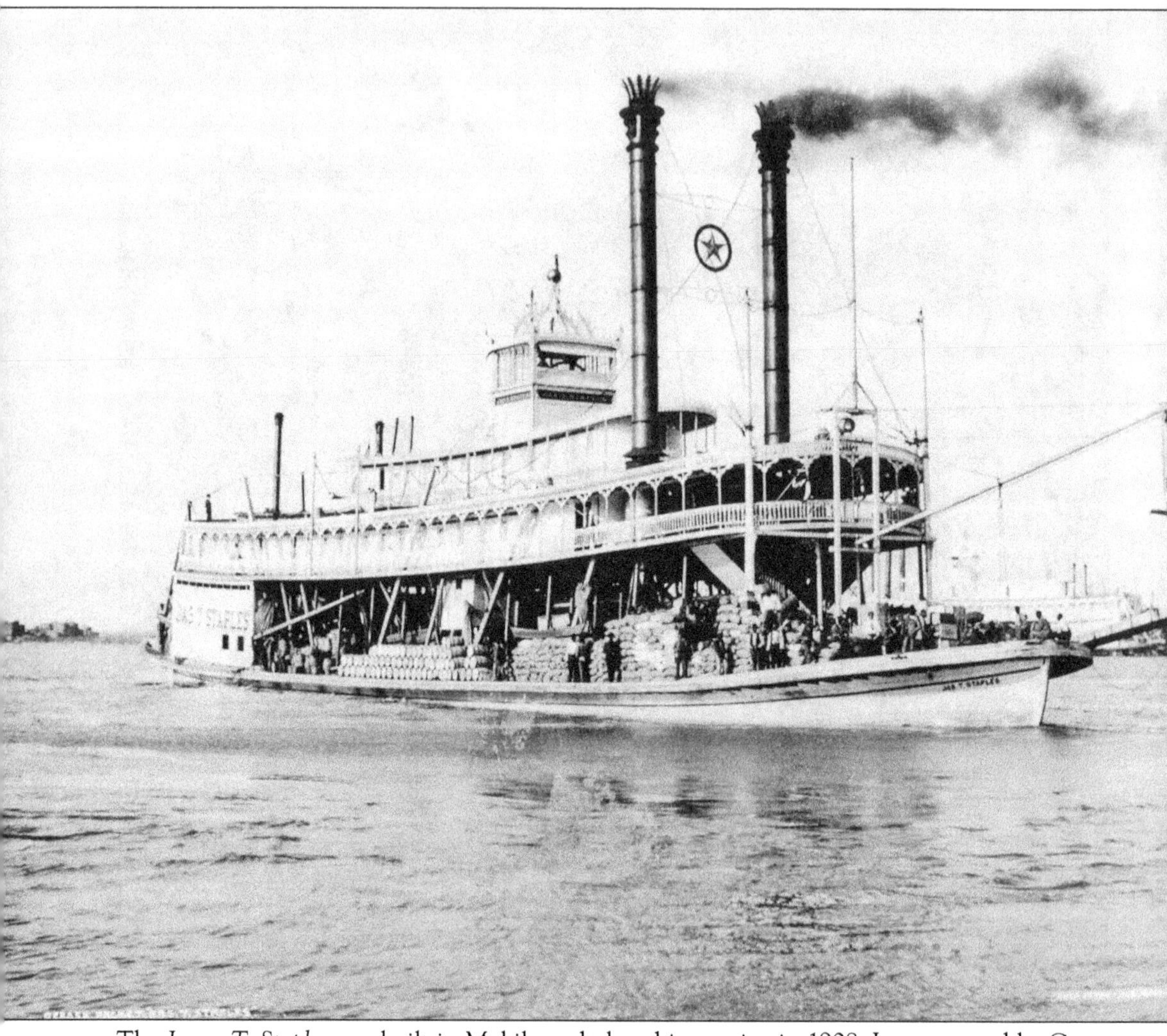

The *James T. Staples* was built in Mobile and placed in service in 1908. It was owned by Capt. Norman Staples and named after his father. The captain had problems with owning the boat since a steamboat company wanted to have a monopoly over all of Alabama's rivers. Creditors took possession of the ship in December 1912. Captain Staples struggled with the loss and committed suicide on January 2, 1913. The new crewmembers reported seeing the former captain still walking the ship after it was taken over. On January 13, 1913, when the ship was docked at Powe's Landing to take on wood, at the exact hour of the former captain's suicide, one of the boilers blew up, scalding the new captain and 25 others to death. The remains of the boat floated down the river and eventually sank. Norman Staples is buried in the Bladon Springs Cemetery. He has reportedly been seen lingering around the graves of his four children, James Alfred, Bertha Jaquetta, Mable Claire, and an unnamed baby.

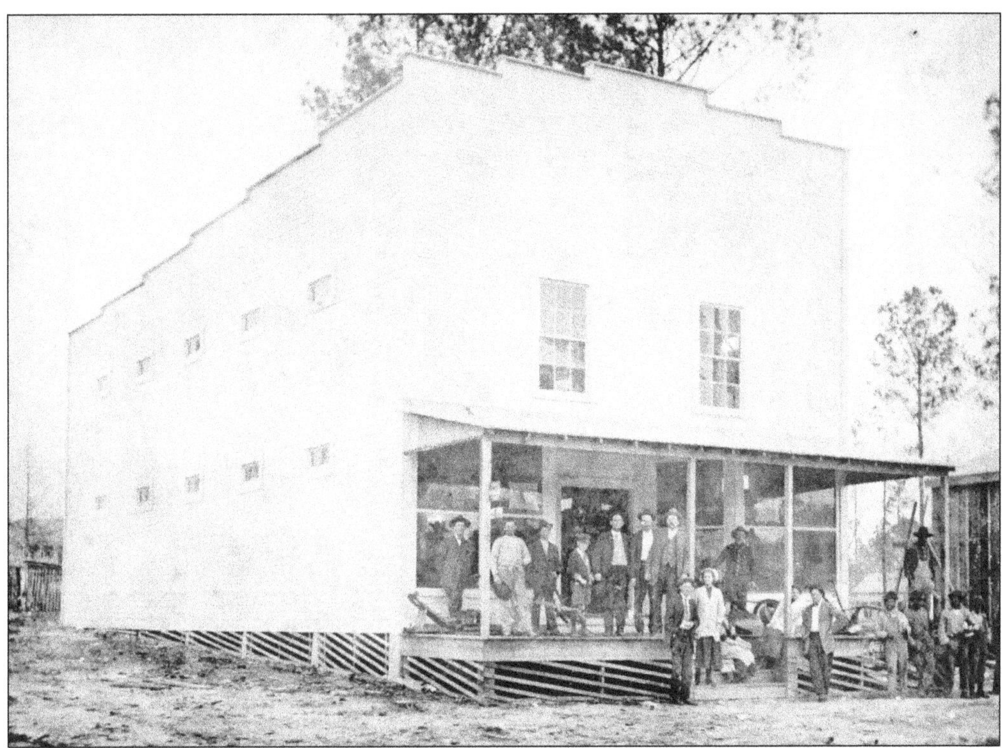

Pictured is an unidentified business that operated somewhere within Choctaw County. The location is not known, nor are the identities of the patrons gathered when this photograph was taken. Locals believe that the business was located in Gilbertown.

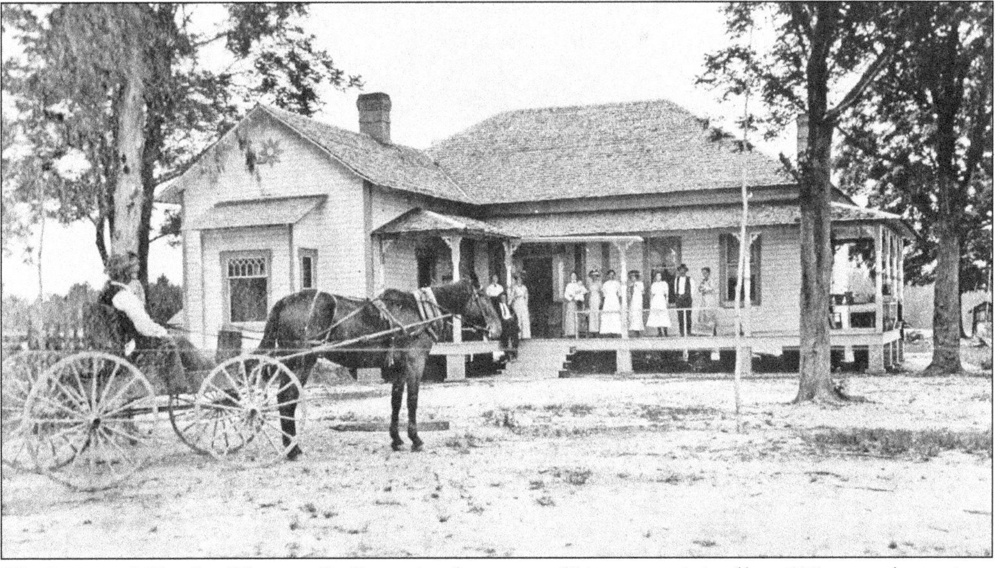

The home of Charles Thomas Ezell was in the town of Lisman, originally a 600-acre plantation. It was inherited by his wife, the former Rosa Anna Smith, from her father, Capt. David Smith of DeSotoville. He was born in 1845 and died in 1916. He fathered a large family, was a successful merchant and planter, and helped establish the town of Lisman. This photograph dates to around 1913.

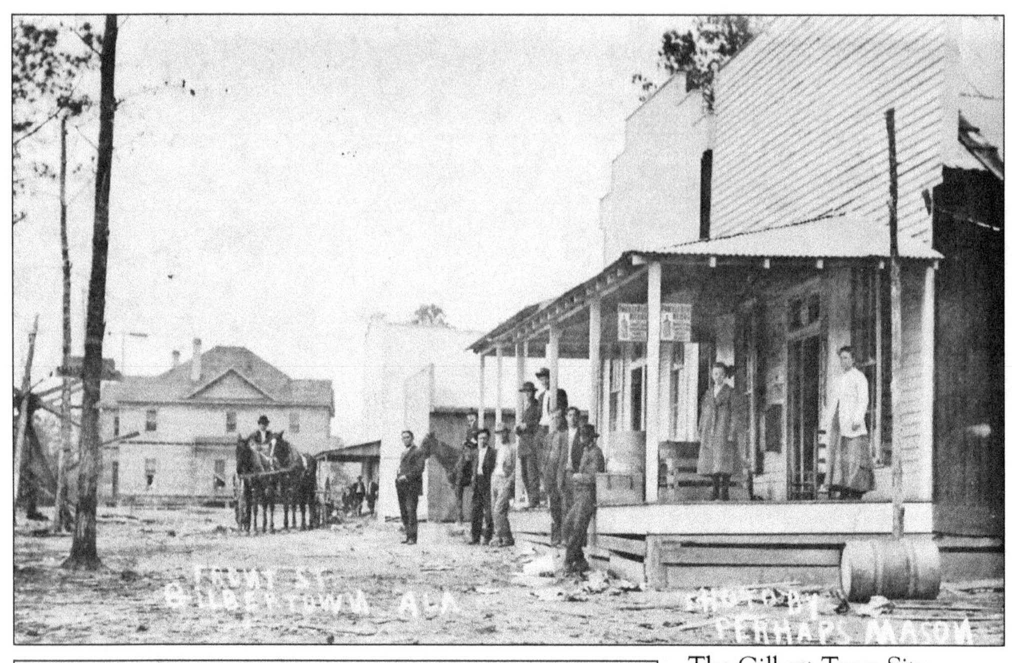

The Gilbert Town Site Company was formed in 1910 by Dr. Sam Alman, S.O. Rogers, and owners B.C. Smith, F.A. Adams, O.B. Gilbert, and Robert Land. Dr. Alman was selected as a manager and given a power of attorney to sell the lots. This postcard photograph shows a portion of Front Street in Gilbertown. It is postmarked April 15, 1912. This street is now part of Highway 17.

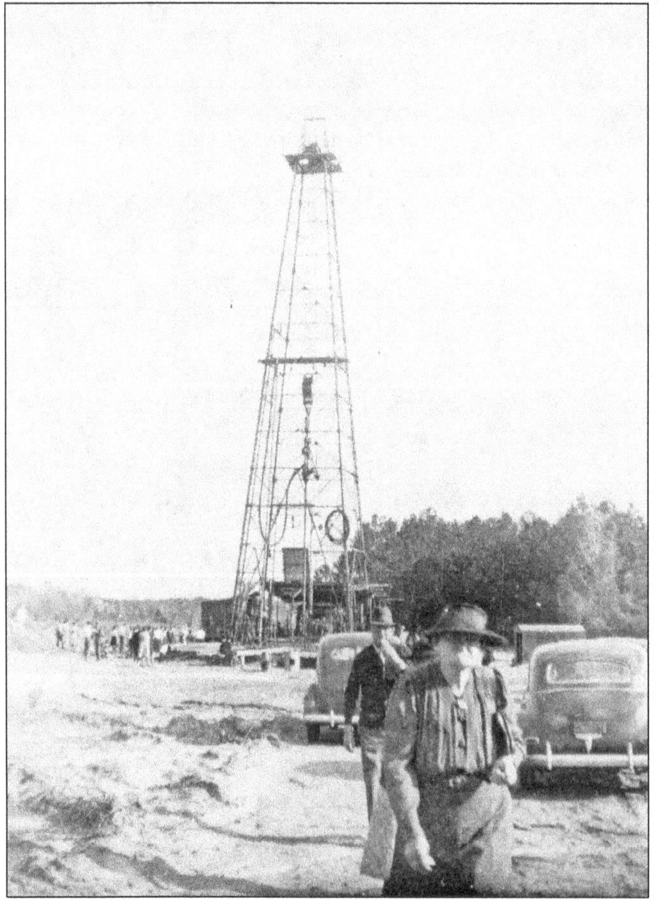

The State of Alabama granted Hunt Oil Company of Dallas, Texas, a permit to drill the A.R. Jackson Well No. 1 on his property west of Gilbertown. On February 12, 1944, drilling struck the Selma Chalk at 2,583 feet, encountering oil. This was the first producing oil well in the state. It produced 70 barrels of oil per day through 1961, when the well was plugged.

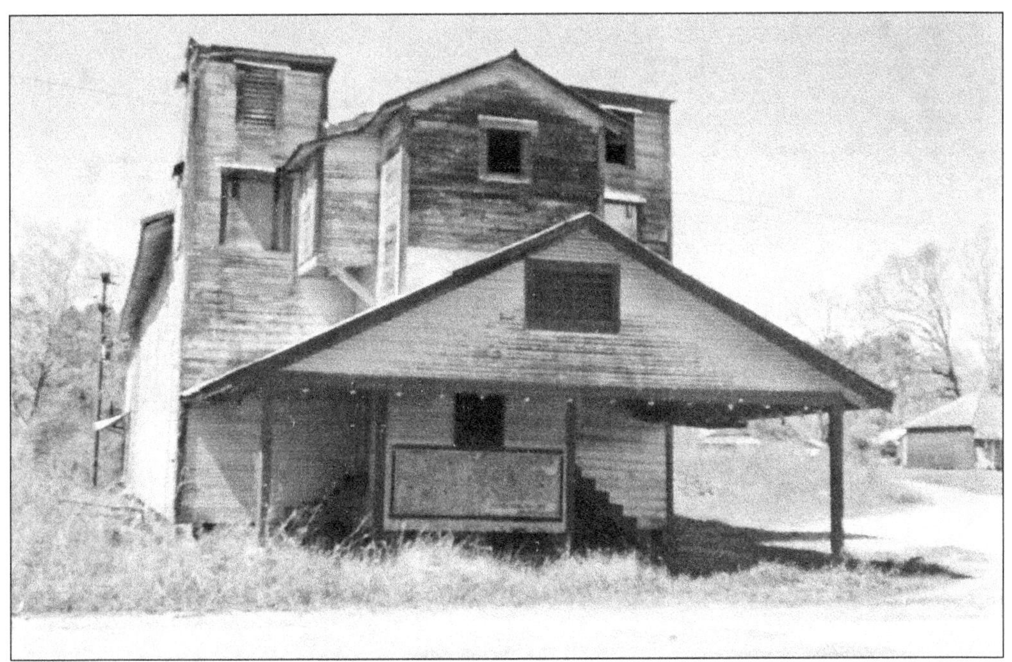

The Bolinger Theater was built by Sanford Henry Bolinger, who owned and operated the Choctaw Lumber Company. The sawmill town that adjoined the northern part of Silas became known as Bolinger. Reginald Stokley was the manager and projectionist in the 1930s and 1940s. The theater would seat about 750 people. It was torn down in late 1977 to early 1978.

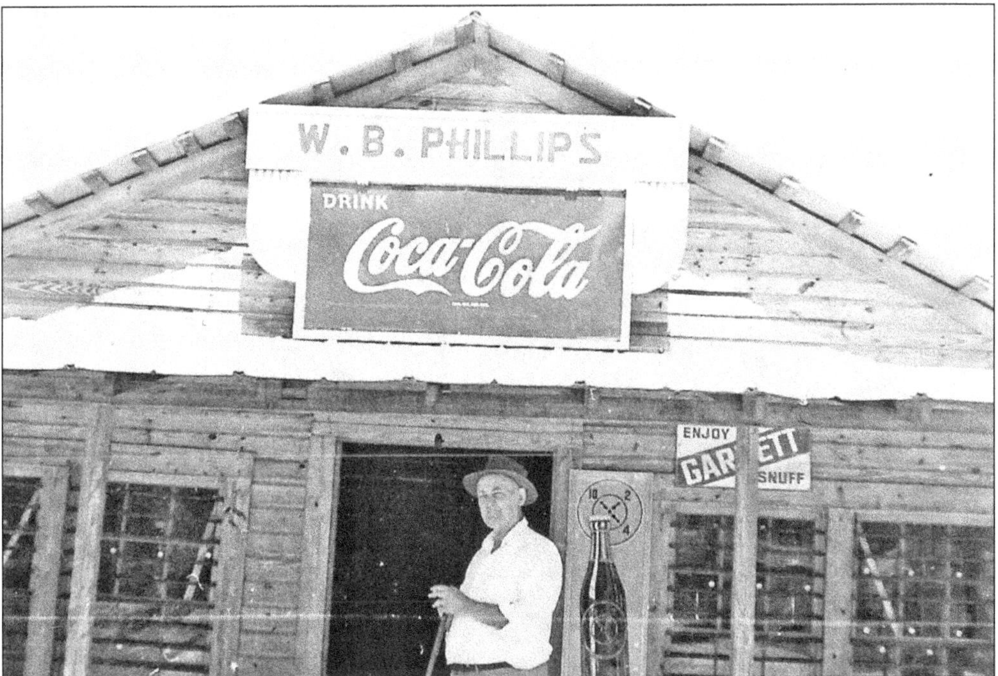

It is believed that the W.B. Phillips store was in or near Yantley. It was one of the many community stores that existed throughout the county. W.B. Phillips is shown on the porch. This photograph was developed in May 1947.

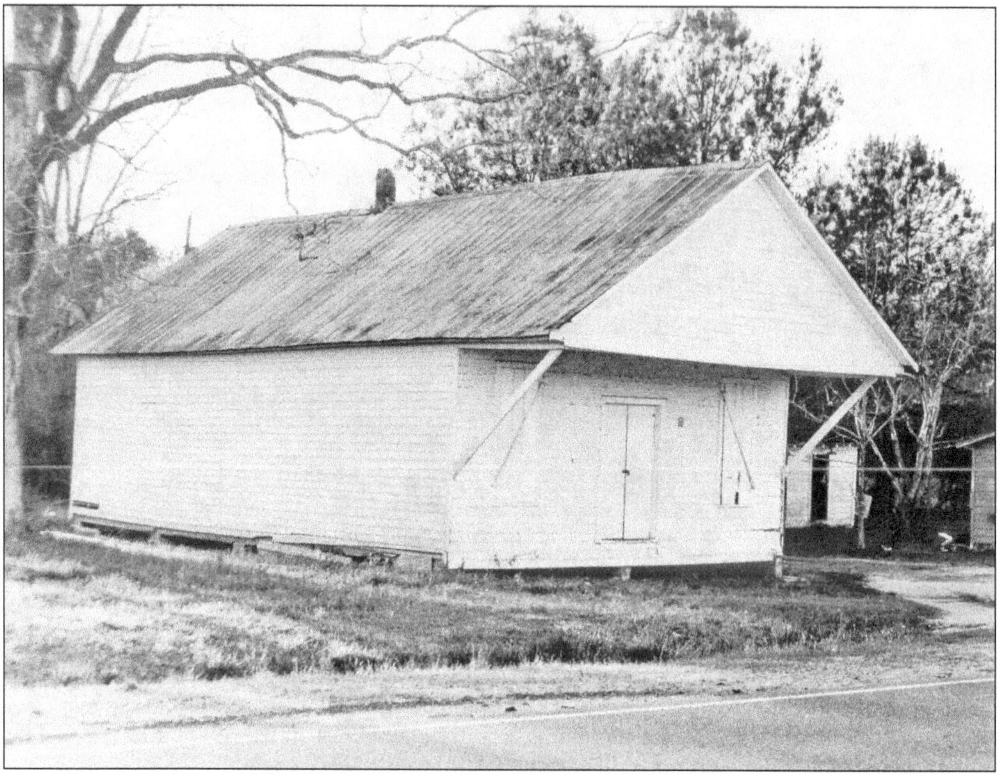

The old Wilcox store and post office was in Lavaca. Hamner C. Wilcox was appointed the postmaster on October 22, 1901. On April 18, 1908, William C. Tillman was appointed postmaster, and he held that position until August 10, 1923, when Hamner Wilcox was reappointed. Wilcox held the position until January 31, 1940; Hazel D. Wilcox was appointed on February 20, 1940.

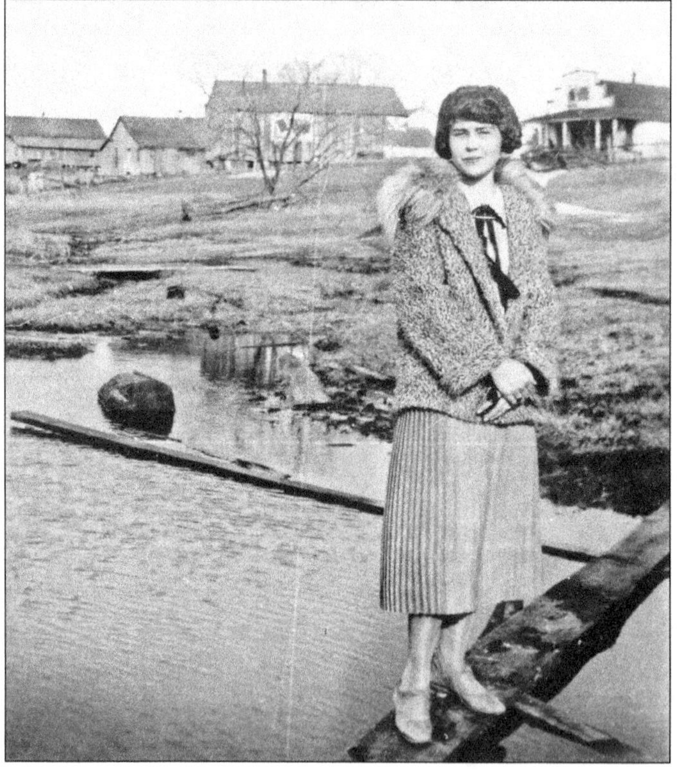

In the foreground of this photograph is Lois Martin. The Womack Hill community buildings behind her are, from left to right, the stores of Dr. T.R. Lenoir and W.S. Powe, the Cox store, and the M.H. Elliott store.

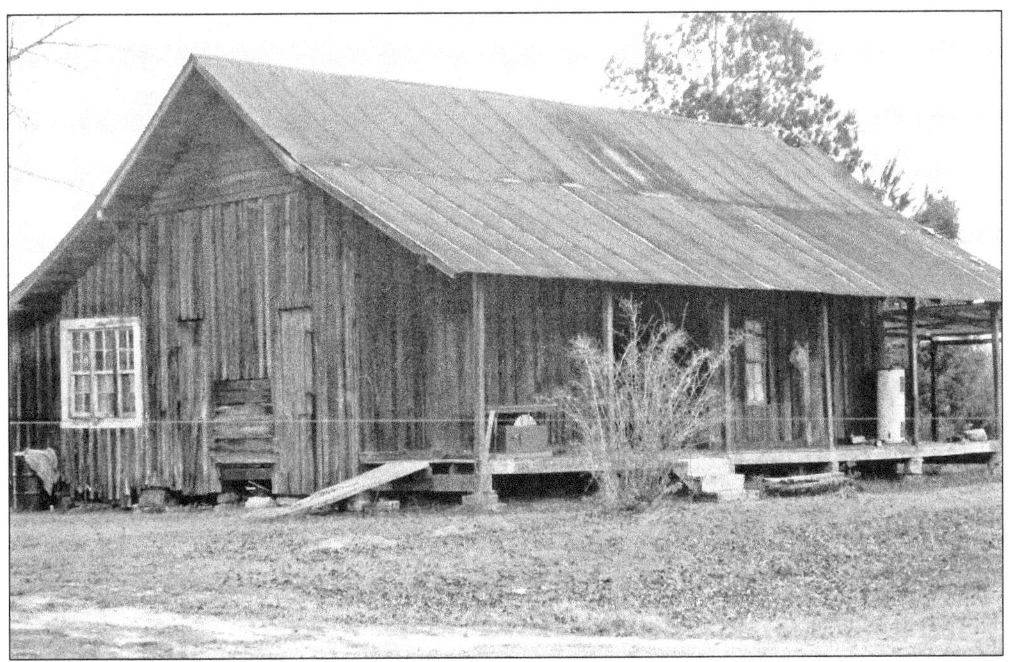

The Walter Felix Wilson dogtrot house was built around 1918. The dogtrot style represented the vast majority of early houses in the county. Walter was born on July 6, 1877, and died on April 10, 1957. He is buried in the Brightwater Cemetery. His first wife was Sallie Turner (1883–1902), and his second wife was Mary Loujean Land (1888–1952).

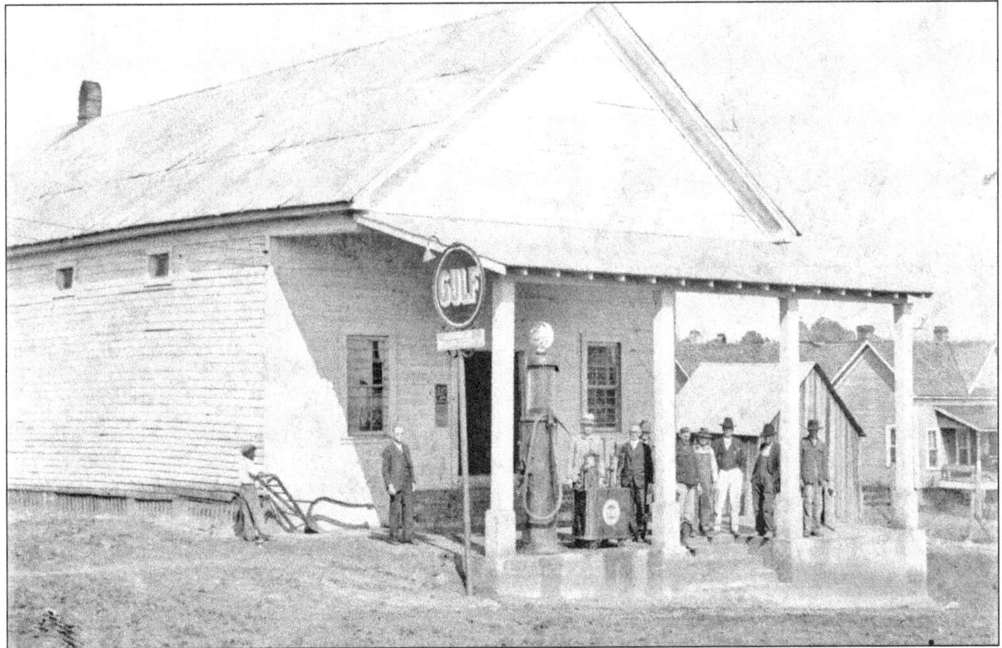

E.C. Robinson built Robinson's store on First Street in Silas in the late 1930s. It became McFadden's store in the 1950s, after the Robinsons retired and moved to Mobile. The store closed in the late 1960s or early 1970s, and the building was torn down in 2014. (Courtesy of Annie Ruth Hutchinson Schleth.)

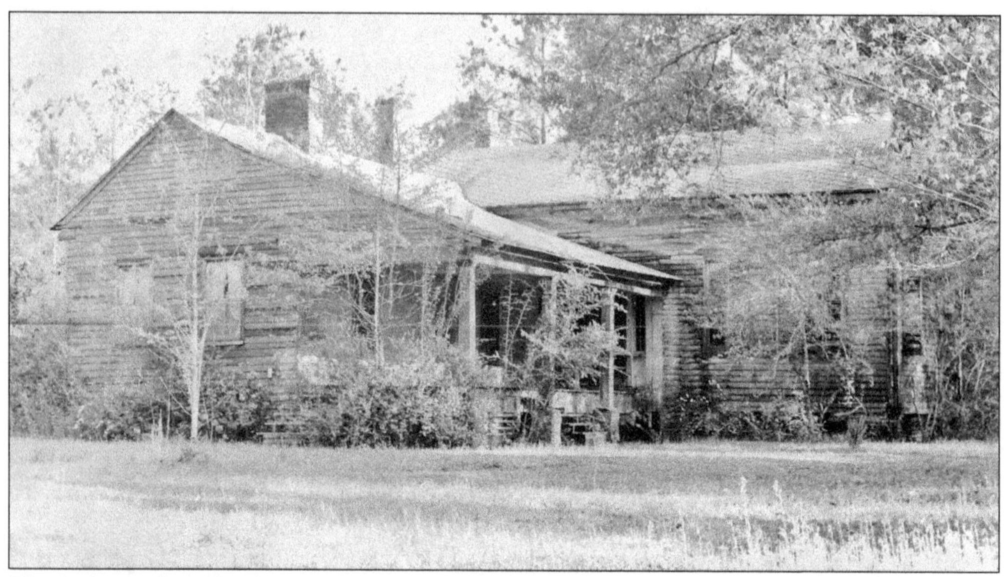

The Seth Smith Mellen home was in Mount Sterling. Professor Mellen came to Choctaw County in 1869 from the Goodman Institute at Pierces Springs, Mississippi. Professor Mellen supervised the Choctaw Male and Female Academy from 1869 to 1877. He used the English boarding system, in which the boys were housed in cabins and the girls boarded with residents around the village. This house was torn down in 1977.

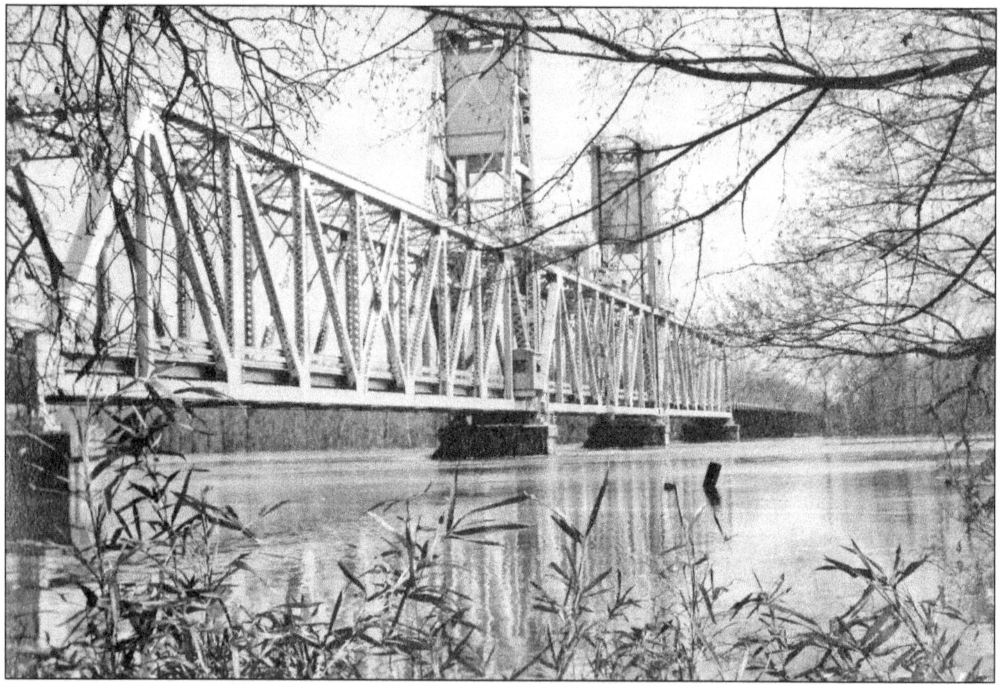

The old Naheola Bridge was near Marathon Southern Corporation in Naheola. It was shared by the Meridian and Bigbee railroad trains and by automobiles. A light regulated the traffic over the Tombigbee River drawbridge so trains and cars did not attempt to cross the one-lane bridge at the same time. A bridge tender was on duty 24 hours a day to make sure the light worked. (Courtesy of Choctaw County Public Library.)

The Butler Mountain fire tower was erected on 5.53 acres on Highway 17 south of Butler. The land was acquired by the Alabama Division of Forestry from Hollingsworth and Whitney on December 16, 1947. Six towers such as this stand 100 feet high at strategic points over Choctaw County. This tower is no longer in use. (Courtesy of Alabama Forestry Commission, Choctaw Office.)

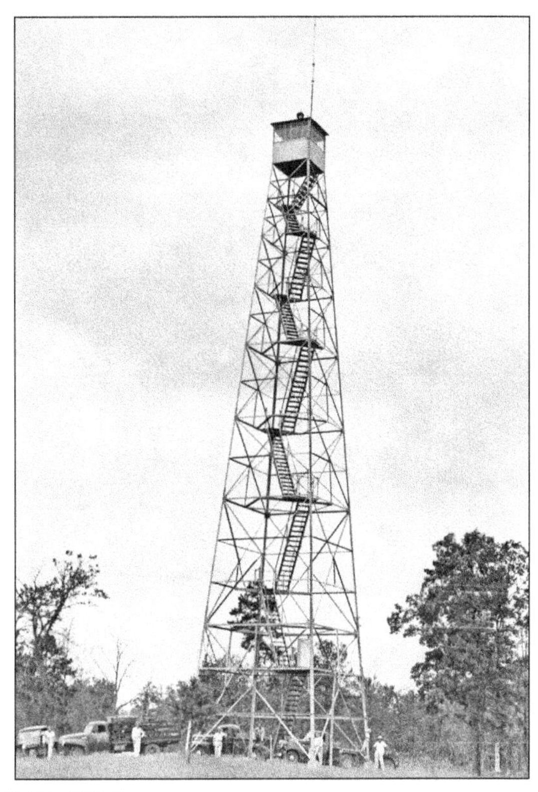

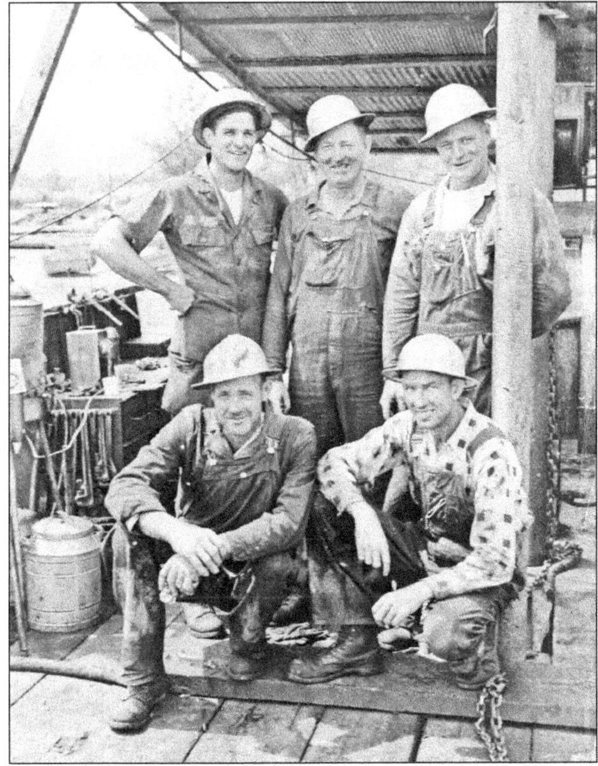

This oilfield crew worked for Hughes Tool Company in Choctaw County during the 1960s. From left to right are (first row) Tony Doggett and L.D. Weaver; (second row) Buddy Lassiter, Amos Kemp, and Max Doggett. The oil well business still played a large part in the Choctaw County economy during the 1960s.

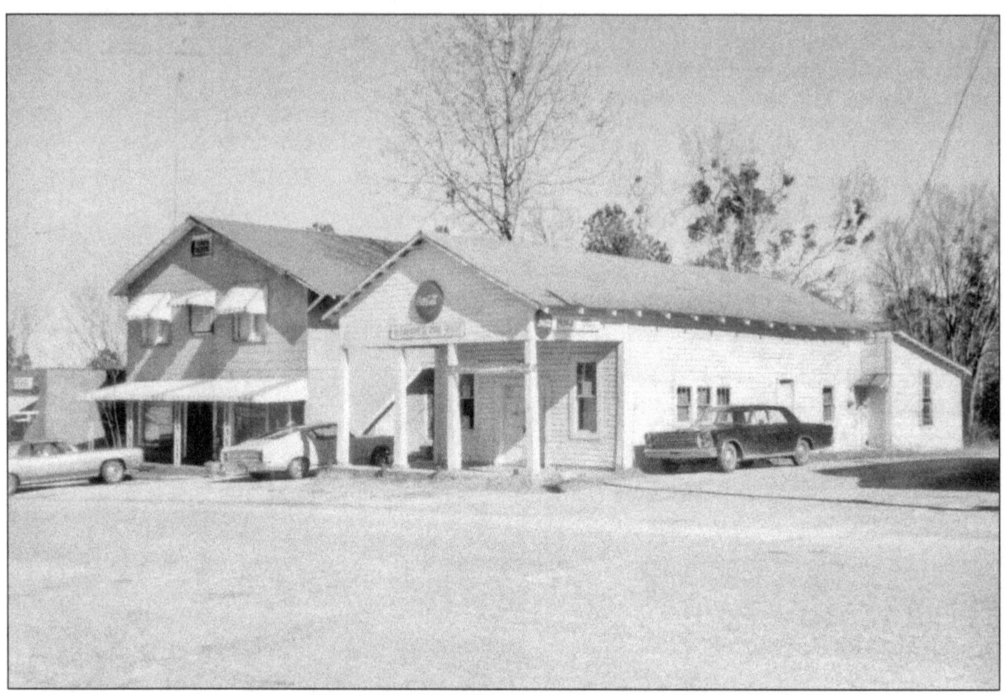

The town of Silas was the home of Odom's Hotel and Minor's Pool Hall. The hotel was owned and operated by Mallie and Almeda Odom. The pool hall was also owned by the Odoms but was operated by Dewey Minor during the late 1930s and early 1940s. The pool hall and hotel closed in the early 1950s. This photograph was taken around 1969.

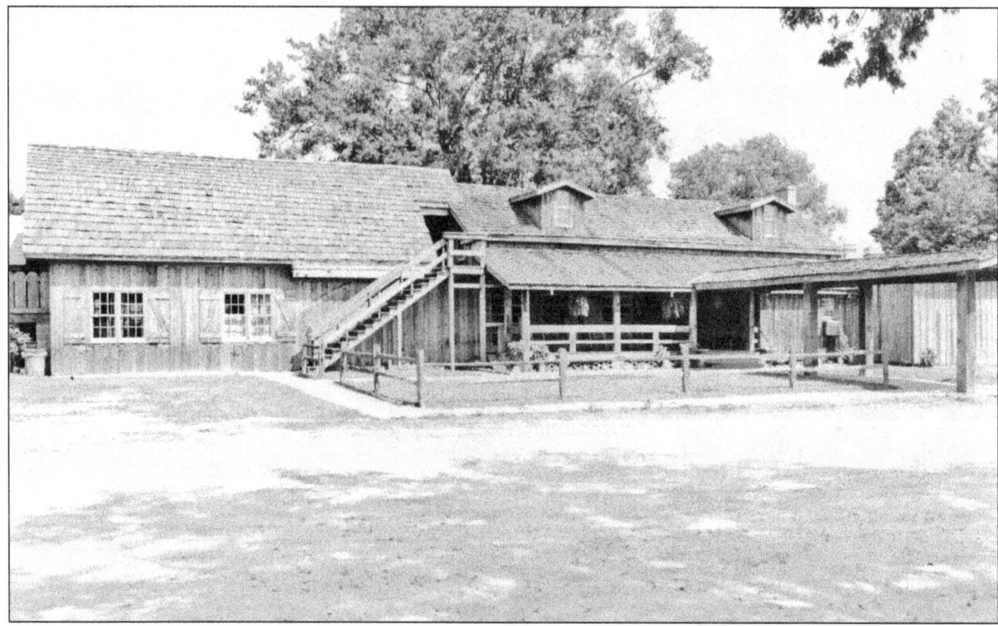

Ezell's Fish Camp restaurant is located off Highway 10 East in Lavaca. It is said to have been built by a French fur trapper over 200 years ago. The original part of the building was a crude log cabin that had two rooms and a wide hall. Charles Thomas Ezell bought it and gave it to his son Charles Agnew Ezell Sr. in 1905. The restaurant has become famous over the years for its catfish.

Three

BUSINESS AND COMMERCE

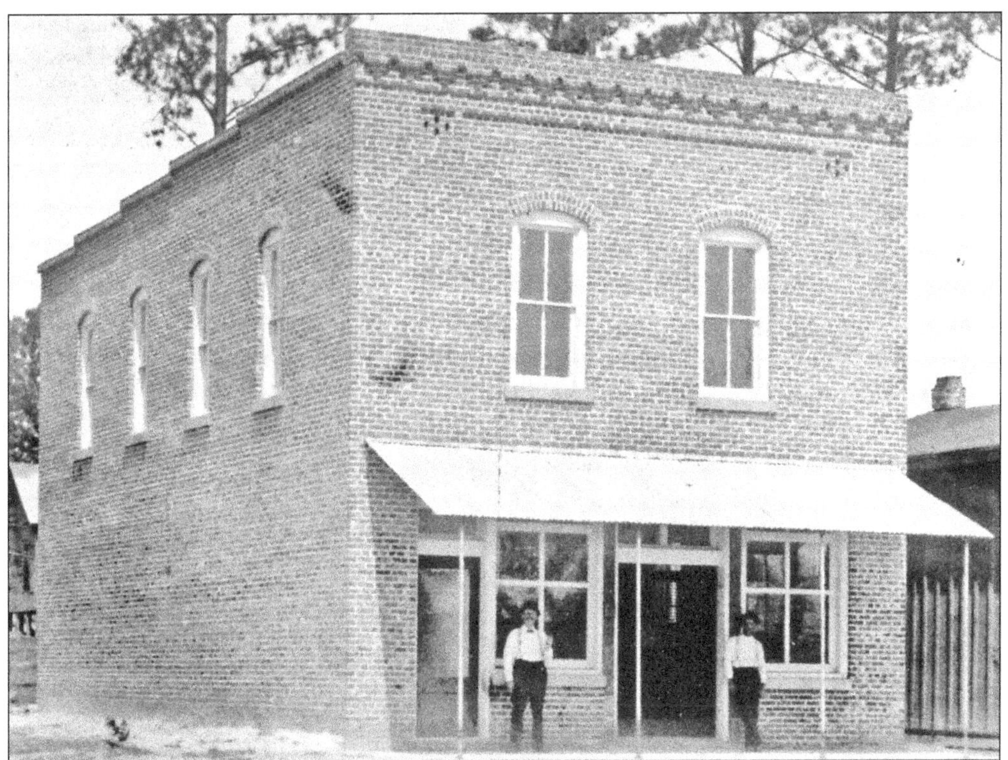

One of Choctaw County's first banks was the Citizens Bank and Trust Company. It operated from 1913 to 1917. After Citizens Bank closed, the building was occupied by the People's Bank of Gilbertown. The Gilbertown building these businesses occupied now houses the offices of Choctaw County's only newspaper, the *Choctaw Sun-Advocate*. (Courtesy of the *Choctaw Sun-Advocate*.)

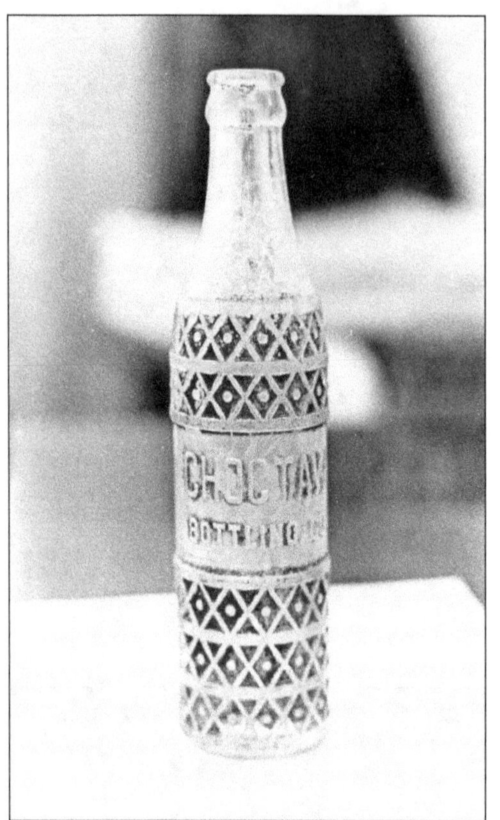

This bottle is one of a few remaining from the Choctaw Bottling Company. The company was started and owned by Dr. Sam Alman in Gilbertown. It operated from 1912 through 1917 as Choctaw Bottling Company. From 1917 to 1924, it operated as the Orange Crush Company, and from 1925 through 1930, it reverted back to Choctaw Bottling Company. The exact location in Gilbertown is not known.

Dr. Sam Alman opened the county's first automobile dealership in Gilbertown around 1916. It was a Ford dealership that was sold in 1921 to G.A. Rentz and G.L. Bonner and later became known as Gilbertown Motor Company. The original business closed in 1947. It was later reorganized and was in operation off and on until about 2010.

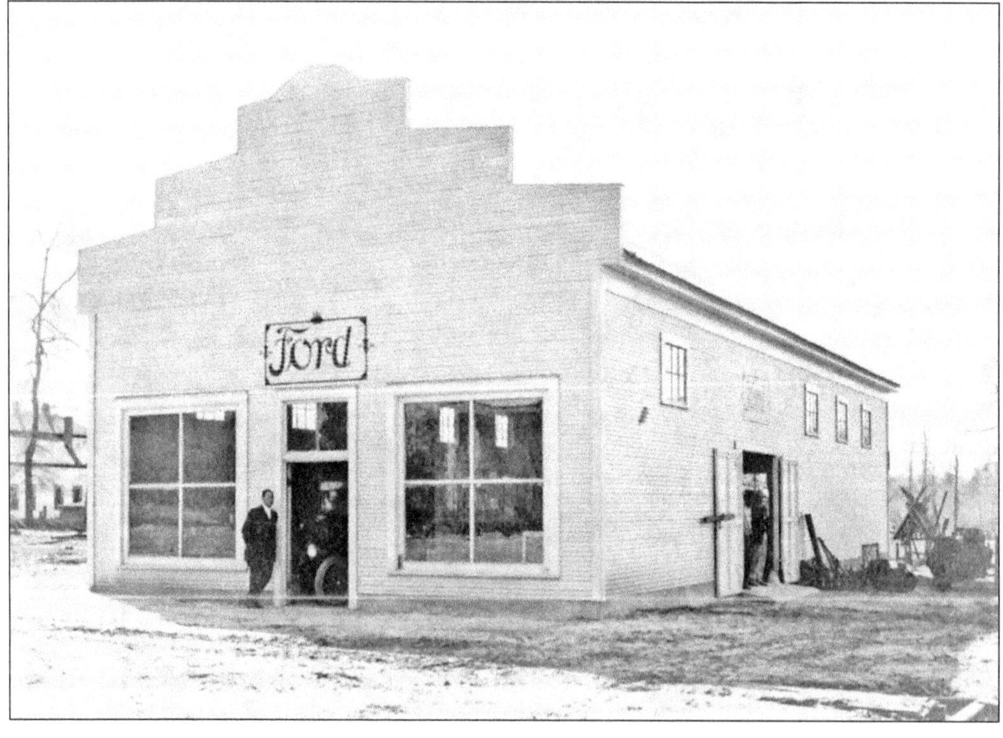

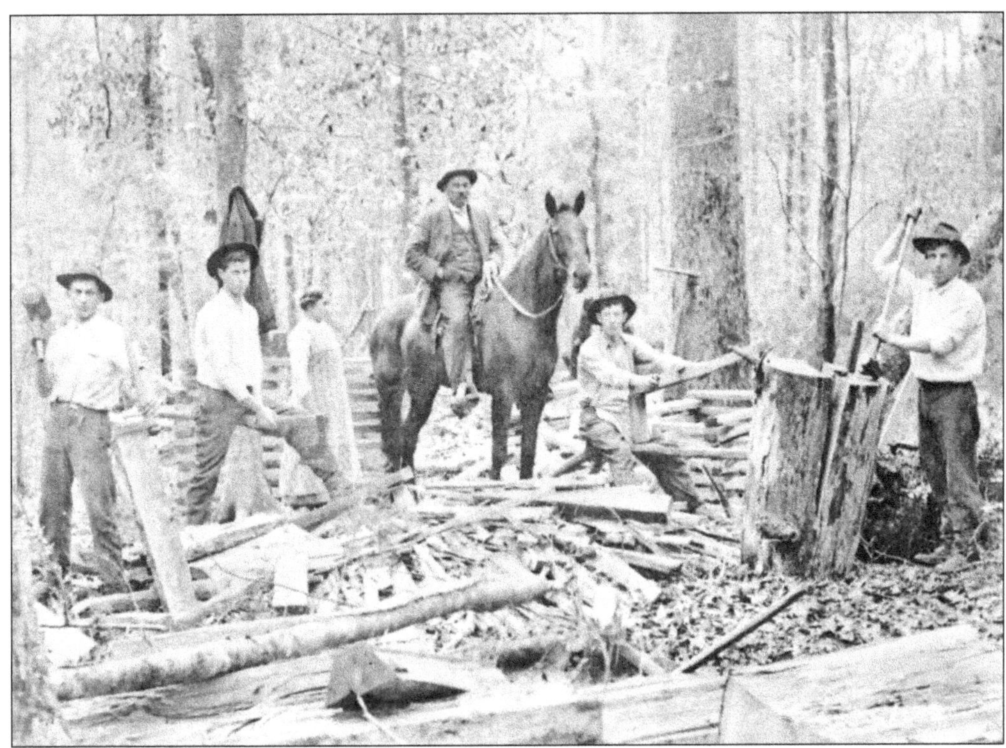

This crew cutting staves for barrels in southeast Choctaw County near the town of Toxey worked for Sam O. Rogers. From left to right are Tony Kovac, Joe Kovac, Amelia Kovac, Sam Rogers (on the horse), Matt Lusk, and John Stinich. Rogers was a local businessman in Gilbertown.

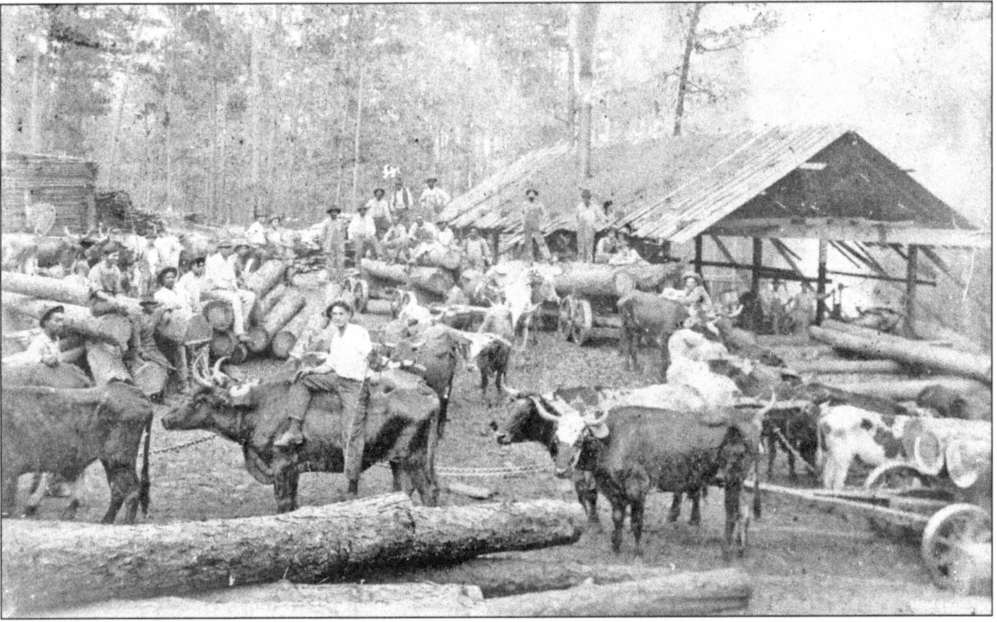

Pictured is one of the many unidentified sawmills that operated in Choctaw County. Logging has always been a large industry in the county. During the early to mid-1900s, there were approximately 50 sawmills in the county.

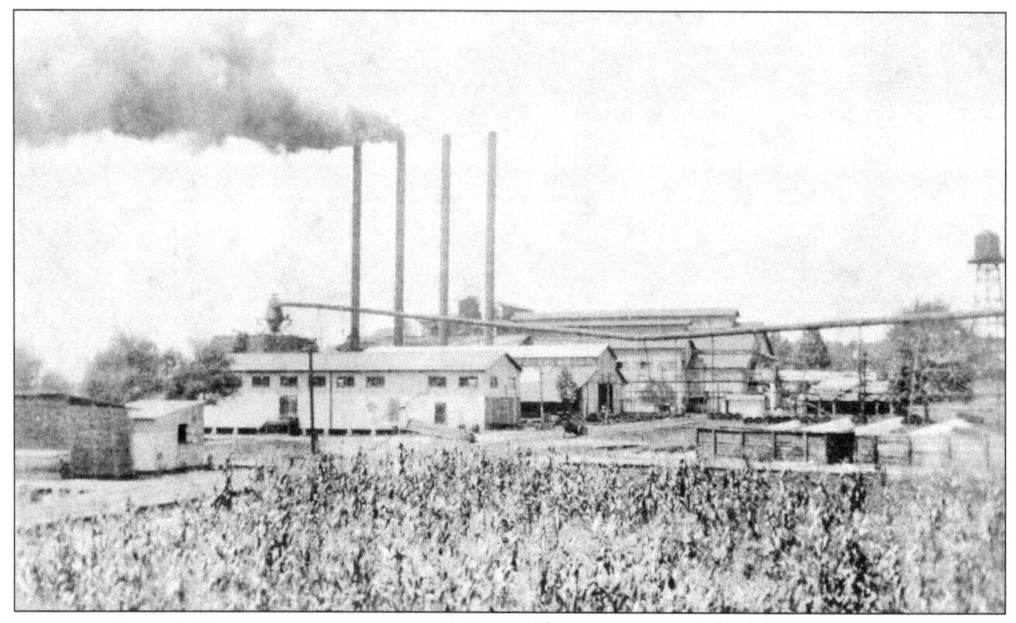

Shown is one of the buildings of the E.E. Jackson Lumber Company, which was in Riderwood during the 1920s to the 1930s. It was the largest employer in the county. It had its own commissary, hotel, and baseball team. The company also built its own church, the Riderwood Church. In its heyday, the lumber company employed approximately 1,500 people.

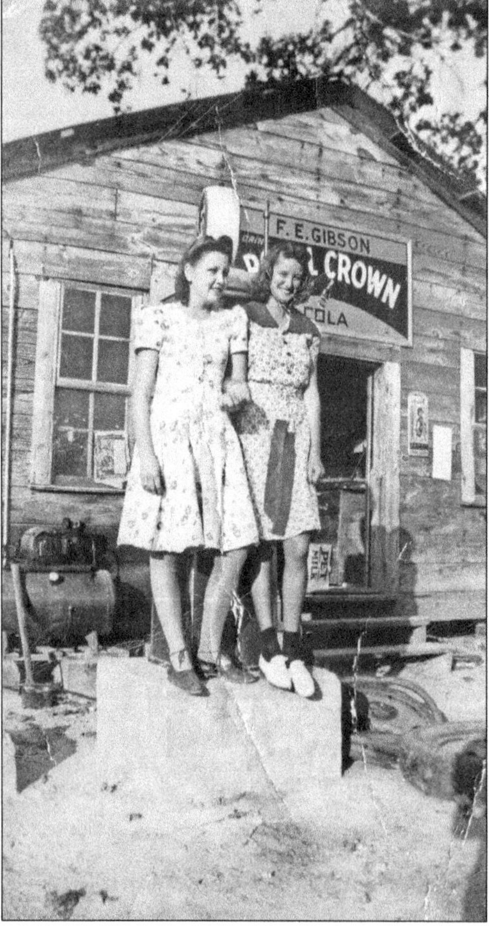

These two young ladies stopped to have their picture taken outside a local store. Mildred McIlwain (right) and an unidentified friend stand in front of the Frank E. Gibson store in Barrytown in the 1940s. (Courtesy of Linda Pittman Mosley.)

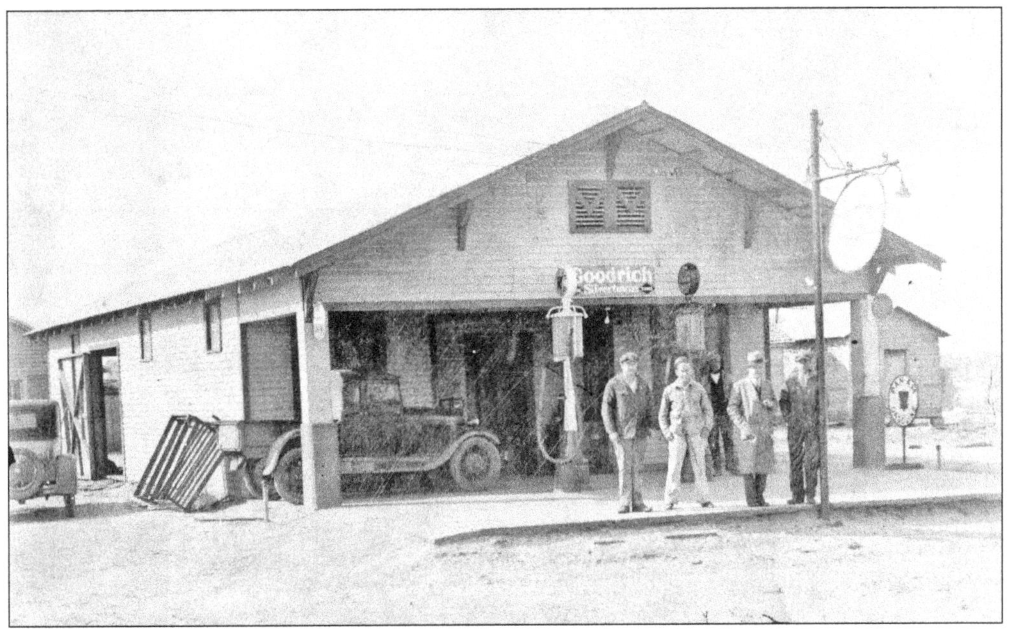

The M.T. Ezell garage was near the current US Post Office in downtown Lisman.

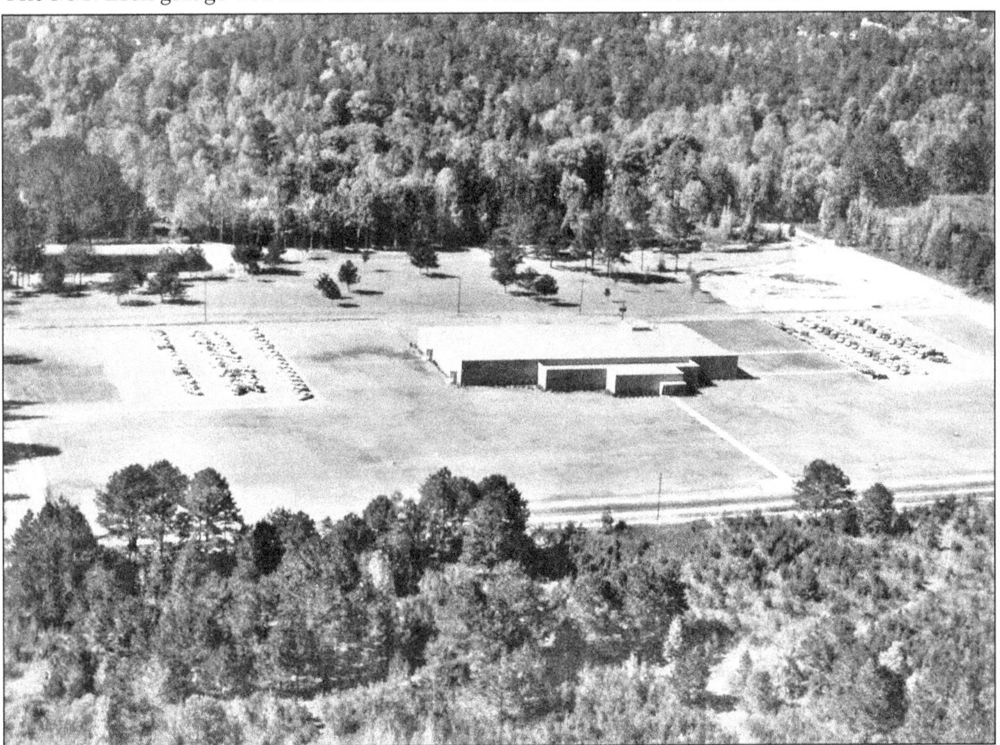

In 1959, members of the local industrial development board met with officials of Vanity Fair at the proposed site of a new business in Butler. When Choctaw Mills/Vanity Fair began operations in Butler on February 6, 1961, the building was 35,000 square feet, housed over 250 sewing machines, and provided 300 jobs. The company announced in October 1995 that the plant in Butler would close in 1996.

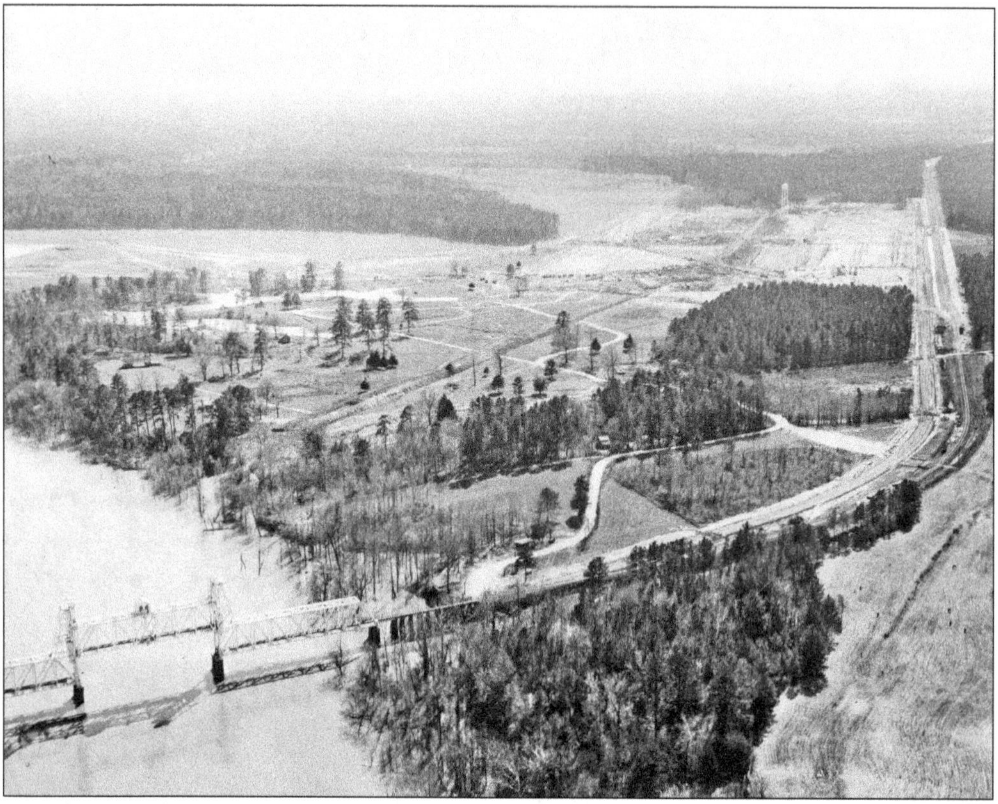

Marathon Southern Corporation announced in August 1955 that the company was building a plant on the Tombigbee River at Naheola. The company purchased 100 acres. This photograph shows an aerial view of the future building site of their paper mill at Naheola. At left is the old Naheola Bridge. (Courtesy of Choctaw County Historical Society.)

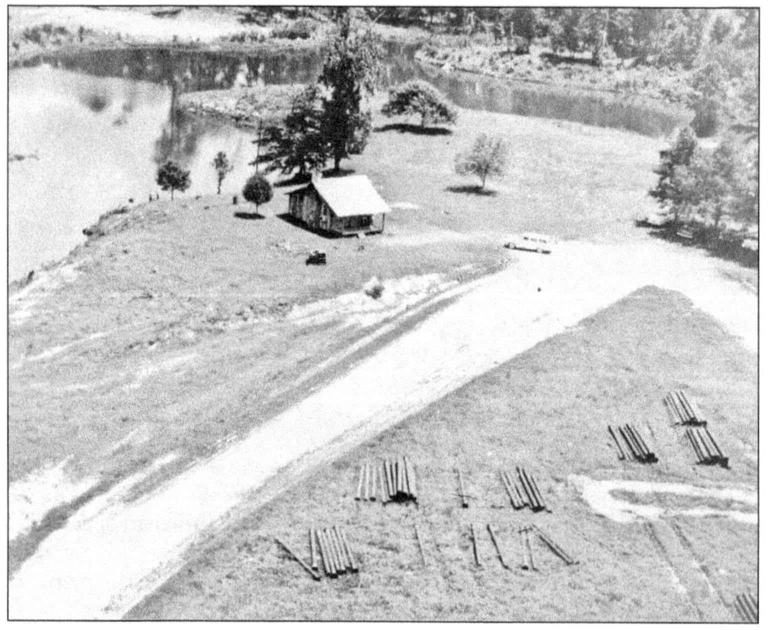

This aerial view of the Marathon Southern Corporation site at Naheola shows the original field office with the lake in the background in 1957. (Courtesy of Choctaw County Historical Society.)

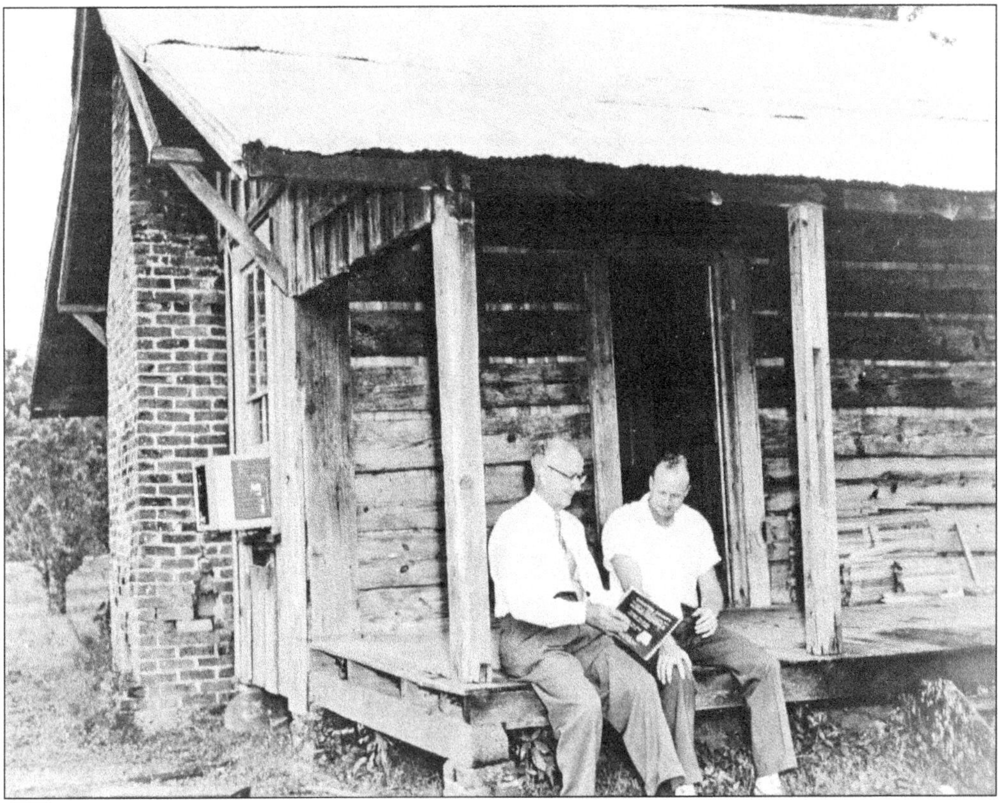

Pictured are Harry Gochnauer (left), chief engineer with Marathon Southern Corporation, and Fred M. Martin Sr. of CRS Sirrine in 1957 at the original field office in Naheola. At this site, the companies initially installed a paper machine, recovery boiler, and power boiler. Sirrine did the site selection and engineering. (Courtesy of Choctaw County Historical Society.)

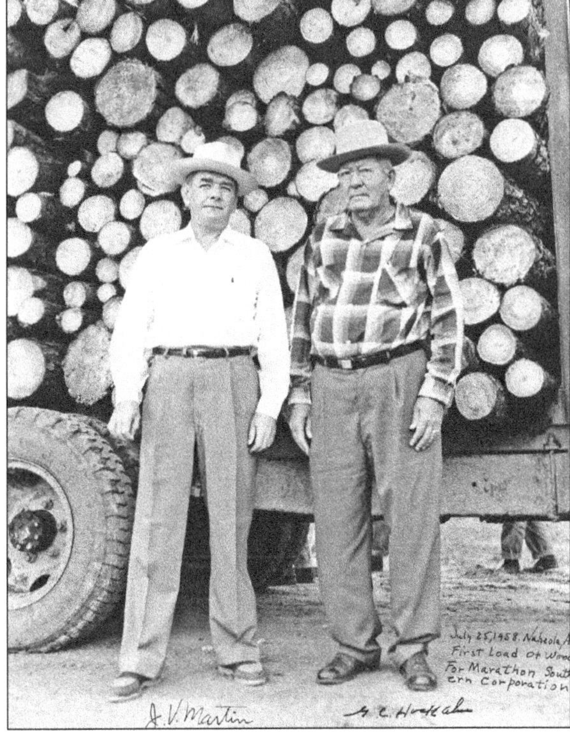

The first load of wood for Marathon Southern Corporation's new Naheola plant in Pennington was delivered on July 25, 1958. Pictured are J.V. Martin (left) and G.C. Huckabee. The paper mill relied heavily on the individuals who made their living in the logging industry. (Courtesy of Choctaw County Public Library.)

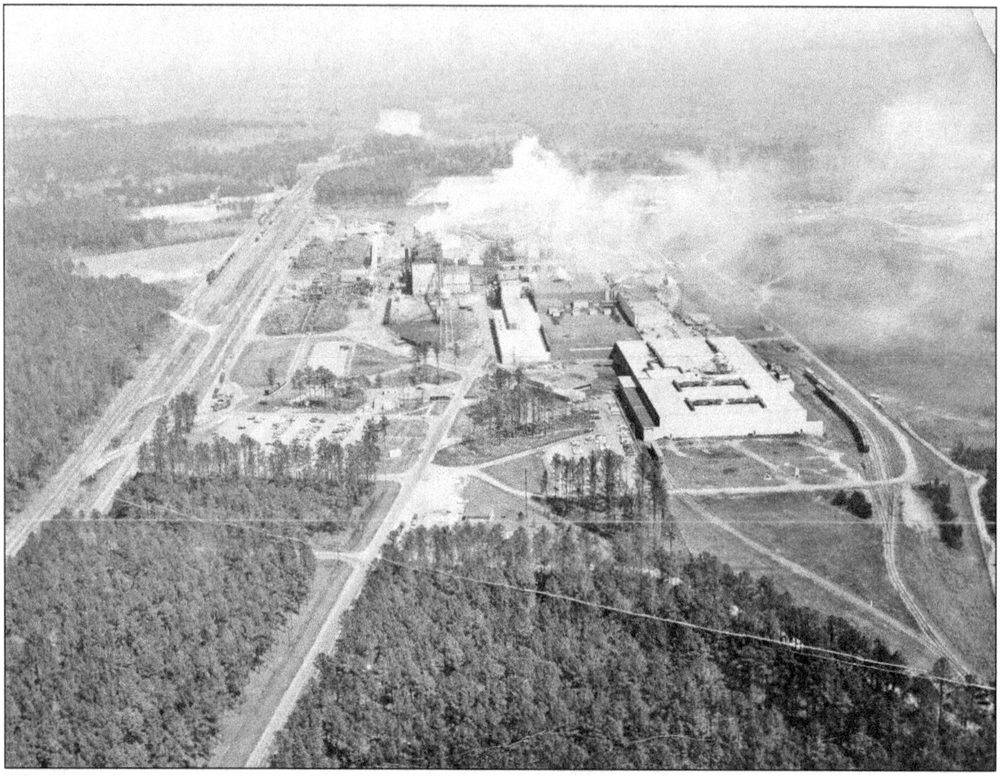

This aerial view shows the Naheola Mill (originally Marathon Southern, a division of American Can) in the mid-1960s, after the new scale house was opened. Throughout the years, the mill was also owned by James River Corporation and Fort James Corporation. It is now owned and operated by Georgia Pacific.

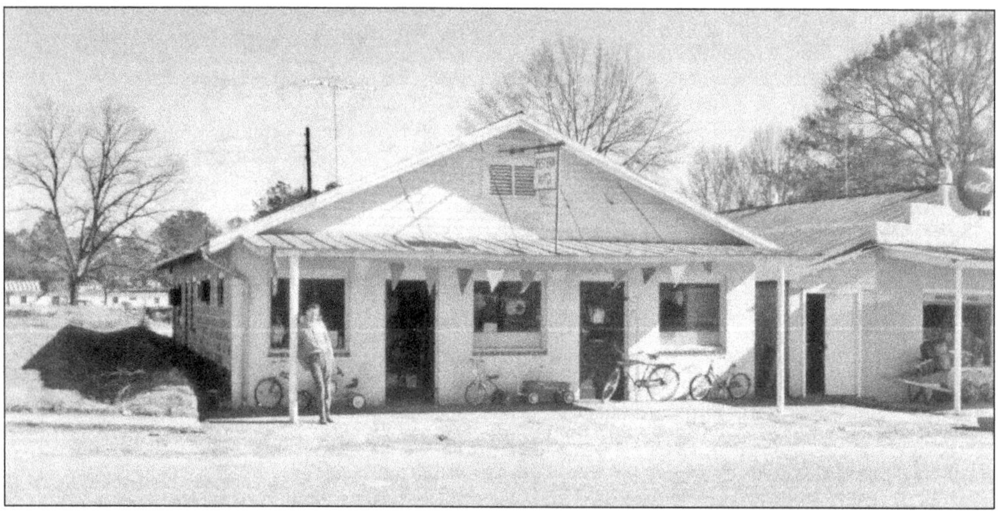

The original building of this business burned down and a new building was constructed in 1948. It was originally Dale's Grocery, run by Asia Cecil DuBose and his son Zack Izar. The business was split into a grocery, bar, barbershop, shoe store, and beauty salon, which were rented out. After Asia's death, the building was rented to Giles Food Store. It changed to a franchise of Western Auto around 1969, as seen here.

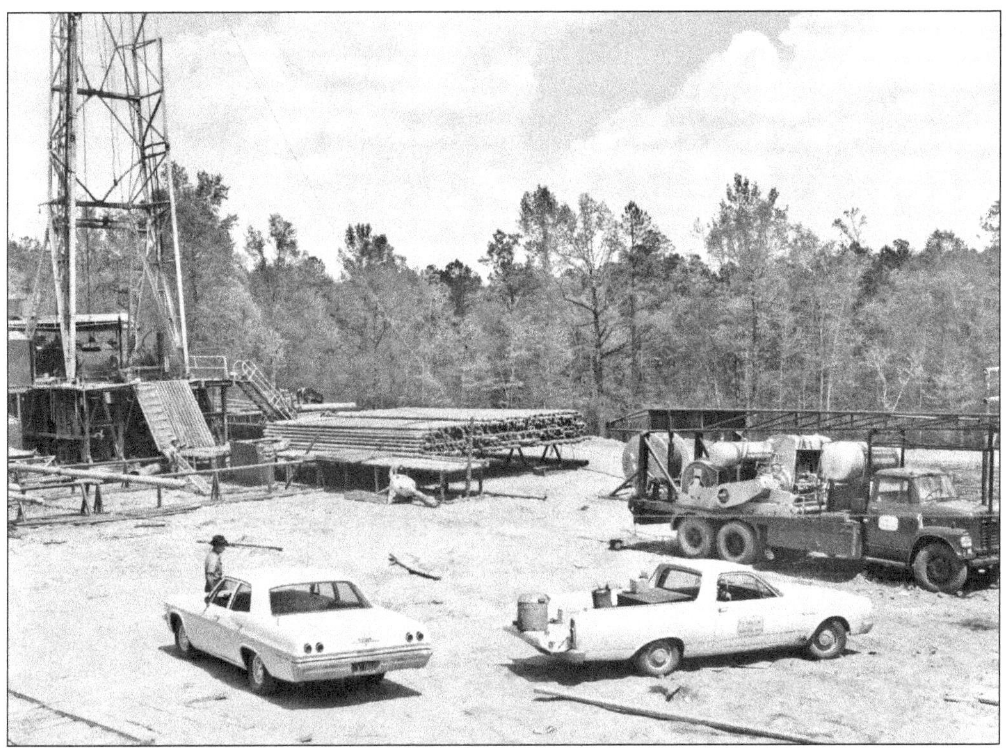
The Toxey Oil Field in Choctaw County was discovered in 1967 by E.L. Erickson. This photograph shows the discovery well, the Scott Paper Company–S.H. Bolinger 4-8 Well. The oil industry was at its peak in the county in the 1960s.

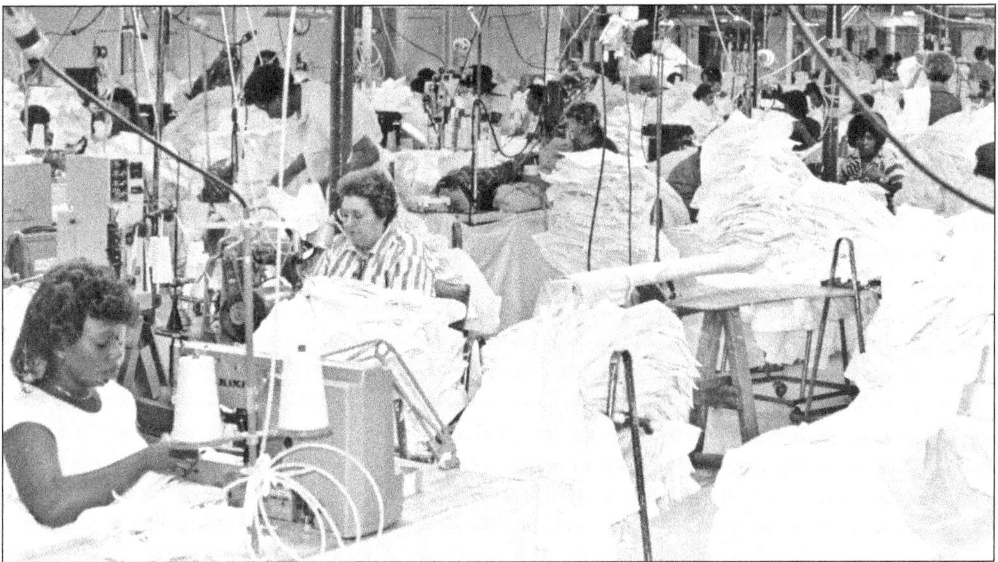
Choctaw Manufacturing Company was in Silas. This photograph shows some workers inside the facility. The 40,000-square-foot plant manufactured military wear. The white uniform used by the US Navy was 95 percent of its product. The plant also made camouflage clothing. In May 1997, it announced it was closing because it did not have any contracts to continue operation. The company had been in operation for 50 years prior to the announcement.

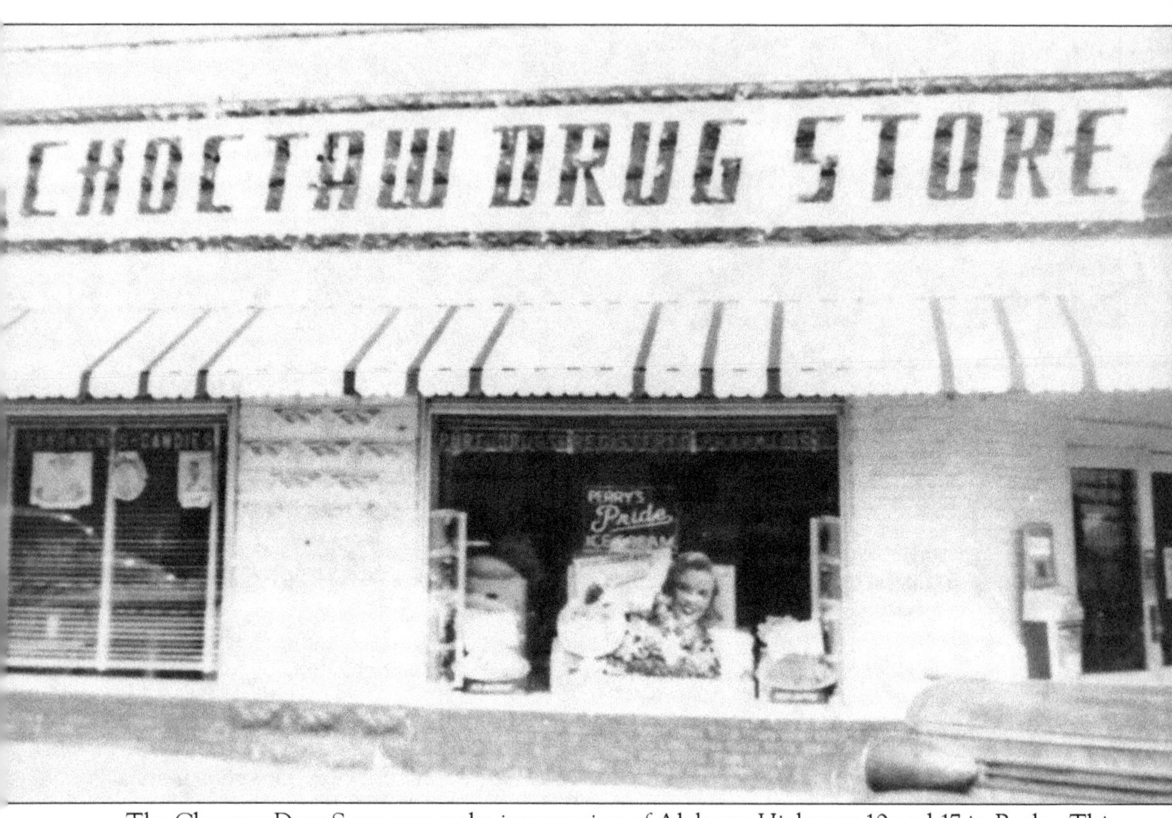

The Choctaw Drug Store was at the intersection of Alabama Highways 10 and 17 in Butler. This photograph was taken in 1951 by Joan Thompson Kelley. She had received a camera that year and was experimenting with it. This building now houses the Verizon Wireless store. (Courtesy of Joan Thompson Kelley.)

Four

SCHOOLS

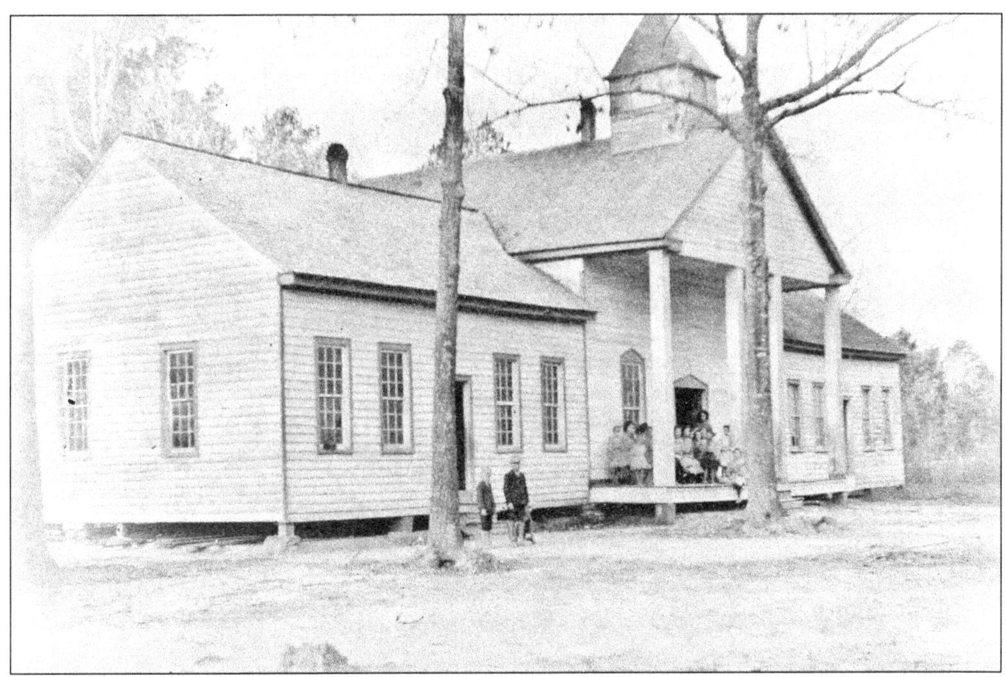

The West Alabama Male and Female Institute at Yantley lasted into the 20th century. Advertisements by the trustees of the school appeared in newspapers as early as February 17, 1851. It attracted boarding students from Mississippi as well as locations in Choctaw County. The principal was John David Phillips. The school was later consolidated with Butler by sending the upper grades there first. The lower grades were later moved to Lisman.

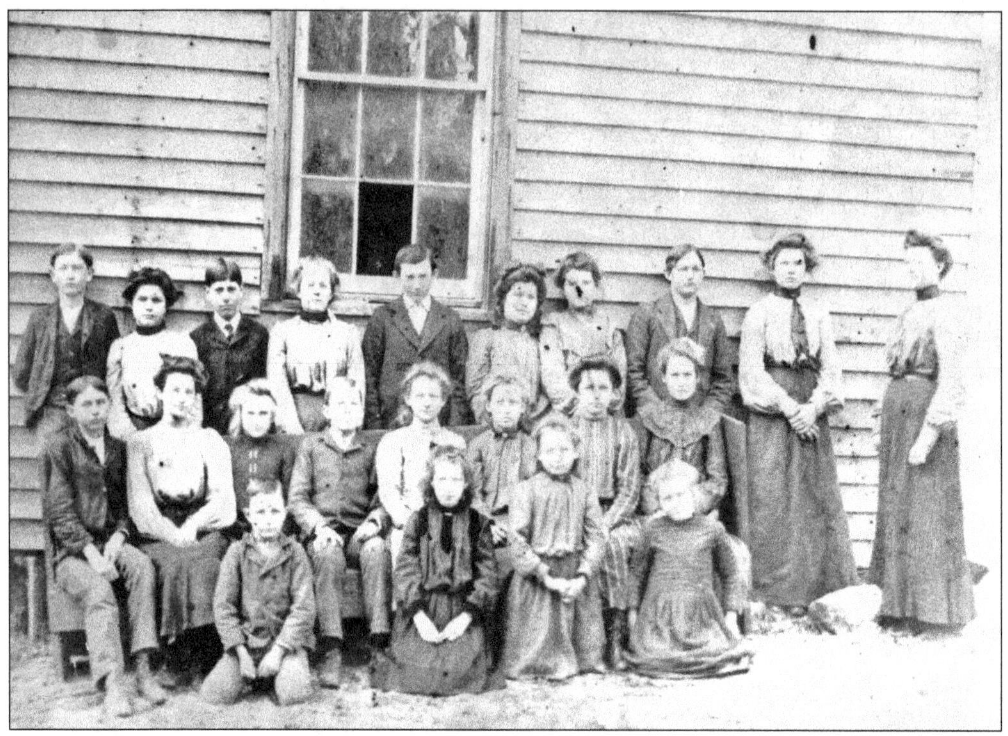

The Womack Hill School class of 1904 is pictured here. From left to right are (first row) John Wimberley, Eula Powe, Geneva Gibson, and Laura Gibson; (second row) Willie Sims, Nora Lee Daniels, Maude Cox, Clarence Elliott, Willie Elliott, Maggie Wimberley, Nettie Wimberley, and Winnie Mills; (third row) Tom Sims, Lucy Martin, John Edwards, Sadie Ray Martin, Bob Sims, Alma Martin, Virgie Odom, Cephus Odom, Anna Martin, and teacher Rena Sims.

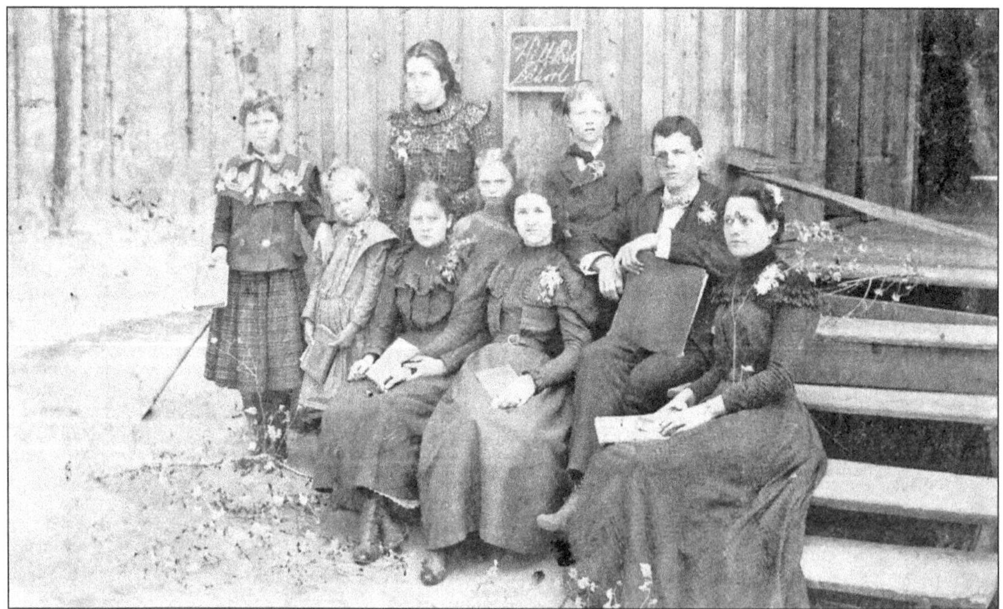

A small group of students from the Hillside School gathers for a picture. The location of this school is not known. The second girl from the left in the first row is Mary Wesley Whitted.

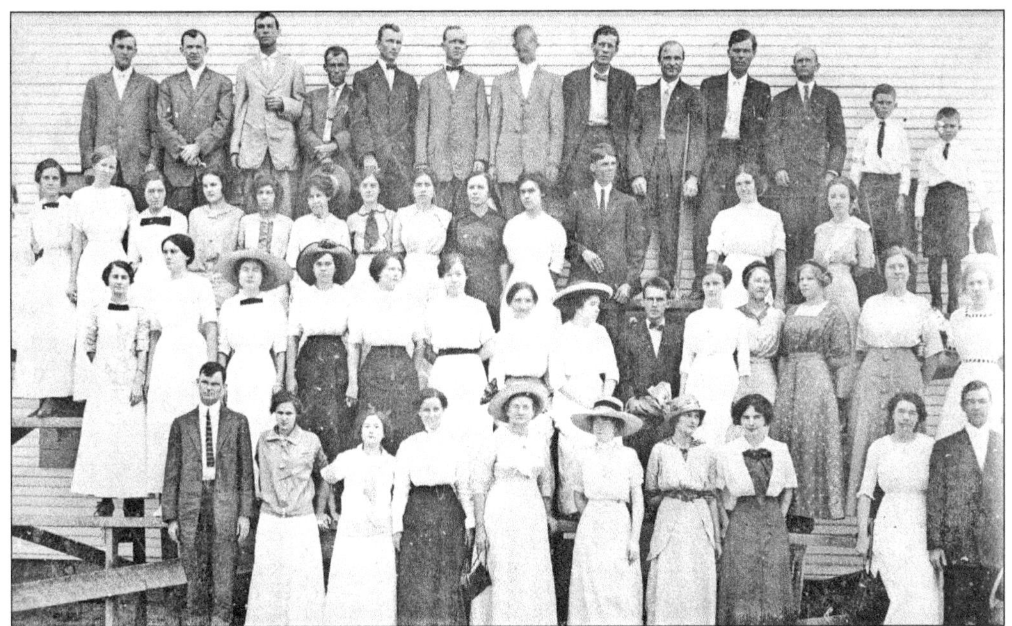

A large group of Choctaw County teachers gathers for a meeting around 1913.

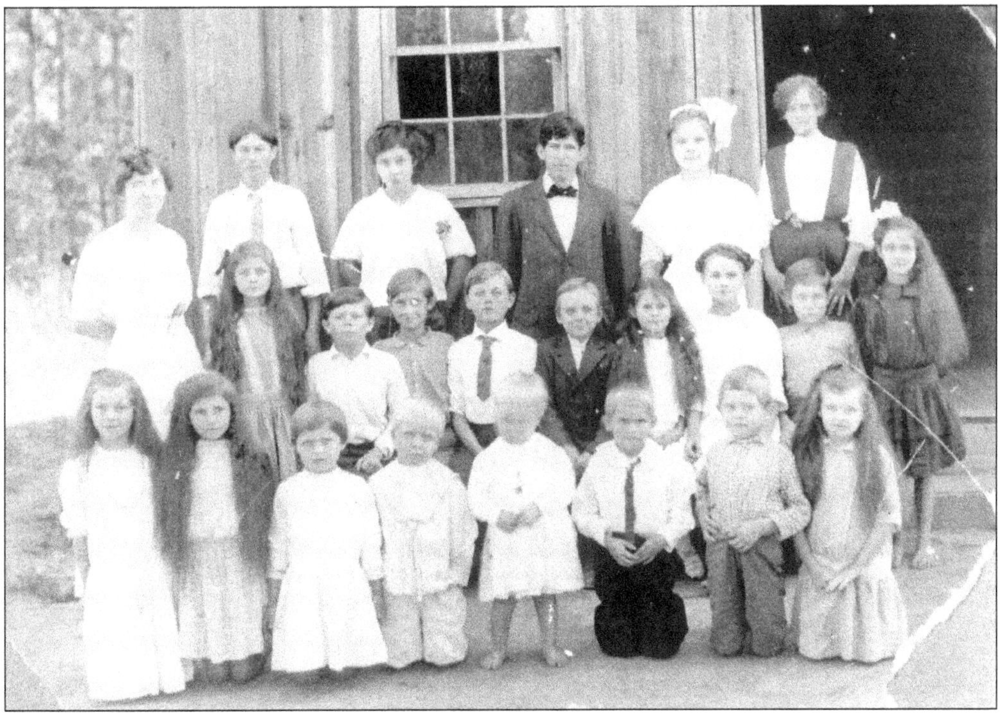

The Hurricane School was located between Melvin and Isney. From left to right are (first row) Ruby Evans, Lula Daugherty, Alma Evans, Roy Donald, Rex Donald, Claude Daugherty, Gilbert Evans, and Daisy McAdams; (second row) Katie McInnis, Jack Evans, Ira Davis, Lester McInnis, Sid Donald, Lola Daugherty, Estelle McInnis, Roshier David, and Agnes Evans; (third row) Eula Dubose (teacher), Audrey McInnis, Eric Davis, Lonnie McAdams, Leila Donald, and Nolie Daugherty. This photograph is from around 1912.

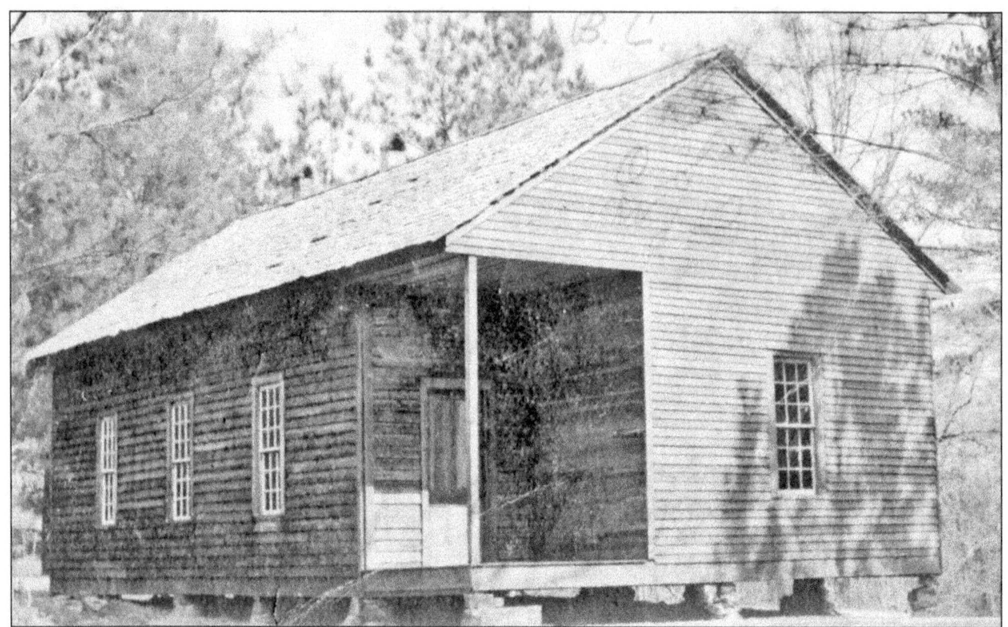

The Black Creek School was near the Black Creek Church off US Highway 84 near Bladon Springs. It was a one-room building that held grades one through six. Students were seated according to their grade level. At the back of the building was a stage. The children drank water that flowed through an iron pipe from the hillside next to the building. The main subjects were reading, writing, spelling, and arithmetic.

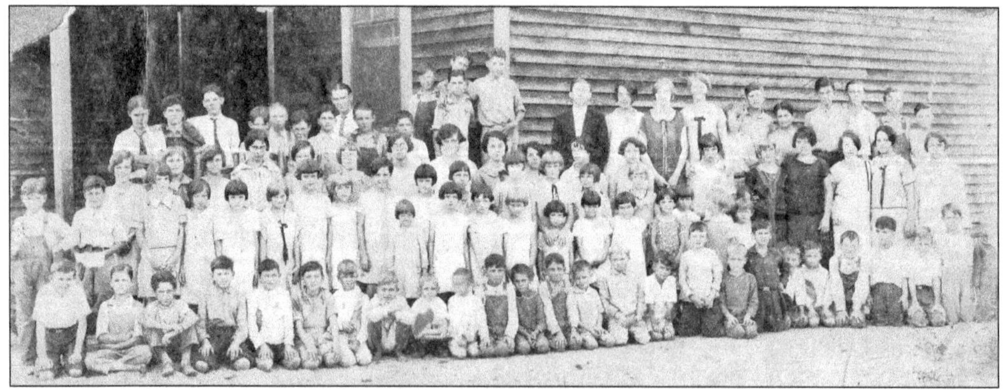

The name and location of this school have not been determined. It was one of the early schools in Choctaw County. This is one of many photographs in the Choctaw County Historical Museum's collection of unknowns.

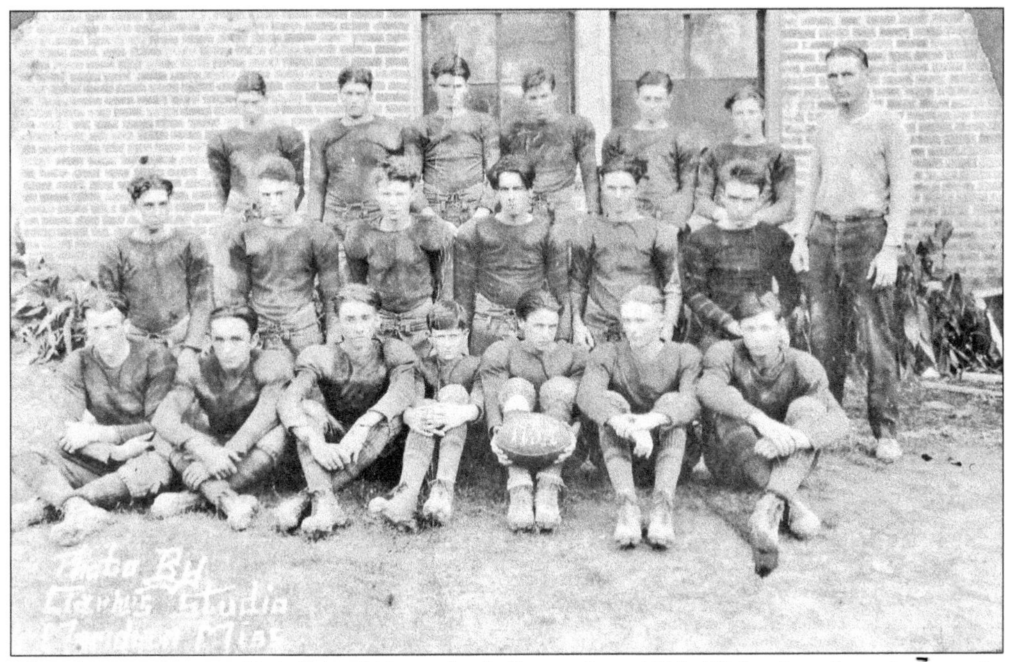

The Choctaw County High School Tigers football team from 1925–1926 gathers for a photograph. From left to right are (first row) unidentified, Buster Plowman, Wilford Jordan, Odis Mitts, Earl Webb, Bryant Lindsey, and Charlie Webb; (second row) George Robinson, W.M. Elliott, unidentified, Gene Moody, Robert Mills, Jack Scurlock, and Coach Lewis; (third row) Ervin Hall, unidentified, ? Bennett, two unidentified, and A.J. Martin.

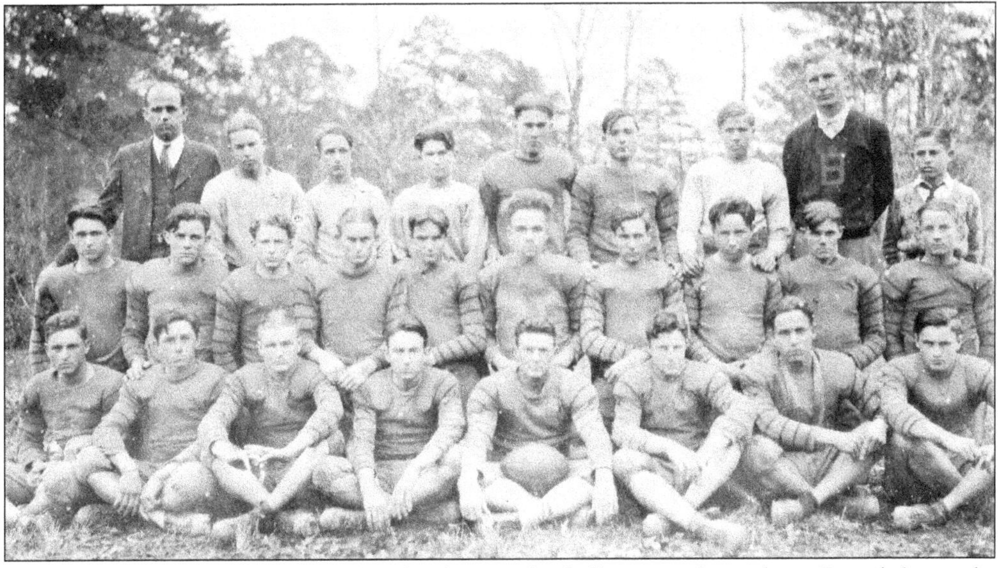

The c. 1928 Choctaw County High School Tigers football team is shown here. From left to right are (first row) John Elliott, Rainer Ezell, Gaines Phillips, Garfield Plowman, Justin Copeland, A.J. Martin, C.A. Ezell, and Earl Webb; (second row) Byron Bailey, Pit Moody, Turkey Hearn, Gilmer Doggett, Winston Edwards, Roy Ezell, Alonzo Combs, John Ezell, Glenn Adams, and Denzel Hollis; (third row) Prof. H.A. Fowler, M.H. Elliott, Max Edwards, Frank Barefield, Massey Goree, Charlie Phillips, Richard Moody, Coach Harris, and J.W. Rudder.

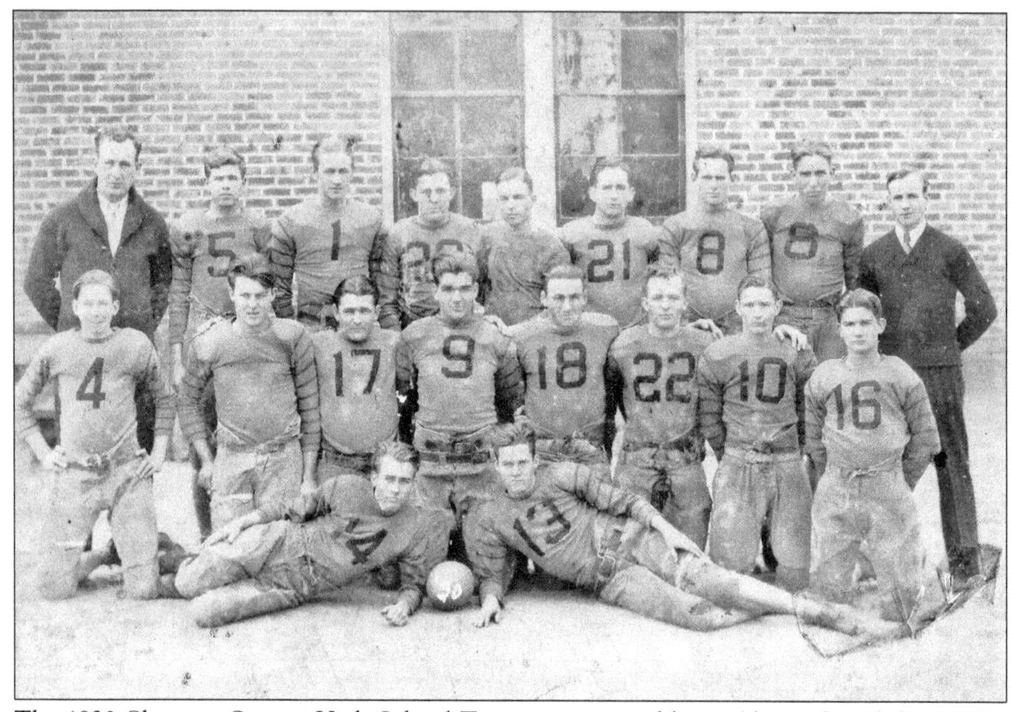

The 1930 Choctaw County High School Tigers are pictured here. Above, from left to right, are (first row) J.W. Wright and Charlie Gavin; (second row) Jack Duncan, Joe Moody, Clayton Fuller, ? Scott, John Williams, Alonzo Combs, Stuart Phillips, and Frank Barefield; (third row) unidentified coach, unidentified, Thomas Arnold, Pitt Moody, M.H. Elliott, ? Whitfield, Aubrey Bush, ? Scott, and unidentified coach.

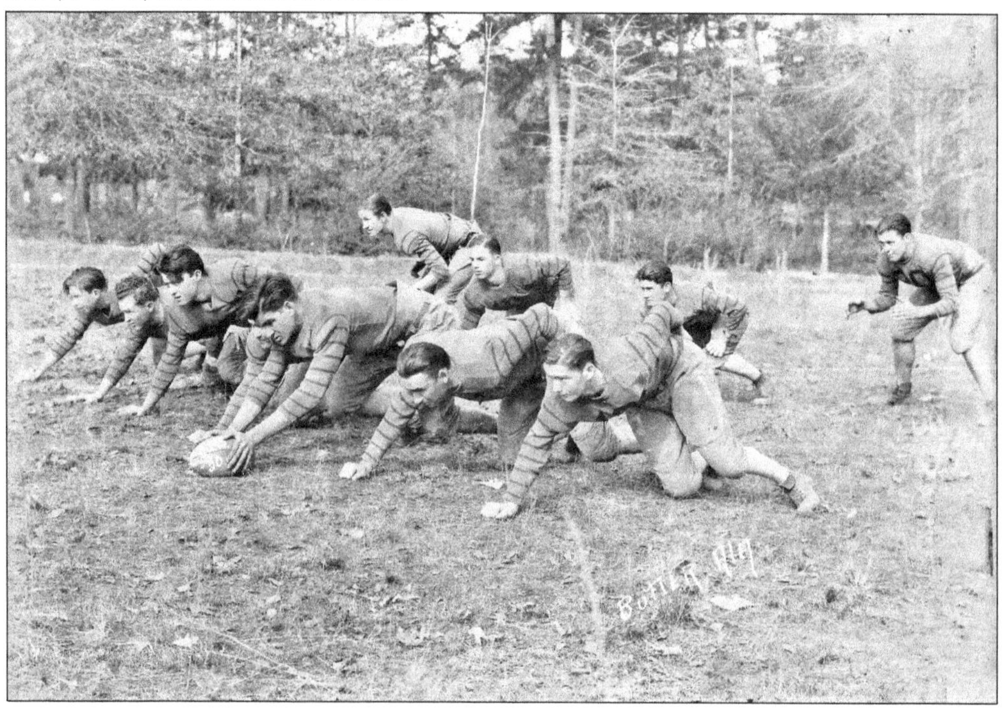

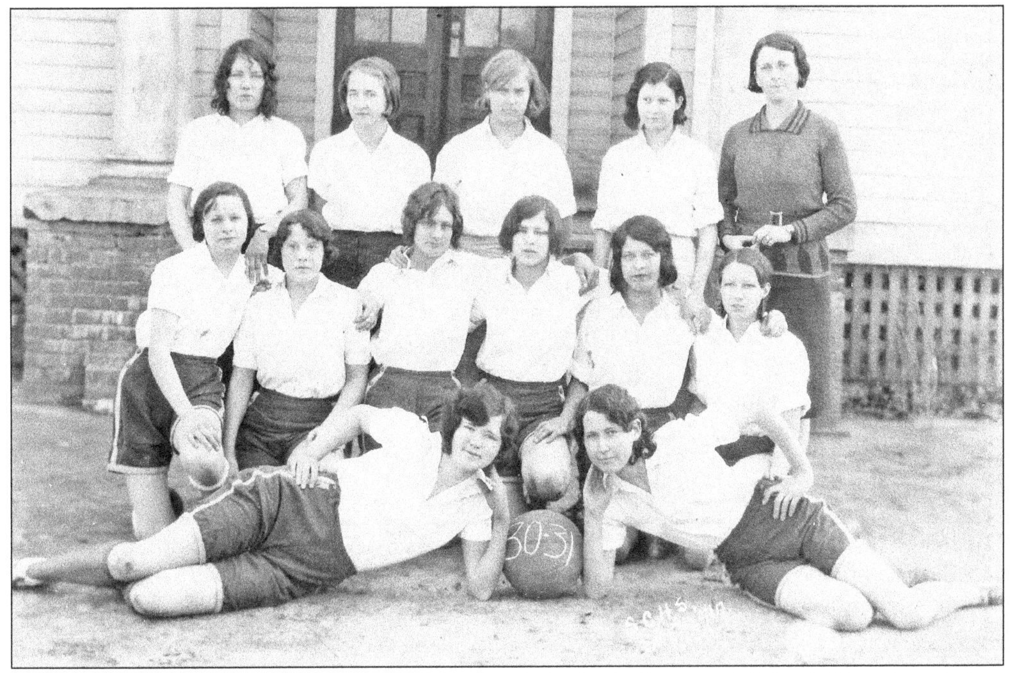

The Southern Choctaw County High School girls' basketball team of 1930–1931 is, from left to right, (first row) May Bell Herring and unidentified; (second row) Trudie Murphy, Myrtle Taylor, two unidentified, Berneice Hutchinson, and Voncille Lassiter; (third row) Mary ?, Jessie Mixon, unidentified, Abbie Powe, and unidentified.

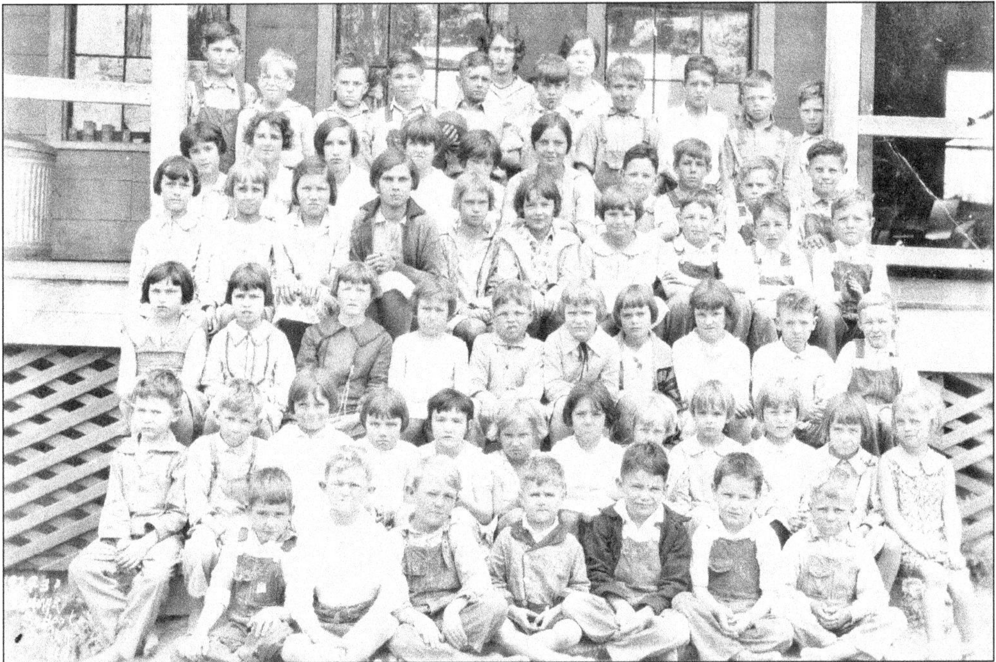

Students of the 1929–1930 Choctaw County Grammar School at Butler are pictured here. It is not known if they are sitting on the steps of the old school or at another location. Alman Jacobs is fifth from left in the third row, and Howard Norton is at left in back. (Courtesy of Ruth Jacobs Corley.)

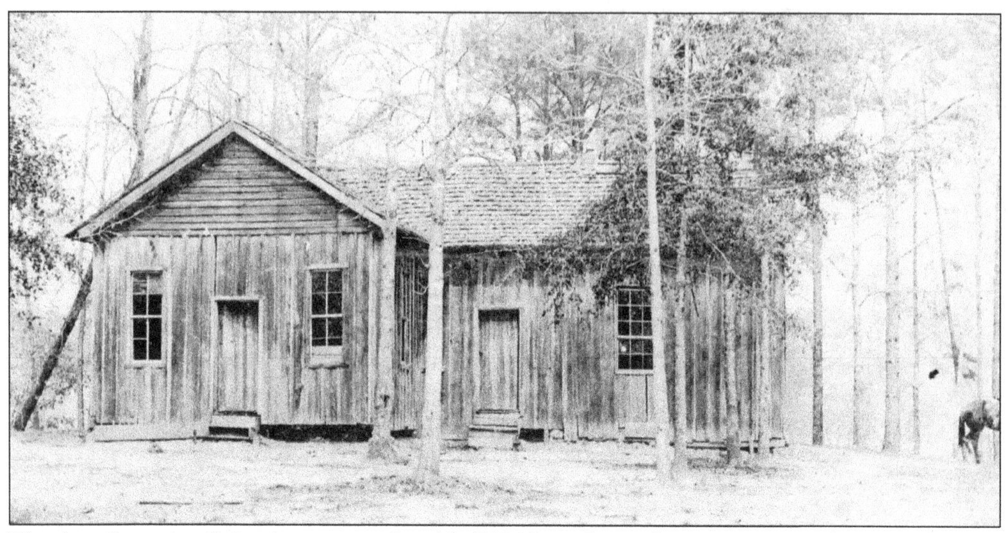

The first Souwilpa School was near the old AT&N tracks in the community of Souwilpa, a few miles south of Gilbertown. The school became too small to accommodate all the students, so a two-story building was constructed near the same spot. The teachers were Mildred Hutchinson, Harold Owens, and Green Edgar. (Courtesy of Thomas Jefferson Campbell Jr.)

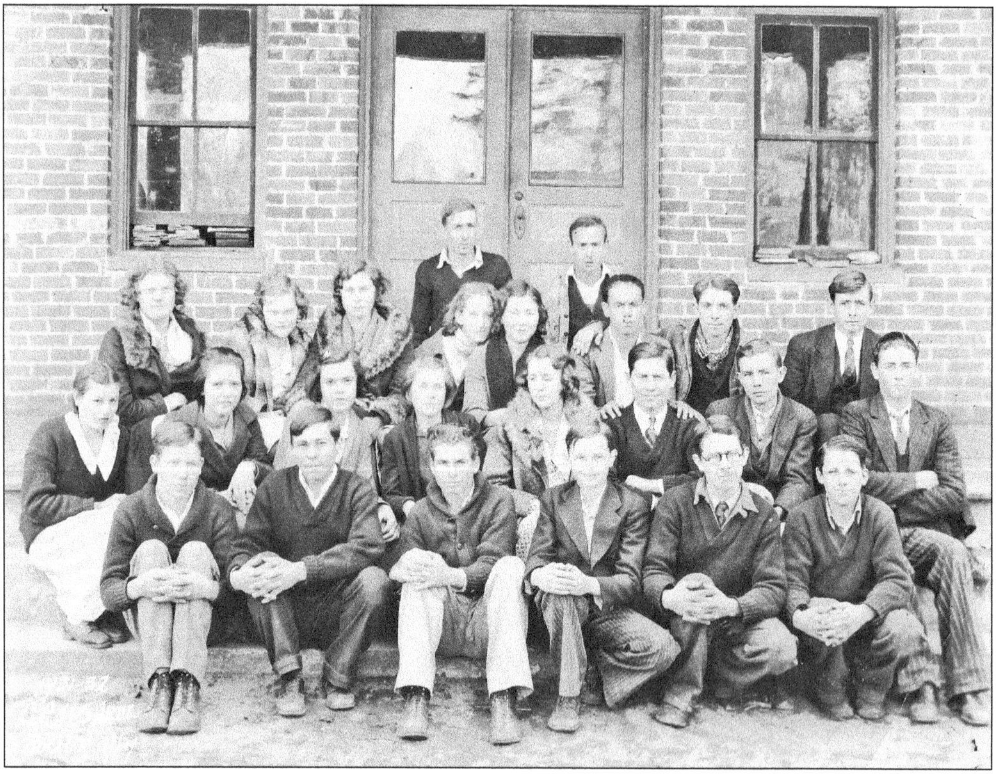

Shown is the Choctaw County High School Junior III class of 1931–1932.

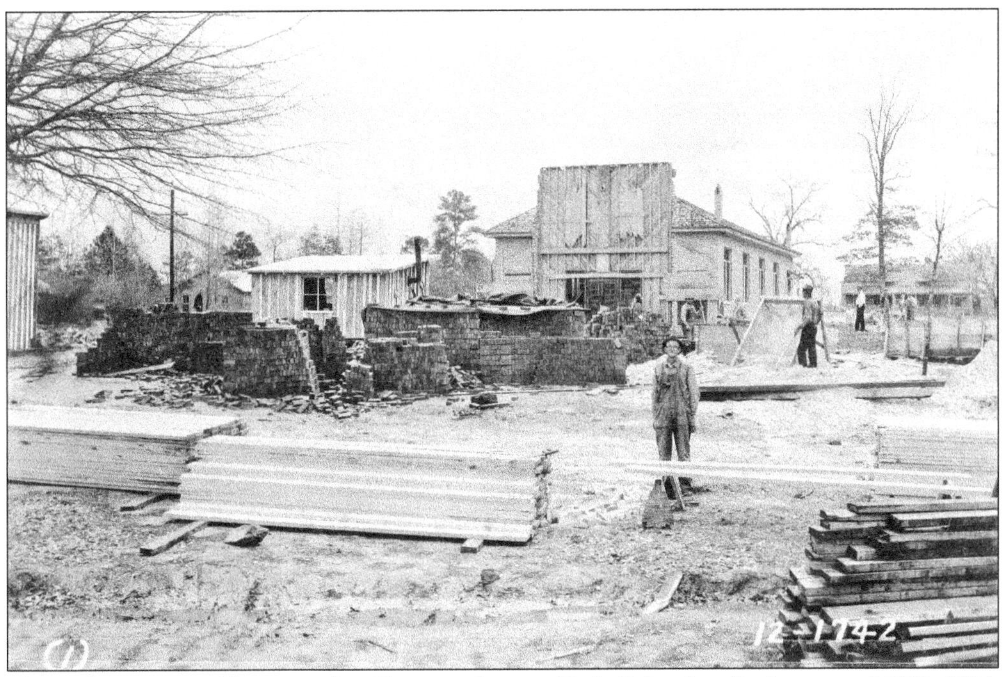

Shown here is an addition to the Choctaw County High School in Butler around 1933–1934. The school was built using funds of the Civil Works Administration that had been established by the New Deal during the Great Depression to rapidly create jobs for millions of unemployed. The Alabama Relief Administration (ARA), a state-run public relief agency, distributed the funds for building the school. (Courtesy of Alabama Department of Archives and History, Montgomery.)

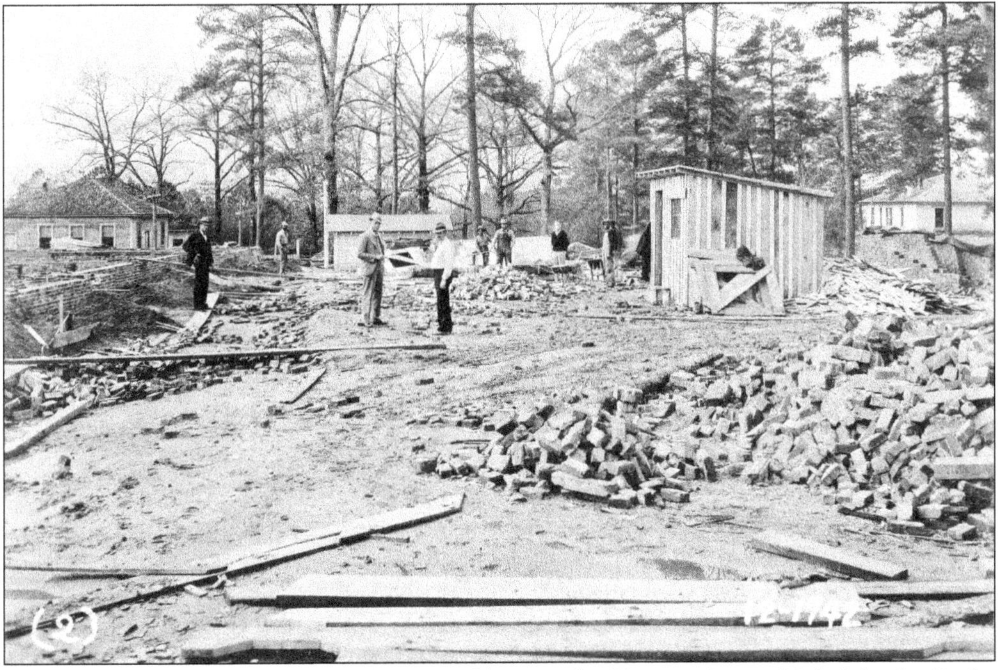

This is another photograph showing the same addition to the Choctaw County High School in Butler around 1933–1934. (Courtesy of Alabama Department of Archives and History, Montgomery.)

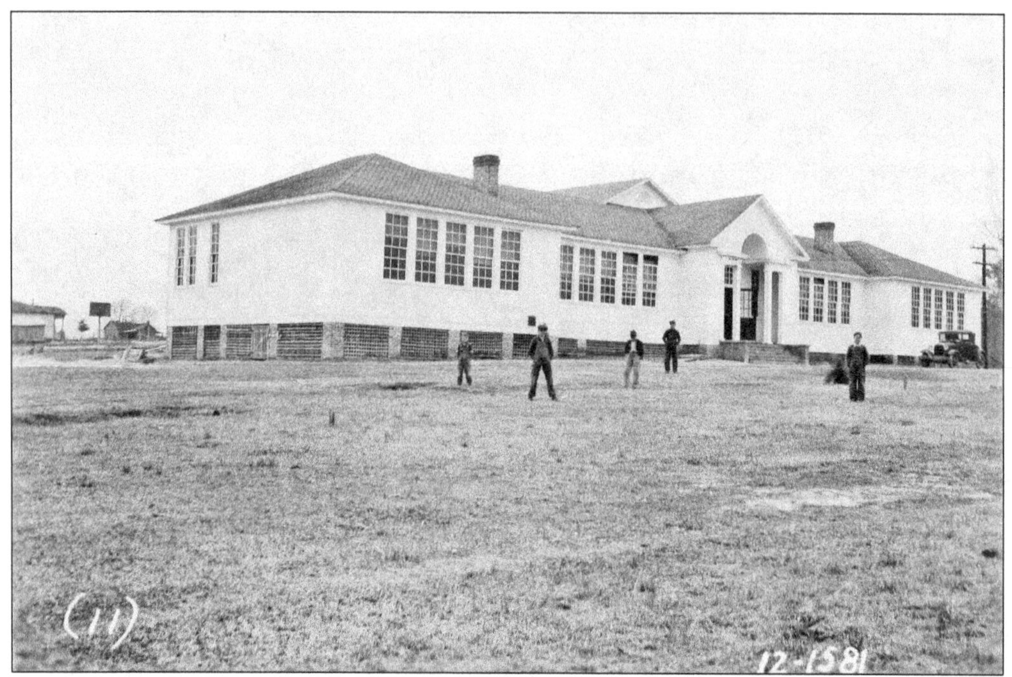

The recently repaired and repainted Gilbertown School is shown around 1933–1934. This school was renovated using funds of the Civil Works Administration as distributed by the ARA. (Courtesy of Alabama Department of Archives and History, Montgomery.)

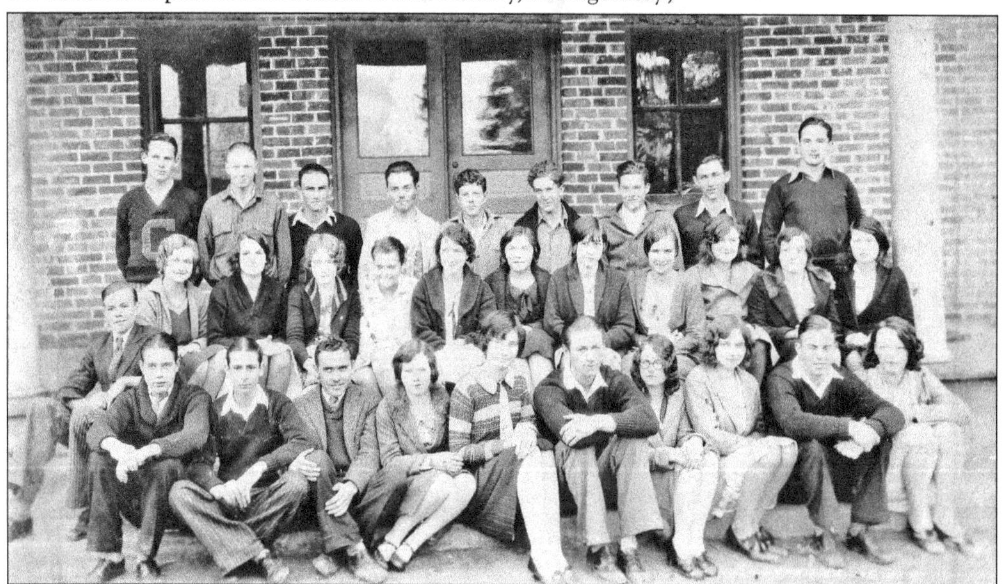

Students of the 1930–1931 Choctaw County High School Senior III class are shown here. From left to right are (first row) Paul Miller, Jeff Stewart, Bill Granberry, Ola Gibson, Lida Bush, Thomas Arnold, Mary Ella Scott, May Bell Fuller, M.H. Elliott, and Ernestine Lawley; (second row) Jack Duncan, Thelma Hearn, Lucille Means, Viva Long, Evelyn Jeffries, teacher Edith Foster, Maggie Lindsey, Ruth Marie Minor, Mattie Irene Morris, Annie Lou Gavin, Eula Gibson, and Sadie Stafford; (third row) Aubrey Bush, Charles McKnight, John Williams, ? Allen, Grady Long, James Carter, Charlie Gavin, ? Hinds, and Glennon Whitted.

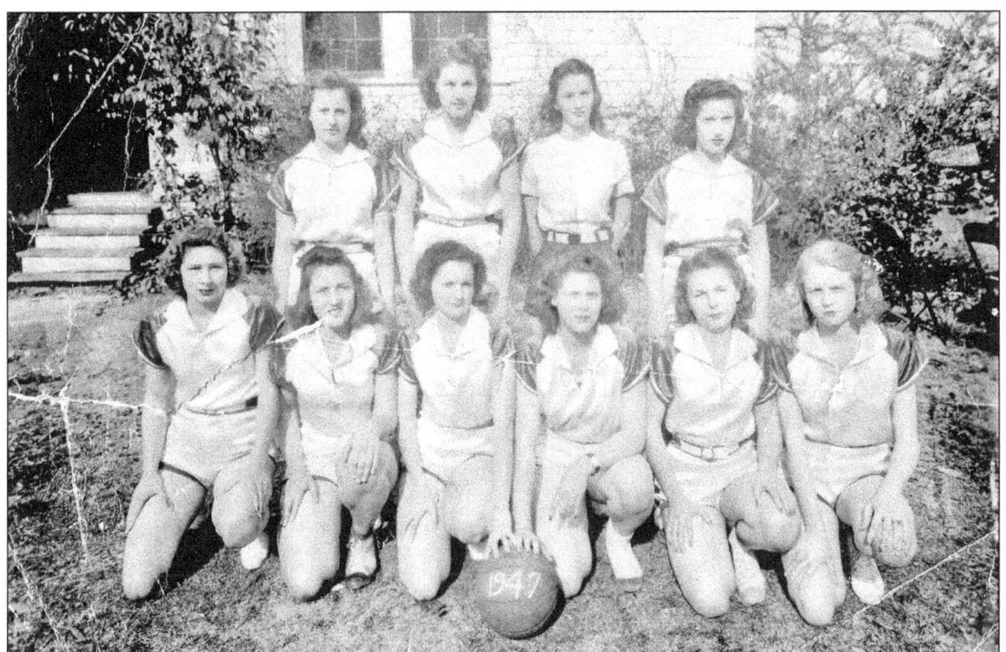

The Southern Choctaw High School girls' basketball team of 1947 gathers for a group photograph. From left to right are (first row) Ruby Lee Jackson, Eda B. Davis, Lillian Murphy, Maxine Gilmer, Joyce Utsey, and Ruby Lee Palmer; (second row) Edith Winslow, Martha Clark, Ruby Lee Powe, and Jean Stanford.

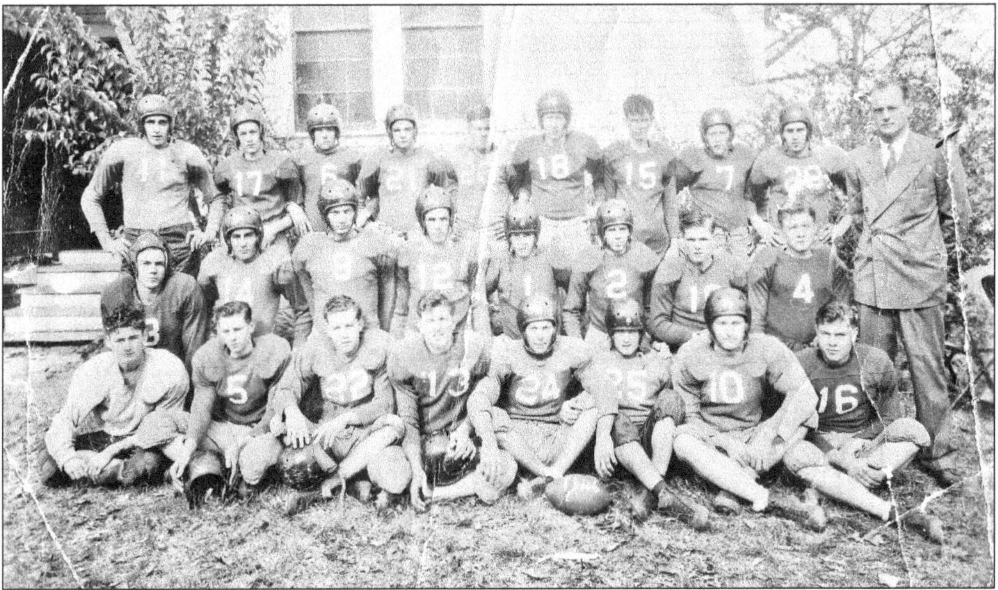

The 1946 Southern Choctaw High School football team is, from left to right, (first row) Casper Carlisle, unidentified, Bill Holder, Jimmy Kennedy, unidentified, Joe Carlisle, Jim Norton, and Joe Harvey Stokley; (second row) Buddy Trice, Max Becton, unidentified, Richard Covington, two unidentified, Jimmy Mixon, and Jim Henry Waite; (third row) Tobe Roach, two unidentified, Earle M. Powe, John Hamrick, Allen Abston, Gary Trice, unidentified, and Edward Gibson. The coach is Lee Singley.

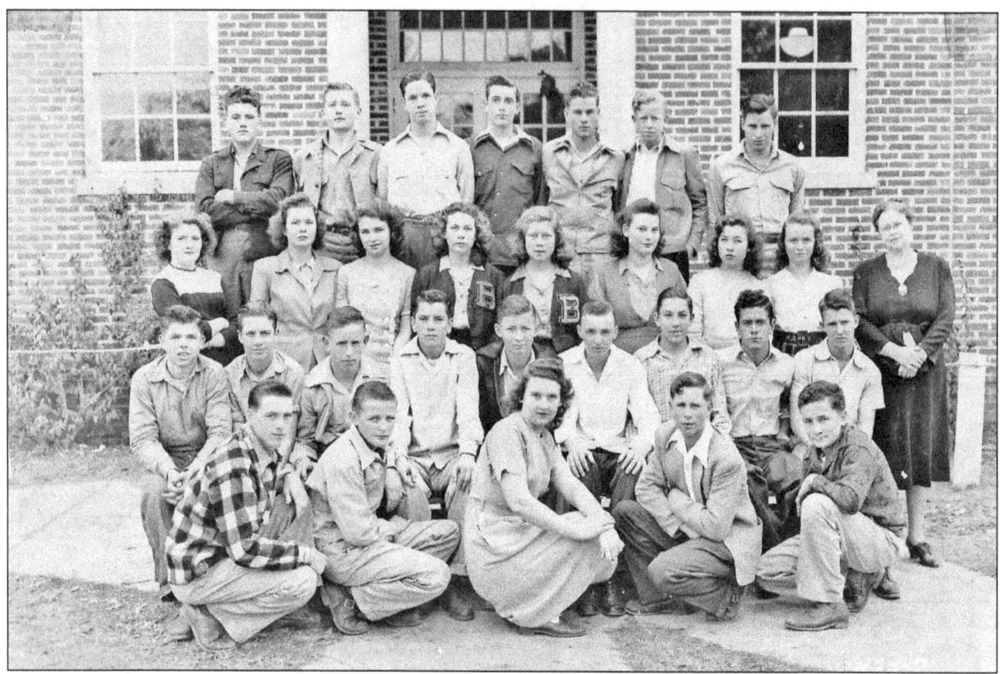

Students of the 1947–1948 class at Choctaw County High School are pictured here. Their names, in no particular order, are Raymond Ford, Johnny Keahey, Buck McDonald, Bailey Powell, Vernon Johnson, James Gilbert, Robert Chappell, Gloria Moody, Lucille Mercier, Miriam Gunnels, Tray Rolison, Annie Jewel McAteer, Ruby Norton, Evelyn Jackson, Jacie Mosley, Messina Scott, Charles Norwood, McMorris Johnson, Charles Ezell, Myles Evaston, Thomas Cummings, Fred Fore, Lyman Bryan, George Wimberley, Billy Summerville, Billie Earl Phillips, Laverne Melton, Billie Joe McDowell, Robert Moody, and Jack Boykin. The teacher is Claudia Scott.

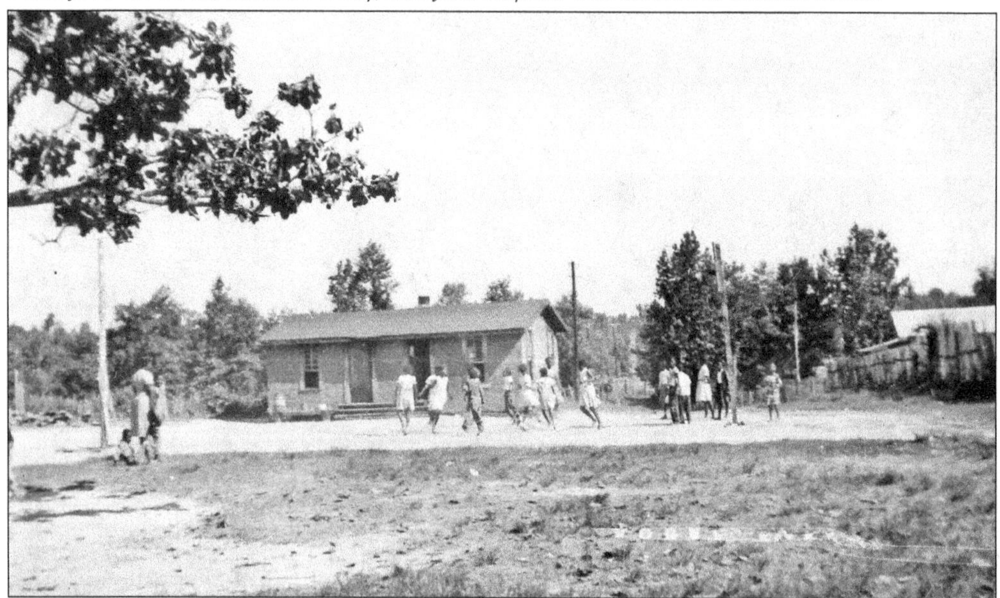

The Shiloh School was a black school in the Bolinger community. It was on Everett Circle next to the Shiloh Baptist Church. The school had two teachers, Eulishia Lindsey and a Miss Edwards. (Courtesy of James Everett.)

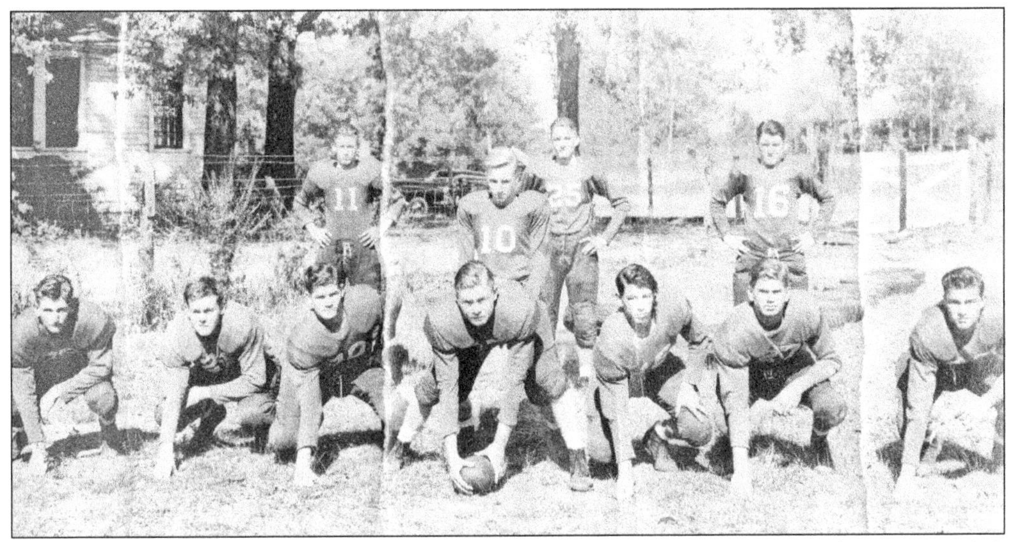

Pictured are members of the 1949–1950 Southern Choctaw High School football team. From left to right are (first row) Paul Bird, John Henry Hamrick, Milton Brown, Jim Henry Waites, Oneal Wright, Eddie Gibson, and Verl Carney; (second row) John Lewis Jackson, Norman Thomas, Don Young, and Billy Carney.

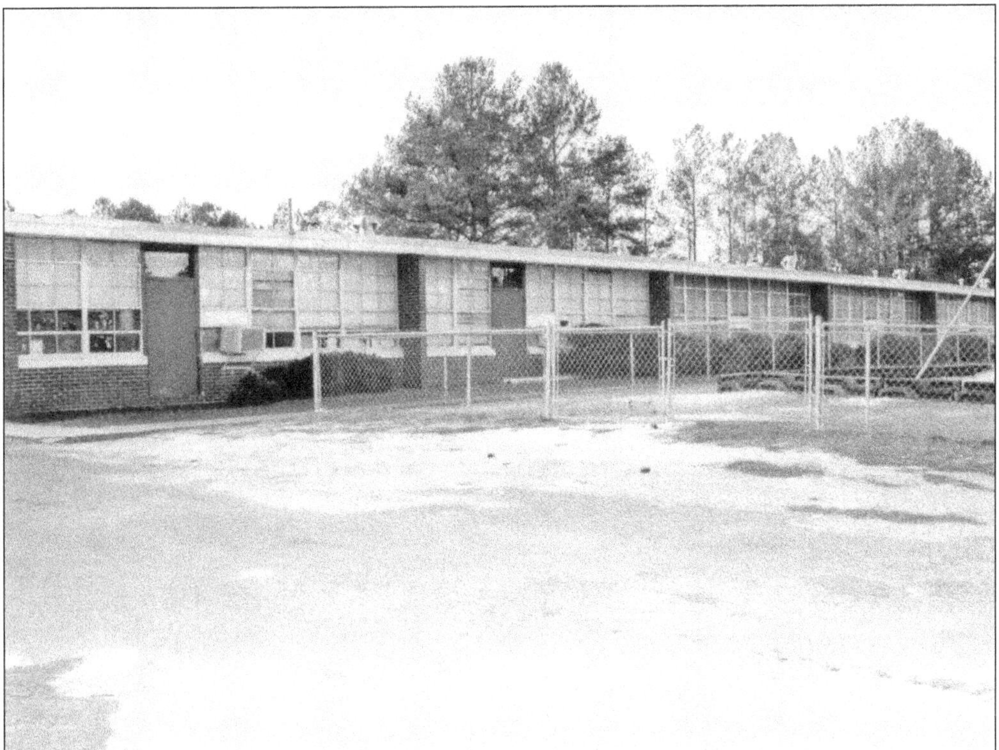

Shady Grove School is pictured in the mid-1960s. In 1959, the school board of Choctaw County approved construction of a new black school at Shady Grove near the town of Silas. The cost for the new school was estimated to be about $90,000. In 1969, high school students were transferred to Silas, and this became Shady Grove Junior High School. (Courtesy of *Choctaw Sun-Advocate*.)

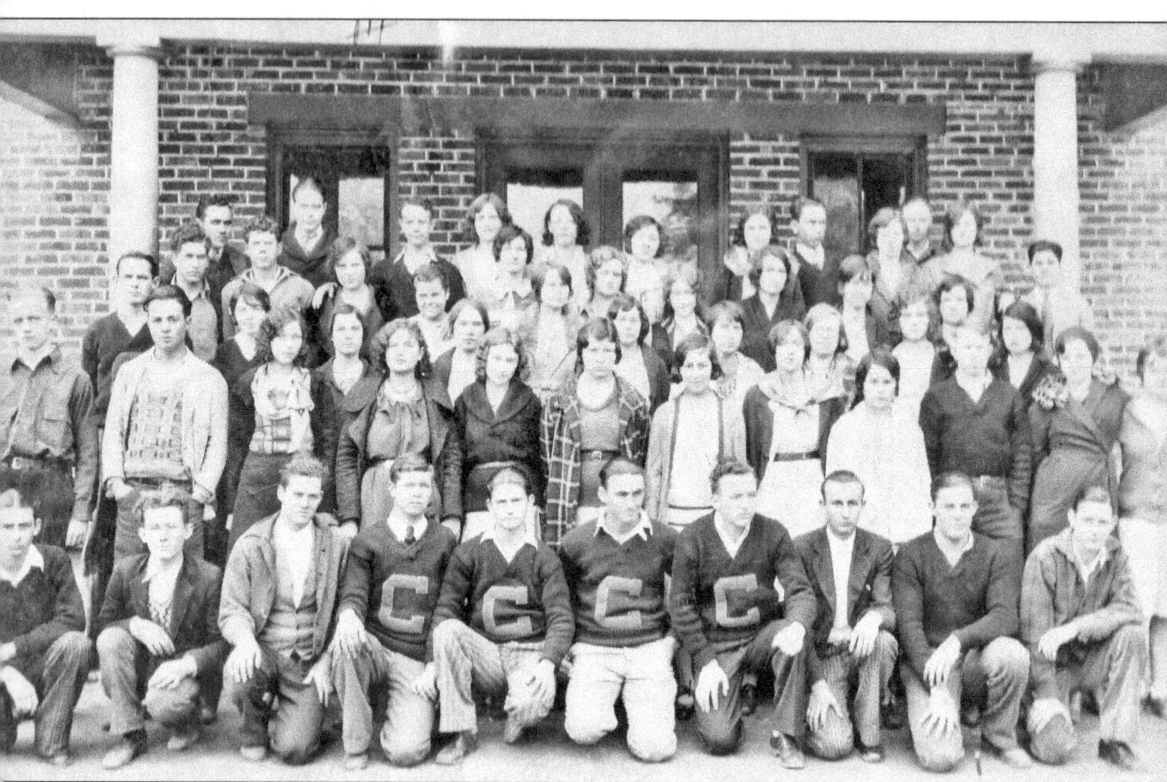

The Choctaw County High School commercial class of 1930–1931 gathers for the annual school photograph. From left to right are (first row) Jeff Stewart, Oscar Goree, Charlie Gavin, unidentified, Frank Barefield, John ?, Bill Granberry, Leonard Boykin, Pitt Moody, and Stewart Phillips; (second row) ? Smiley, ? Allen, Mary Ryan Sparrow, unidentified, Ruby Stanford, Frances LeNoir, Hermia Sparrow, Emma Lee Roson, ? Edwards, Hardy Ferry, Sadie Stafford, and two unidentified; (third and fourth rows) Aubrey Bush, James Carter, ? Sparrow, ? Phillips, Elaine Williams, unidentified, Evelyn Jeffries, Mary Ellen Morris, Louise Boswell, Lyda Bush, Ruth Minor, Thelma Hearn, unidentified, Viva Long, Lelia Banks, Lucille Means, unidentified, Marie Minor, Eula Gibson, Ola Gibson, Robert Martin, and Anna Lou Gavin; (fifth row) Bill Granberry, Paul Miller, Belk Dickerson, Mary Bell Fuller, Ernestine Lawley, teacher Mavis Cole, Mary Melton, Bruister Day, and Edward McKnight.

Five

CHURCHES

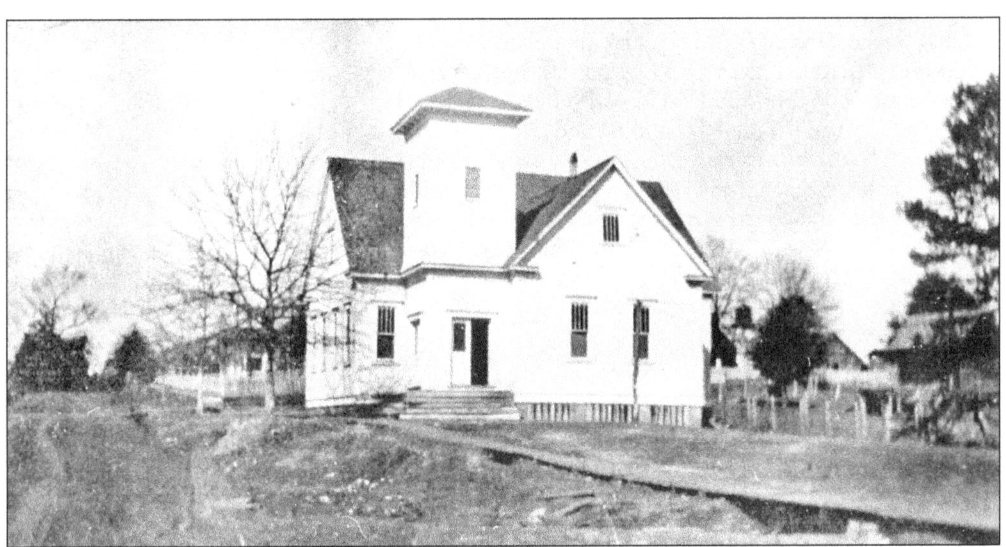

The original First Baptist Church in Butler stood on the corner of Mulberry Avenue and Alabama Street. The main structure was started in 1906. Paul and Ledonia Miller deeded the church the lot on January 22, 1905. The church was built by James Bush and completed in 1907. This photograph shows the remodeled building with additions as it appeared in 1950. A new church was built and dedicated on Highway 10 West on August 21, 1960.

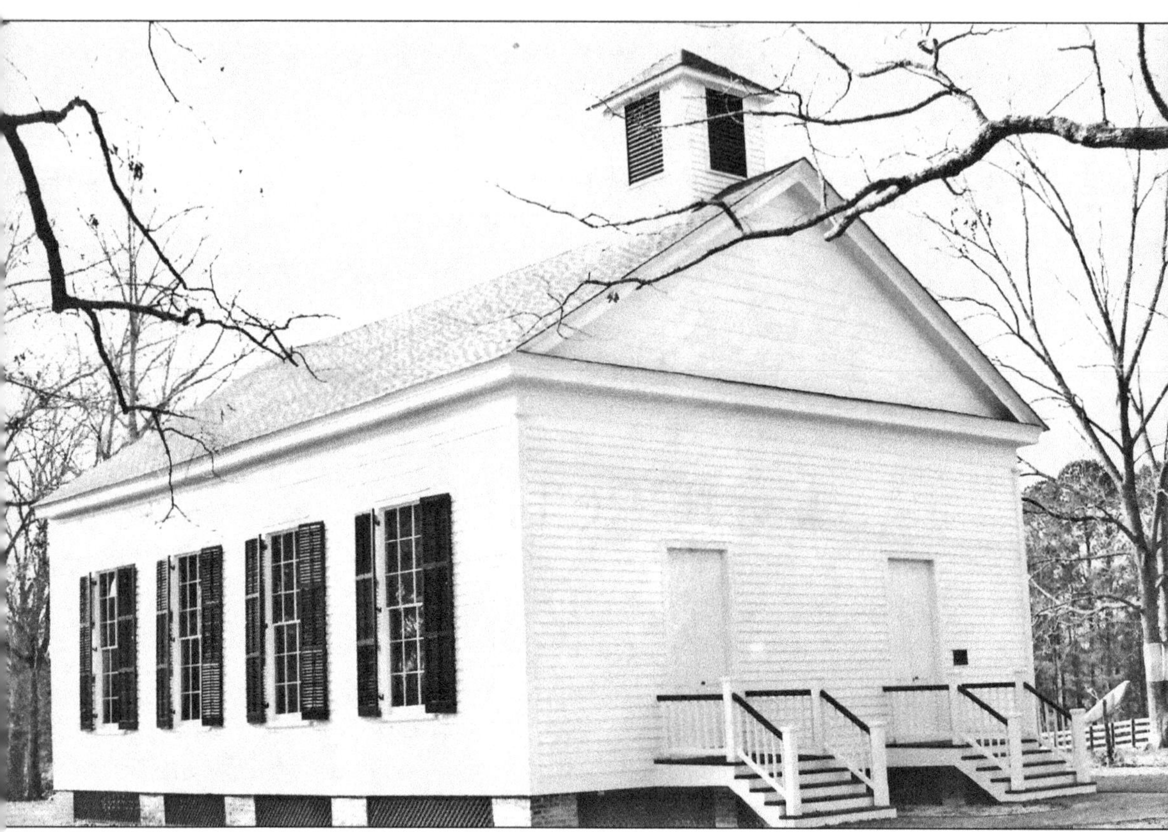

The Mount Sterling Methodist Church was organized in 1854, and in 1859, the deed to the church lot was given by Sanford E. Catterlin. Gabriel Hawkins was the first pastor in 1855. The building was constructed in 1859 and remained in continuous service as a Methodist church until it closed in 1976 due to lack of participation. In the early days, the church never had a fulltime pastor; it was served by circuit riders who held services once a month. In 1980, the Methodist Conference deeded the church building and two acres to the Choctaw County Historical Society. The church is historically significant in that it is the only remaining structure of a once-wealthy and popular area. When the town of Mount Sterling was surveyed and laid out in 1847, a public square was left for a courthouse, because it was believed that the town would be selected as the county seat. On May 8, 1986, the Mount Sterling Methodist Church was listed in the National Register of Historic Places.

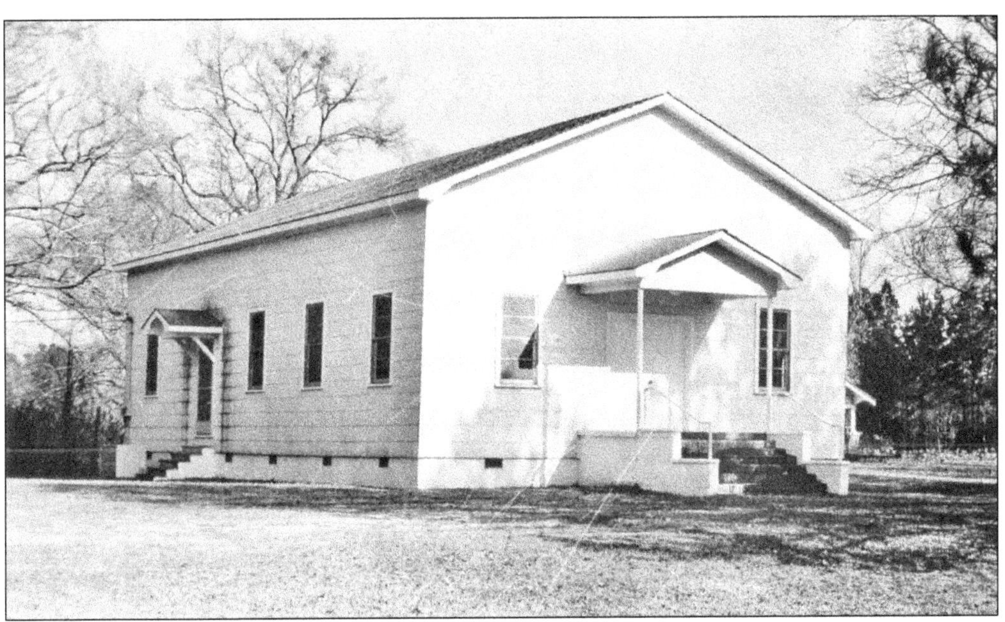

The Rehoboth Baptist Church at Pushmataha was organized on November 18, 1851. The pastor was W. Jacob Parker. Many slaves held membership in Rehoboth Church because permission had been granted by their owners. In 1869, the black members moved to another church. In 1943, Rehoboth was received into the Choctaw County Baptist Association. It had formerly belonged to the Bigbee Baptist Association.

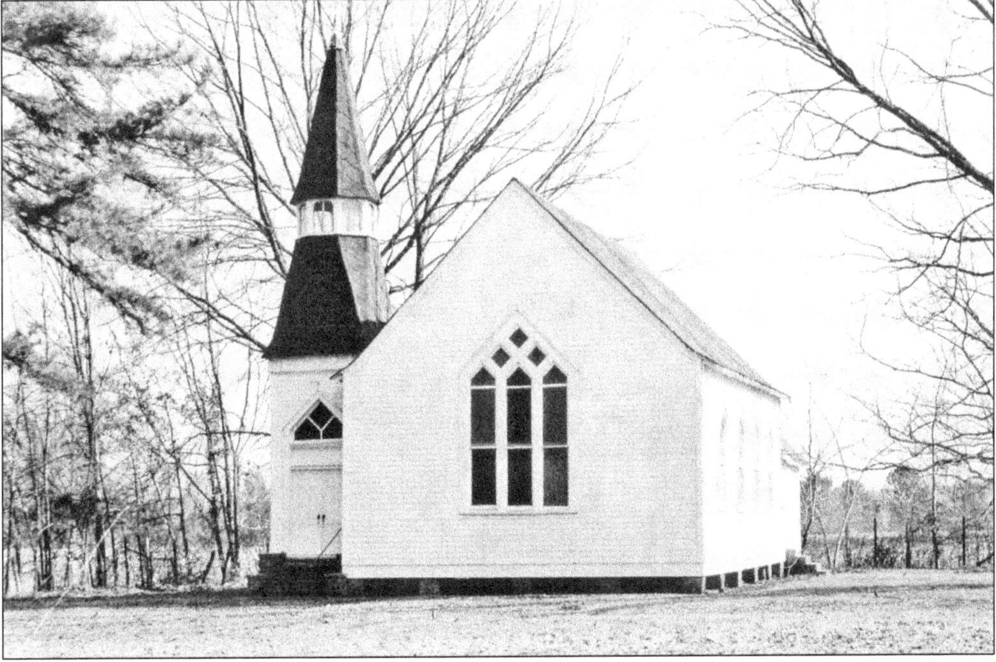

The present building of Pushmataha United Methodist Church was built in 1911 on land deeded to the church by Mary Gilder Bruister on August 27, 1908. The building was a frame structure with three Sunday school rooms. The records of the church date to January 1871. C.B. Dubose was the first pastor.

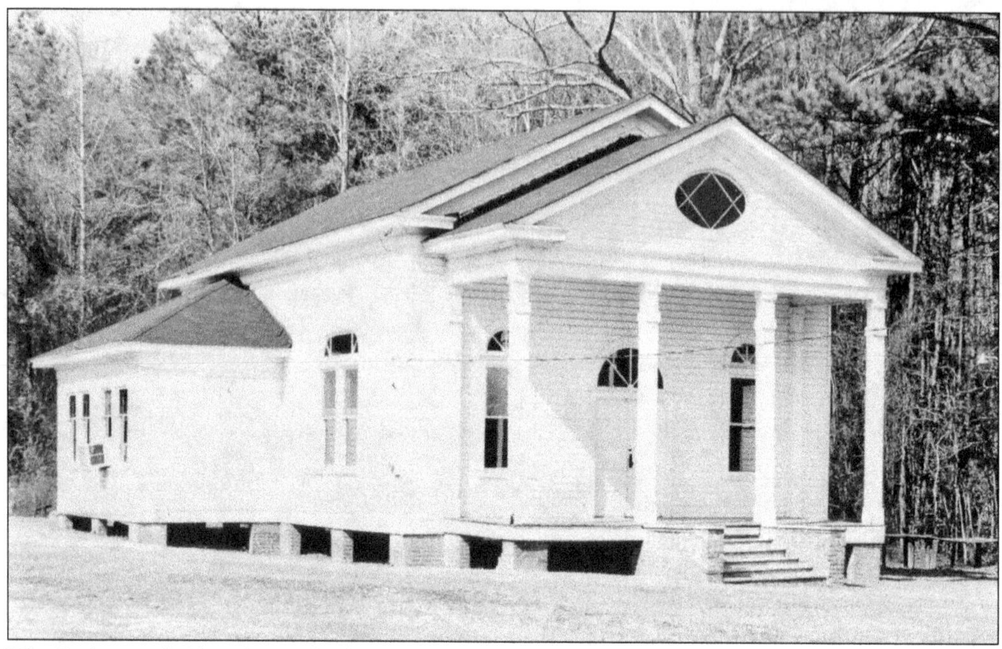

The Riderwood Church was built in the early 1920s by the E.E. Jackson Lumber Company. It is composed of a main auditorium and Sunday school rooms with a porch across the front. The church was used by all denominations until the mill ceased operations in 1931. In February 1961, Scott Paper Company, which had purchased the land, drew up an agreement giving the people of Riderwood permission to use the church building indefinitely for religious purposes.

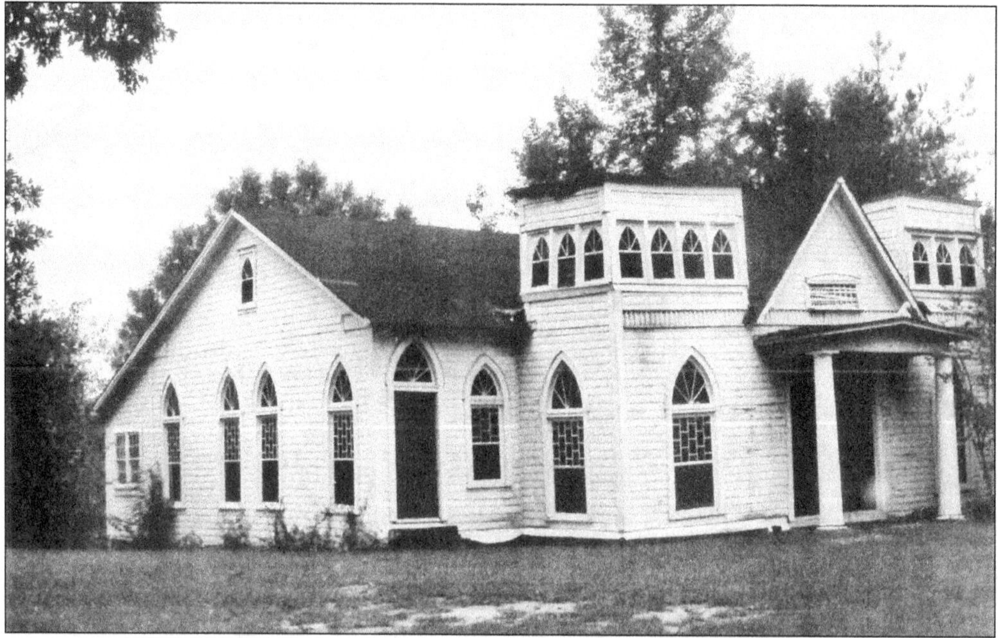

Members of the Gilbertown United Pentecostal Church first had to attend church in Meridian, Mississippi. When the Seventh-Day Adventist Church members were going to build a new church, the old one was purchased by Hubert Mosley for use by the Gilbertown United Pentecostal Church. Mrs. John Moore was the pastor until May 21, 1971.

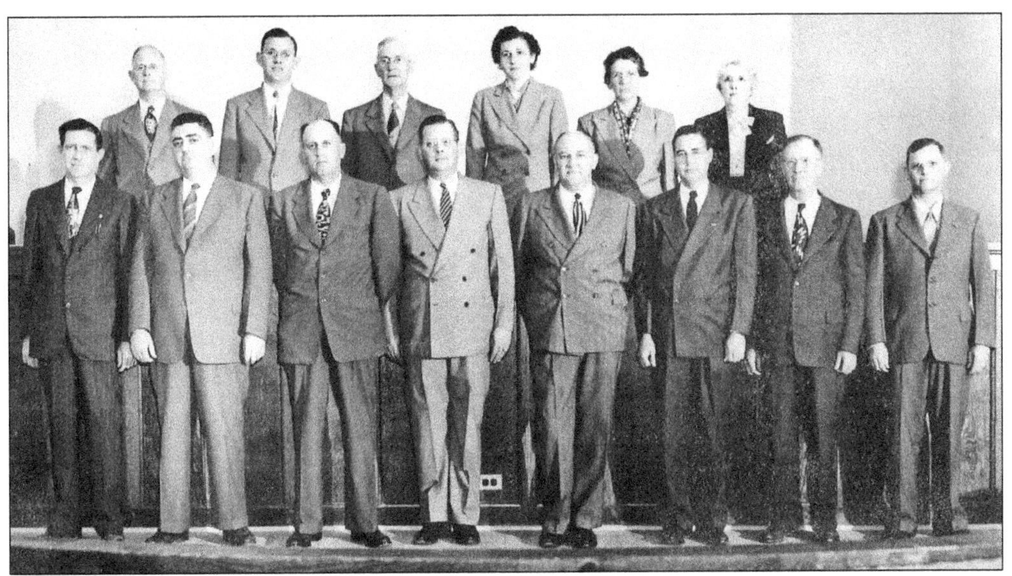

The board of stewards gathers at the new First United Methodist Church for the dedication in 1950. From left to right are (first row) Claude Sanderson, Wallace Lindsey, Lenoir Whitted, Albert Evans, Dr. William J. Barber, Paul Miller, Austin Swann, and Matthew Sexton; (second row) Willie Tew, Oscar Christopher, Olin Adams, Marguarite Moody, Minnie Whitted, and Ethel Liddell. Two members of the board are not shown: J. Massey Edgar and Idrain Doggett.

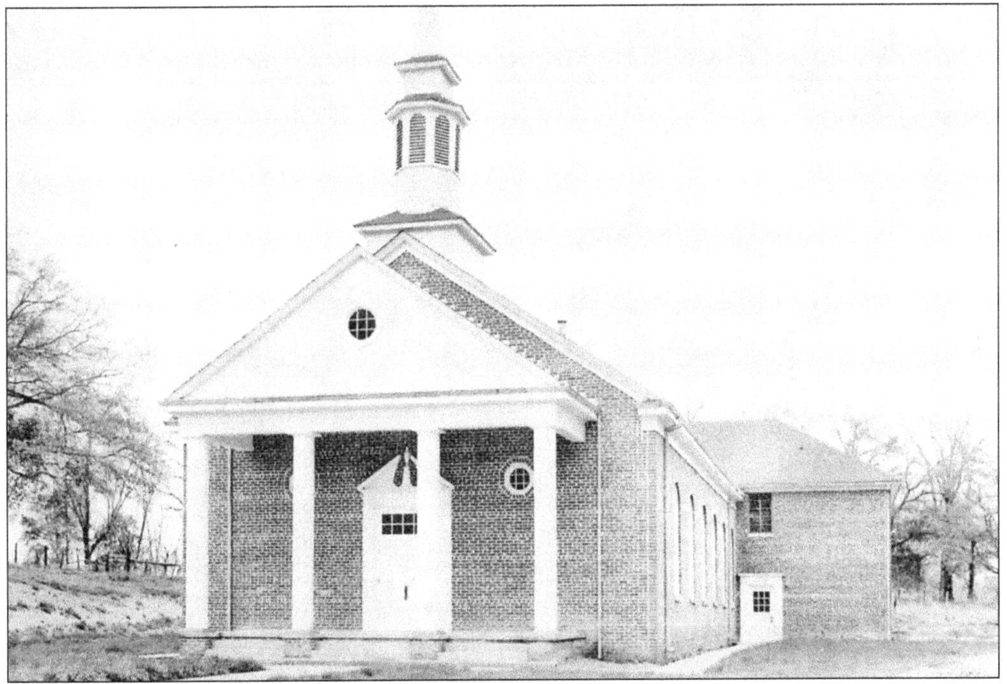

The First United Methodist Church in Butler is on Highway 17 South. This photograph shows how it looked in 1950. The general chairman and construction chairman for the project was Lenoir Whitted. The work on the new building was supervised by Dr. W.J. Barber. Construction started in 1949, and the church was dedicated on Sunday, March 5, 1950. Clare Purchell, resident bishop of Birmingham, officiated at the dedication.

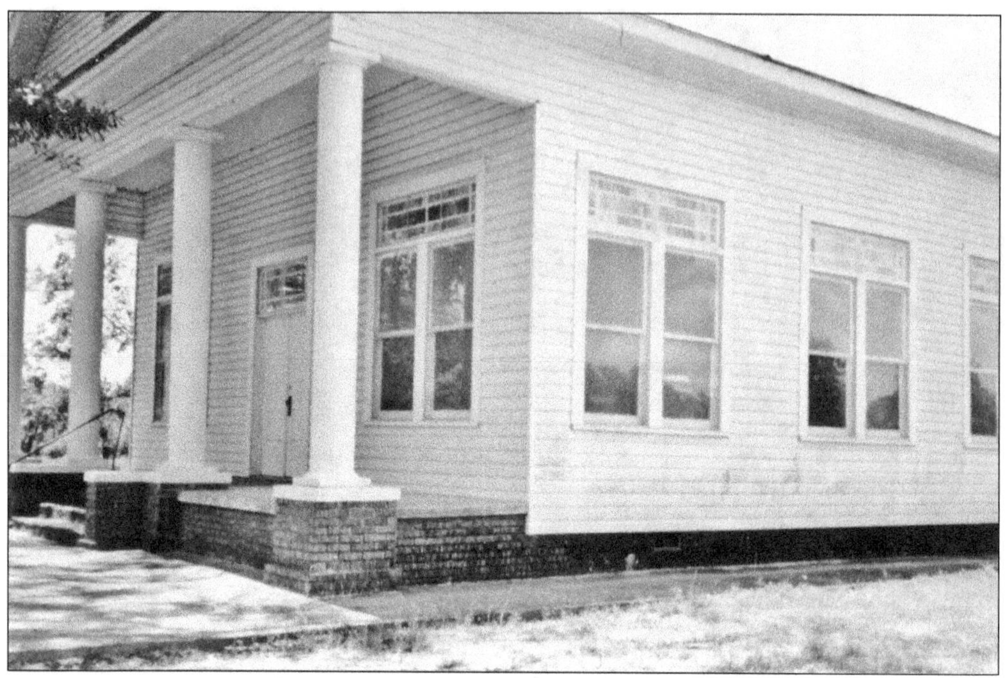

The Lisman Baptist Church was organized by J.E. Vaughn and C.H. Morgan on June 25, 1915, with charter members J.O. Phillips, G.R. Allen, J.H. Atkinson, R.M. Sims, Baker Ezell, J.A. Ryne Jr., Taylor Ezell, Mrs. W.L. Atkinson, Eva Allen, Mrs. R.M. Simmons, Nora Rainer Ezell, Leona Hearn Ezell, and Mrs. J.A. Ryne Jr. J.O. Phillips furnished lumber to build the church.

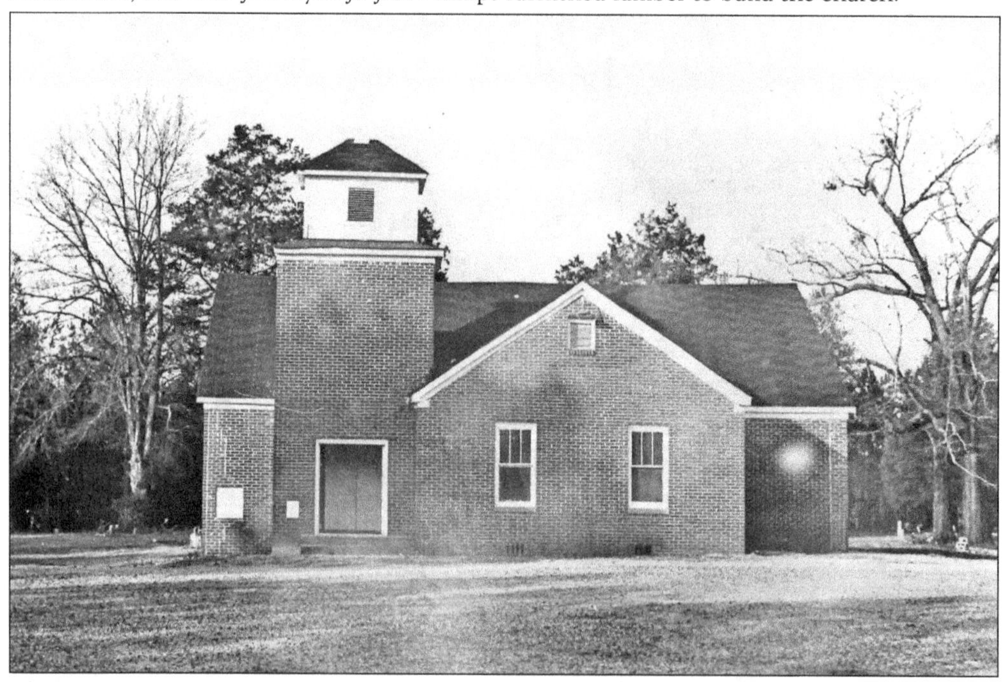

The Butler Chapel AME Zion Church was founded in 1867. It is across from the Robert Locke Park in Butler. All ministers were called elders. John Chaney was the "grandfather" of the church. In 1919–1920, a new church was built. During this time, school was also taught there.

David Chester Mason was referred to as the "Abraham of Choctaw County." He was born in Isney on May 11, 1890, and preached his first sermon in 1904 at the Isney Methodist Church when he was 14 years old. Reverend Mason was also licensed to teach, having graduated from Livingston State Normal School. In 1917, he was selected to draft plans for the beginning of the Choctaw Association. In 1918, he was selected as the first moderator.

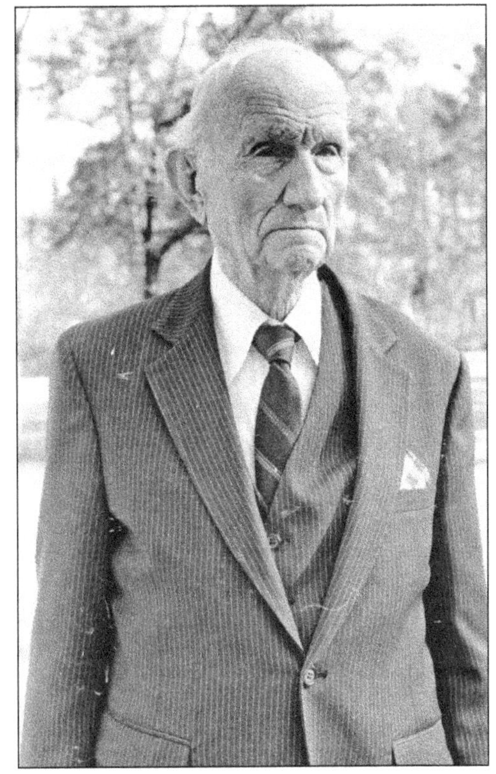

Pictured is Bethel United Methodist Church. On August 13, 1872, Caswell Felts and his wife, Linsey, sold and conveyed land to trustees James A. Gilder, John N. Hamran, and John C. O'Hara and their successors in office for the purpose of erecting a church. The original box-like church was constructed in 1873. The present church was constructed by Lorenzo Camp in 1902 on the same foundation.

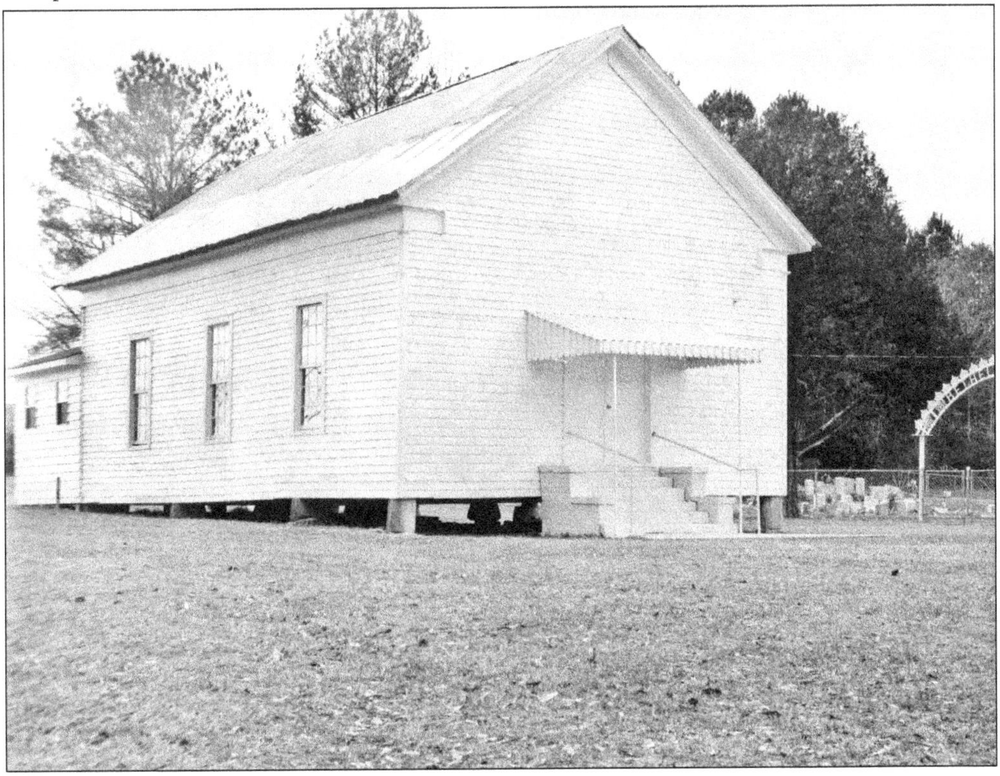

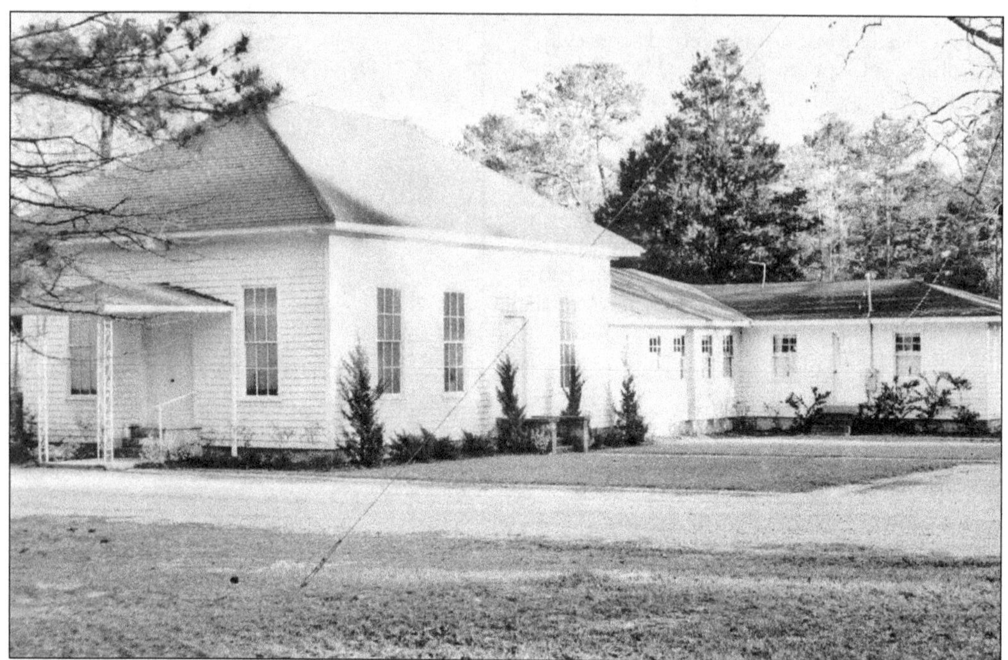

Shown here is Hopewell Baptist Church. In September 1850, a deed was received by the church trustees from Thomas Bleakley from Greene County, Alabama, for two acres between the communities of Sunshine and Lavaca. An auditorium was built that served as a house of worship until 1885. Freeman Dicks built the present auditorium, which was furnished in 1885. Hopewell joined the Choctaw County Baptist Association from the Bigbee Association on August 18, 1919.

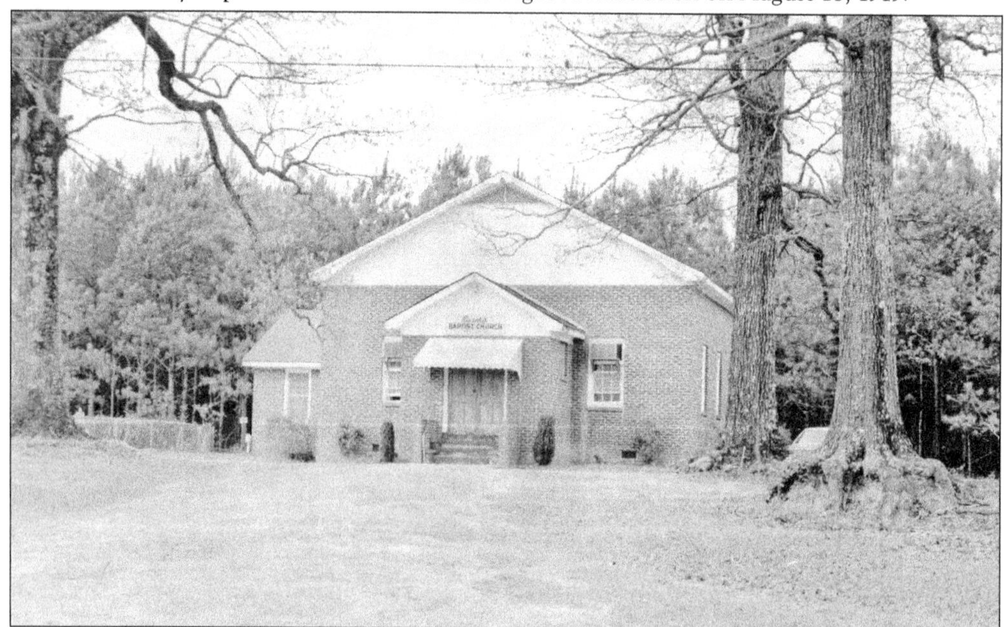

Eureka Baptist Church was organized in 1903 under the direction of James E. Vaughn. The church was without a pastor from 1905 until 1909. The building committee received a land deed from T.W. and Annie K. Allen and built a 32-foot-by-32-foot building. The first sermon in this building was on April 9, 1910. The church was renovated with brick veneer in 1960.

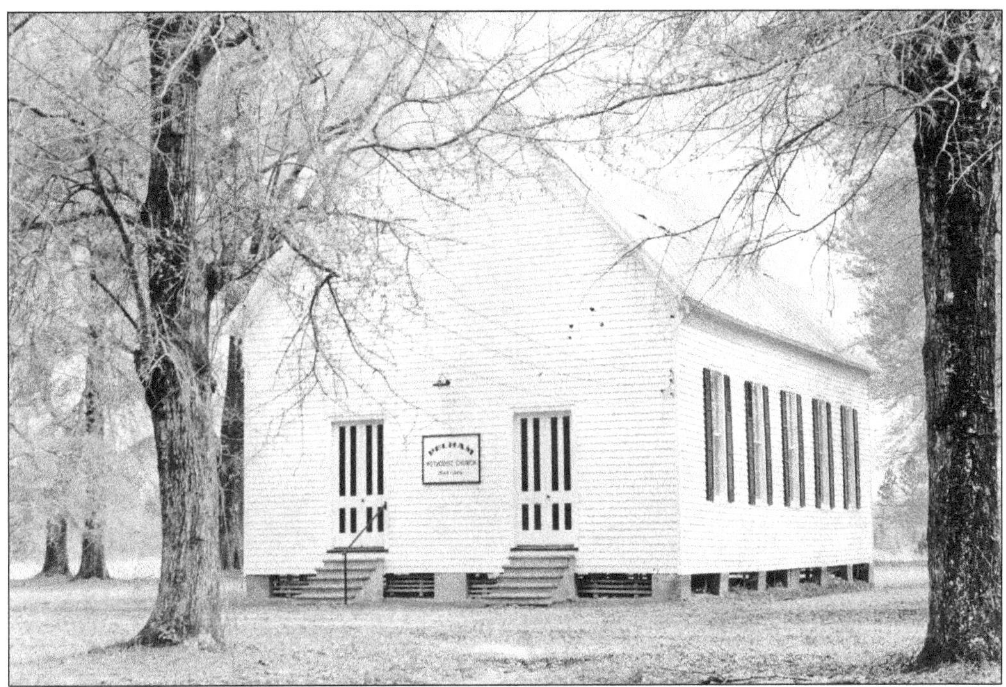

Pelham Methodist Church is one of the oldest Methodist churches in Choctaw County. Although little is known about Pelham until 1845, the congregation's history dates to 1838. In 1845, a deed was made by Robert Young and Nathan Johnson giving land to the church. The second site was given by T.J. Gilder and his wife on December 11, 1888. This is the present site. Pelham was formerly known as Bethlehem Church.

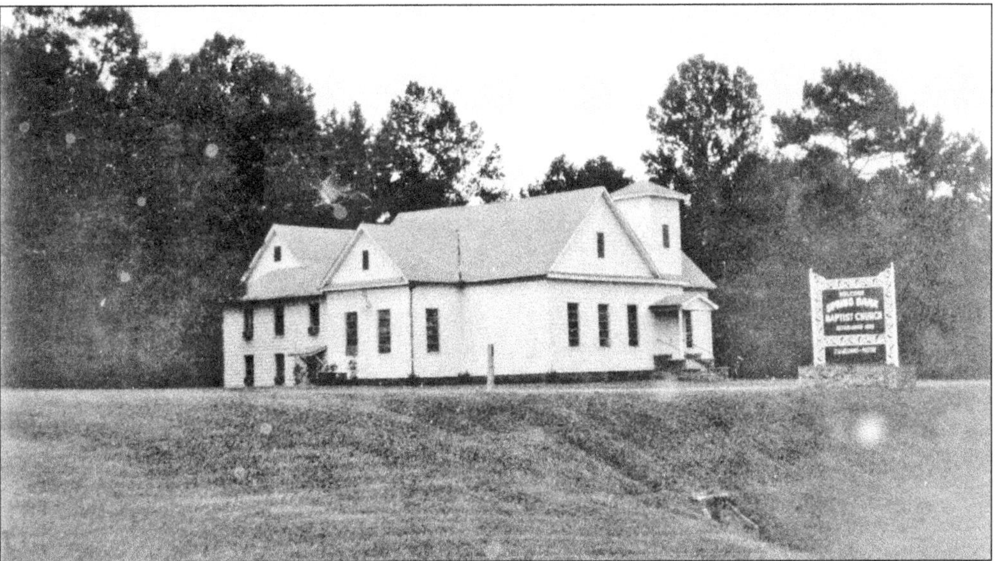

In 1825, a group of men and women met and organized Spring Bank Baptist Church. The original church was about five miles southwest of its present location. It is not known when the church moved to its present site near Silas. Spring Bank was changed from a Wayne County, Mississippi, location to a Choctaw County location in 1849. Church records show that A. Daugherty was pastor from 1837 until 1885.

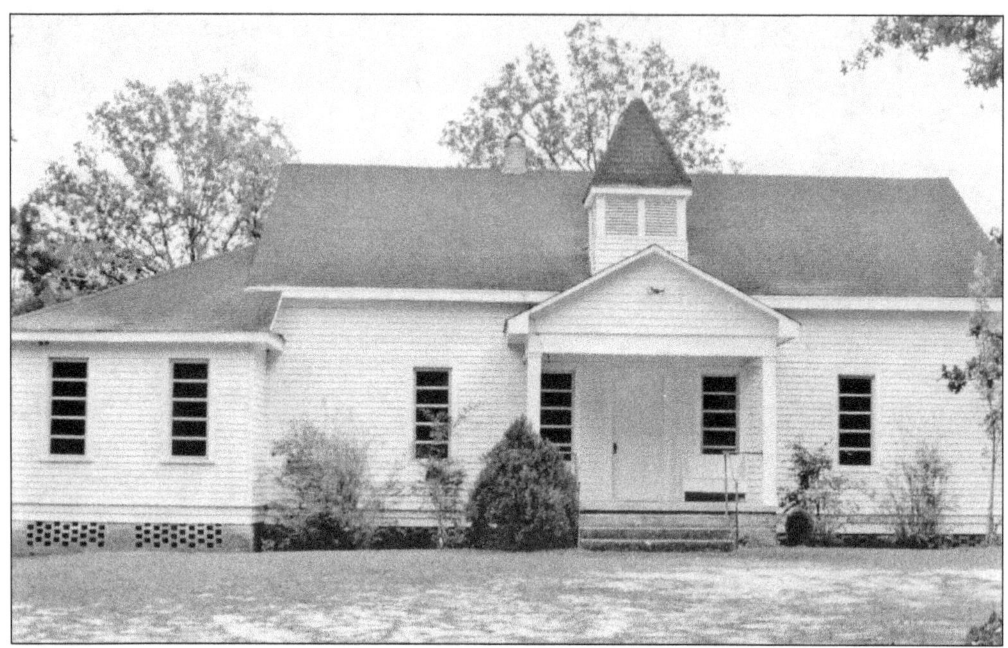

Black Creek Baptist Church was constituted in 1829. It was a log building near the Dennis Powe house, organized with six members and a preacher. It is believed that William Hall was the organizer. Little is known of the church until 1850. It was known as New Prospect until 1850, when it was renamed Black Creek. Records show that A. Daugherty was pastor from 1850 to 1853.

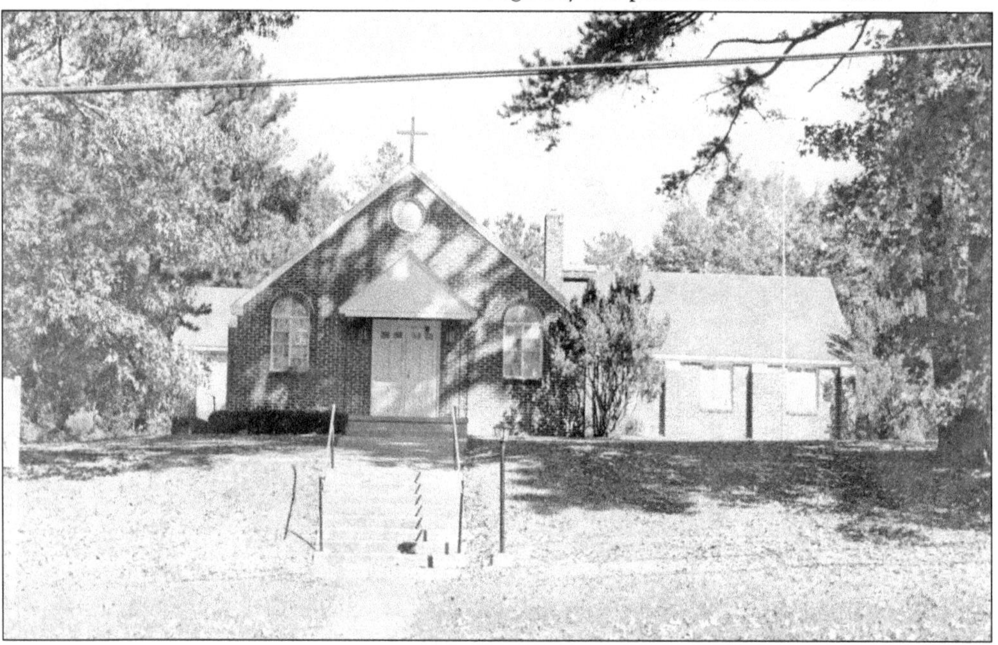

Construction of St. John's Catholic Church in Butler began in 1956. The first mass was celebrated in October 1956 with 35 people in attendance. On March 31, 1957, Archbishop Thomas Joseph Toolen dedicated this the mission chapel of the Grove Hill missions. It remained part of the Grove Hill missions until January 1972, when it was established as a separate parish with Fr. Thomas Leonard as the first resident pastor.

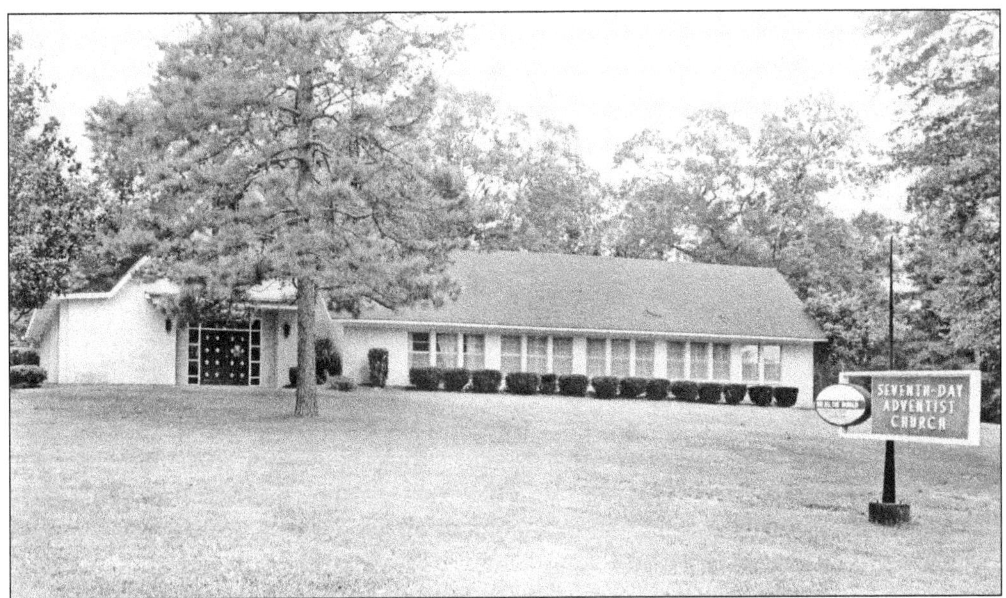

The Gilbertown Seventh-Day Adventist Church was organized on October 31, 1922, with 15 charter members. The original building was used until the spring of 1970. The present building started construction in September 1969. It was largely due to the efforts of Mr. and Mrs. O.B. Clark that erection of the new building was possible.

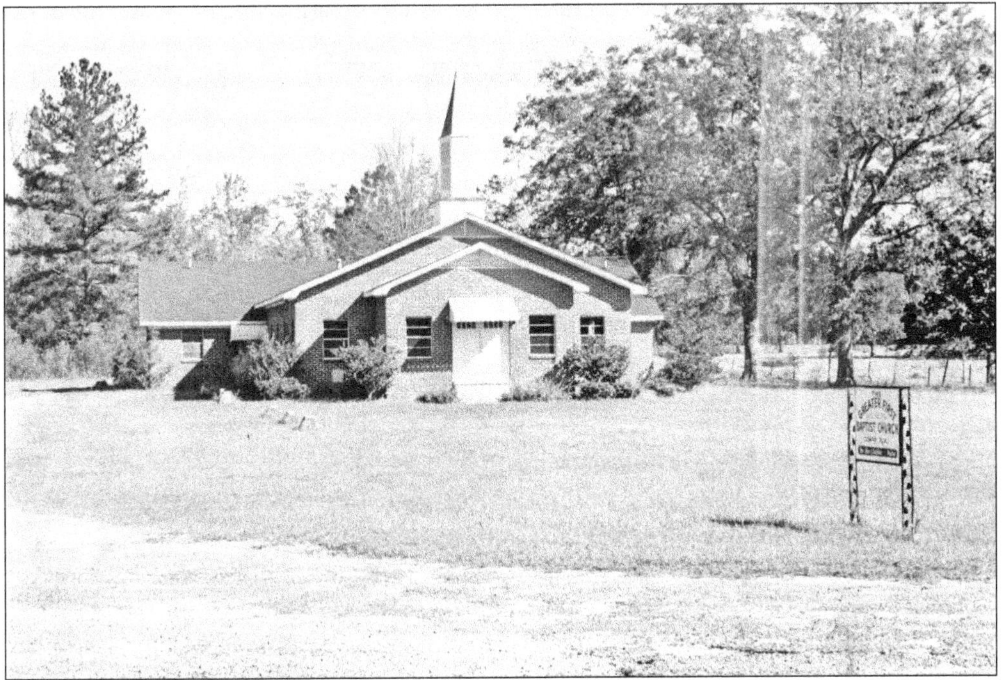

The Greater First Baptist Church of Lisman was organized in September 1913. The organization took place in an old school building known as the Gilfield Baptist Association School. This building was used until members built a church. The church was originally named St. Paul Baptist. In 1938, the church constructed its second building. At this time, the church's name was changed to Greater First Baptist Church.

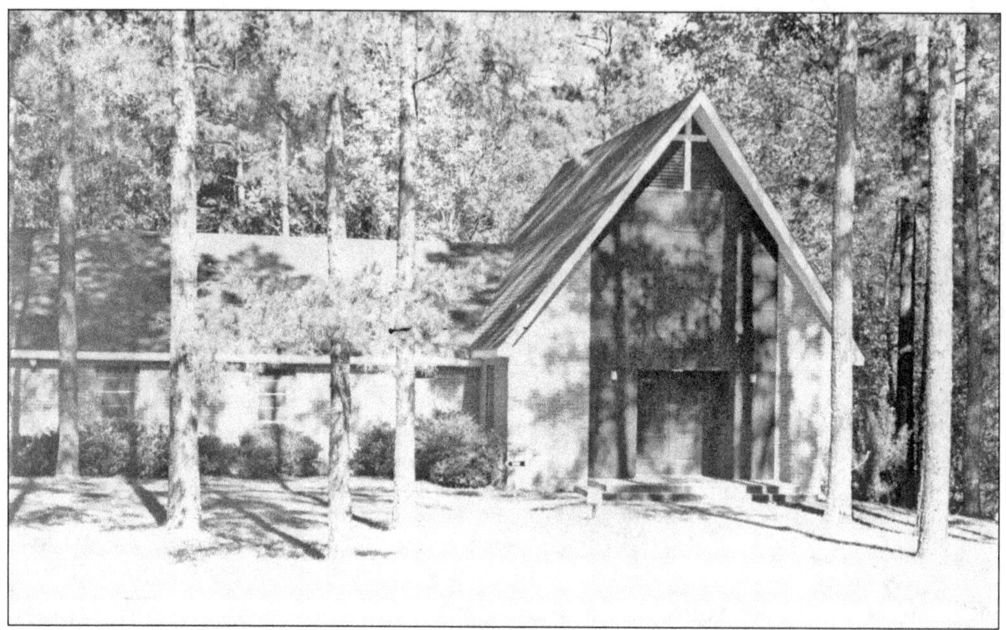

In the summer of 1957, an organization of women formed to begin Presbyterian work in Butler. The original group was composed of Sadie Smith Grimes, Laura Hudson, Cleo Laird, Nan Rogers, and Mildred Scott. On September 18, 1961, the Butler Presbyterian Church was organized. The church building was dedicated on March 18, 1965. Due to dwindling membership, it was disbanded on December 18, 2011.

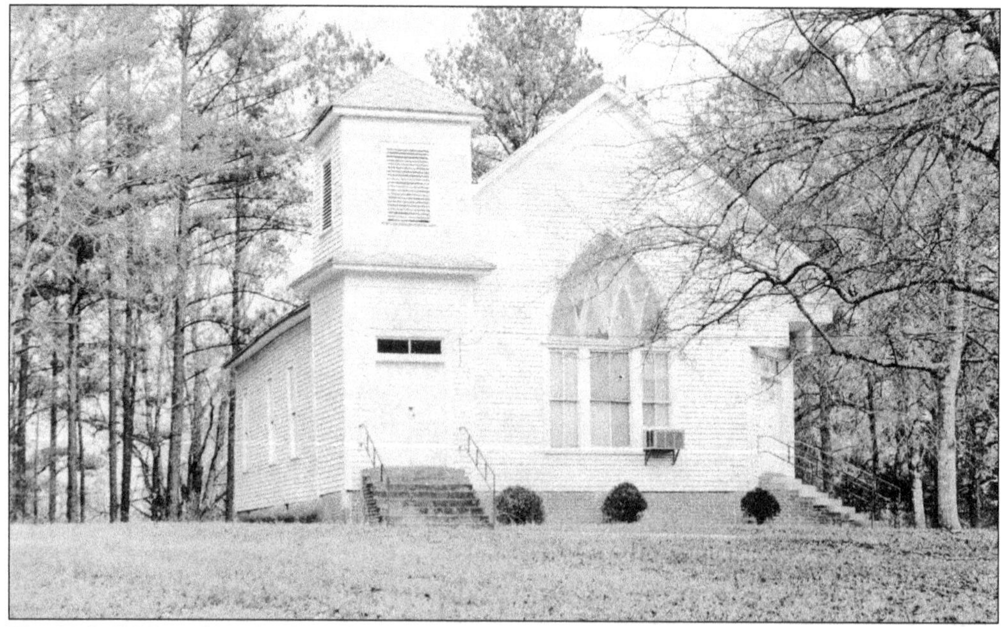

The Halsell United Methodist Church was founded in 1872. The original church was known as the Sharon Methodist Episcopal Church, South. The Sharon church was moved to a new location about 1901. The new church was known as Oak Grove Church. On January 19, 1916, the land on which the present church is located was deeded to the church by Mr. and Mrs. C.W. Bailey and Mr. and Mrs. J.T. Cochrane.

Six

Life and People

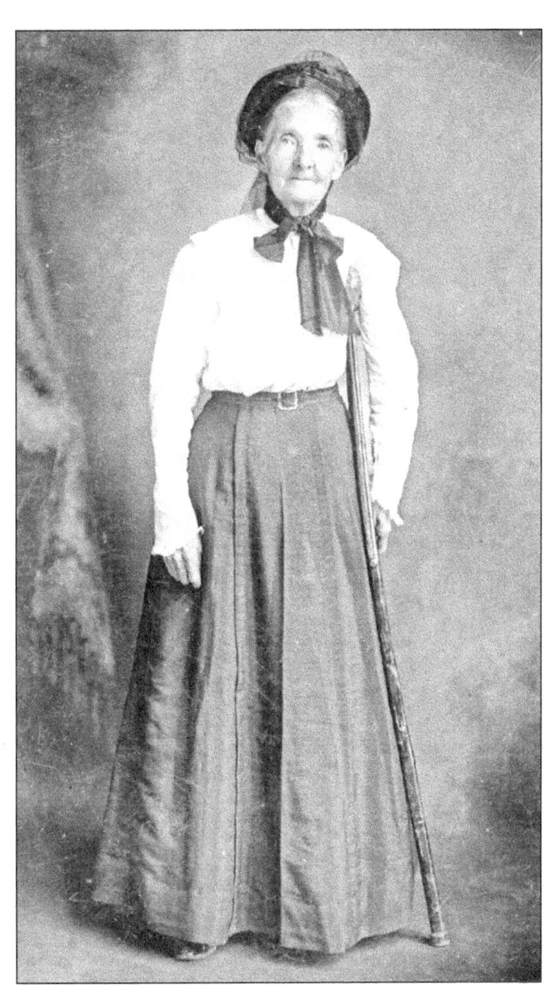

Martha Ellen Hurst is shown in this undated postcard photograph. The daughter of Joseph and Martha Sabray Hurst, she was born around January 1852. She married Albert M. Watson on November 19, 1873. He passed away in June 1914. In 1920, she was living with her son John, and her age was reported as 72. It is unknown when she died.

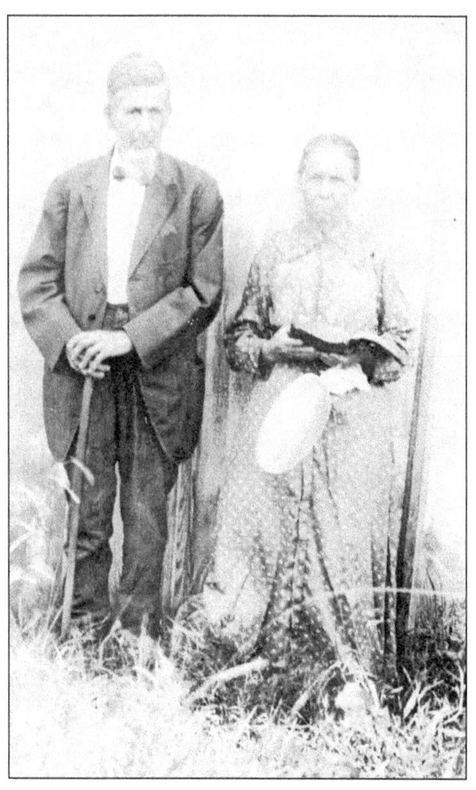

Rev. William A. Campbell, a Baptist minister, and his wife, Martha Ann, are pictured in this undated postcard photograph. He came to Choctaw County from Abbeville, South Carolina, sometime between 1845 and 1849. He lived in the Bladon Springs area but pastored at churches in Clarke County and throughout Choctaw County. Reverend Campbell passed away on December 14, 1877, after a lingering illness. (Courtesy of Sandra Jenkins Little.)

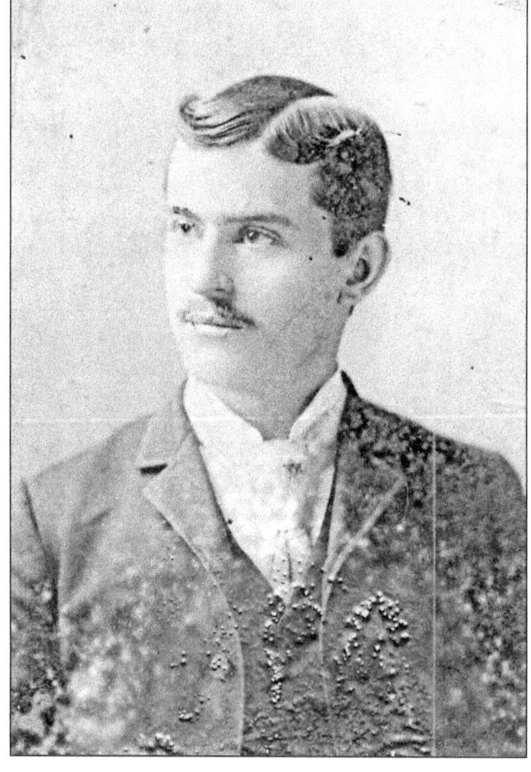

Dr. Alfred Bettis Pugh was an innocent bystander who was killed during a rescue of Bob Sims by his brothers, son, and three other Simsites from deputy marshals at the Bladon Springs Hotel in 1891. Dr. Pugh was 25 years old when he stopped by to talk with his future brother-in-law, Frank Dahlberg, who was guarding Bob Sims during Choctaw County's infamous Sims War period. (Courtesy of Lora Jane McIlwain.)

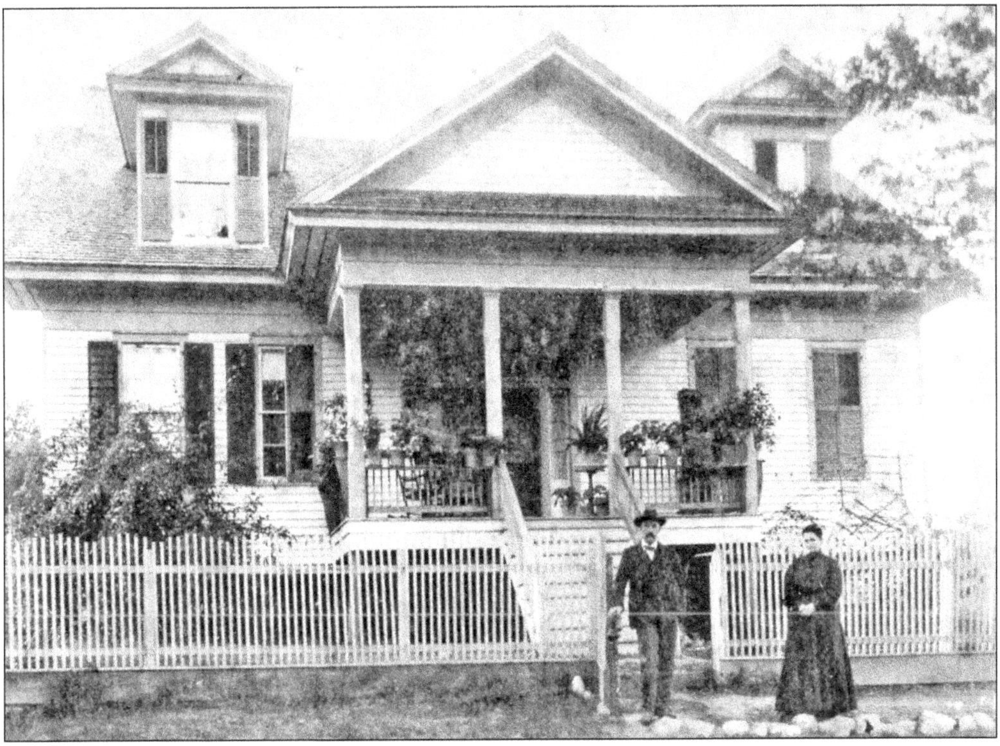

The Samuel Godwin and Alfreda Caroline Olivia Dahlberg Barnes home was across the road from the famed Cullom Springs Hotel. Sam and Alfreda are pictured here. (Courtesy of Lora Jane McIlwain.)

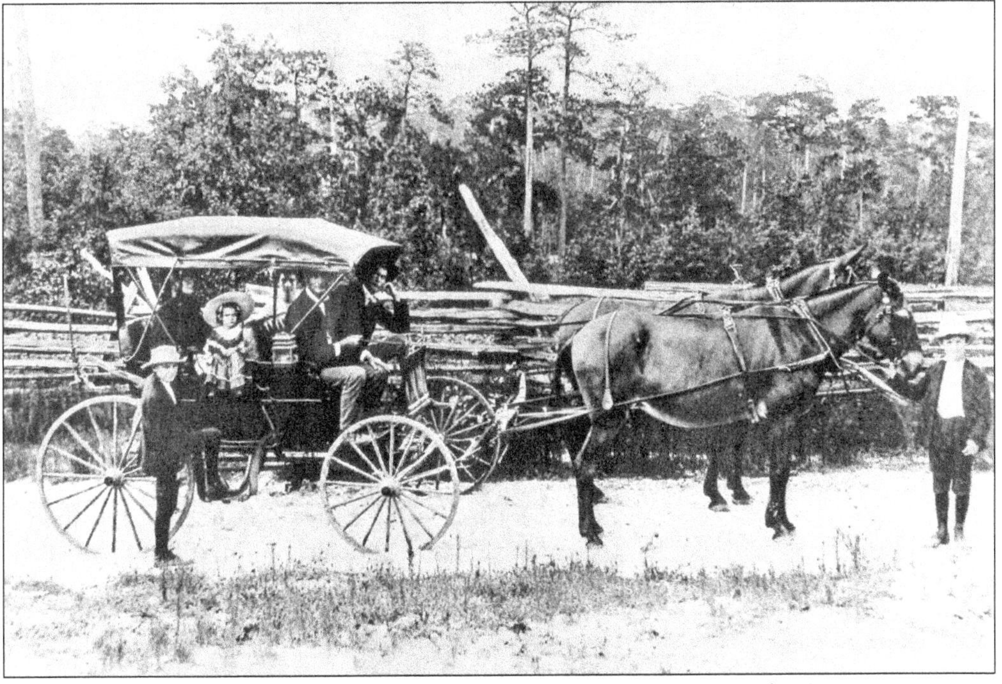

This is a typical Choctaw County family scene from the late 1800s or early 1900s.

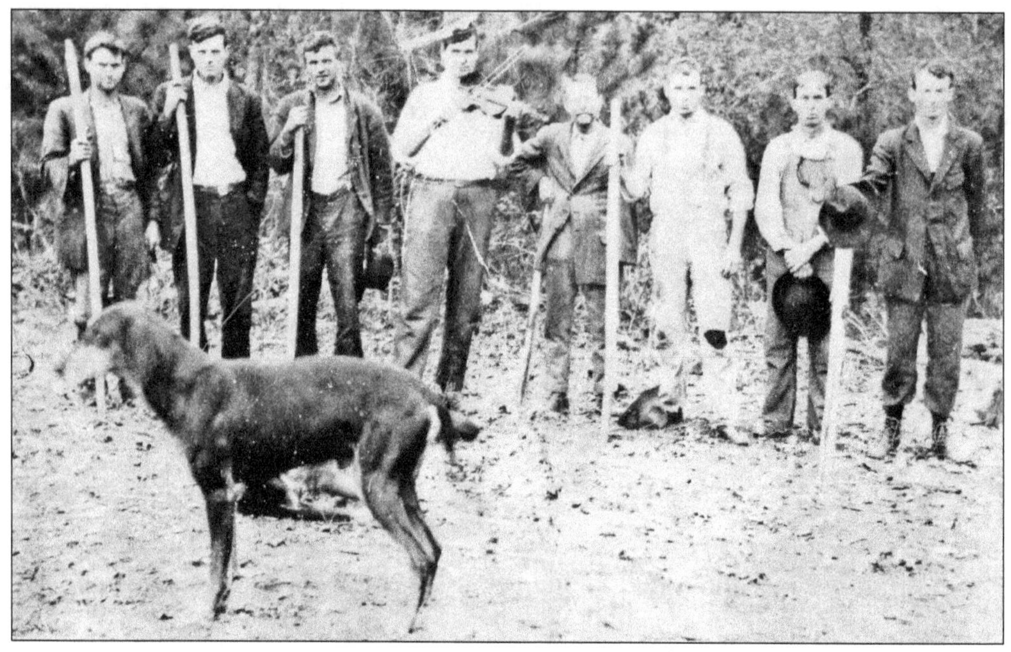

These men were gathered for a log rolling contest near the site of the Country General Store on County Road 23 near Ararat around 1890. From left to right are Dan Morgan, John Mosley, Ira Carlisle, Leamon Mosley, Tom Morgan, Robert Morgan, Will Land, and John Gibson.

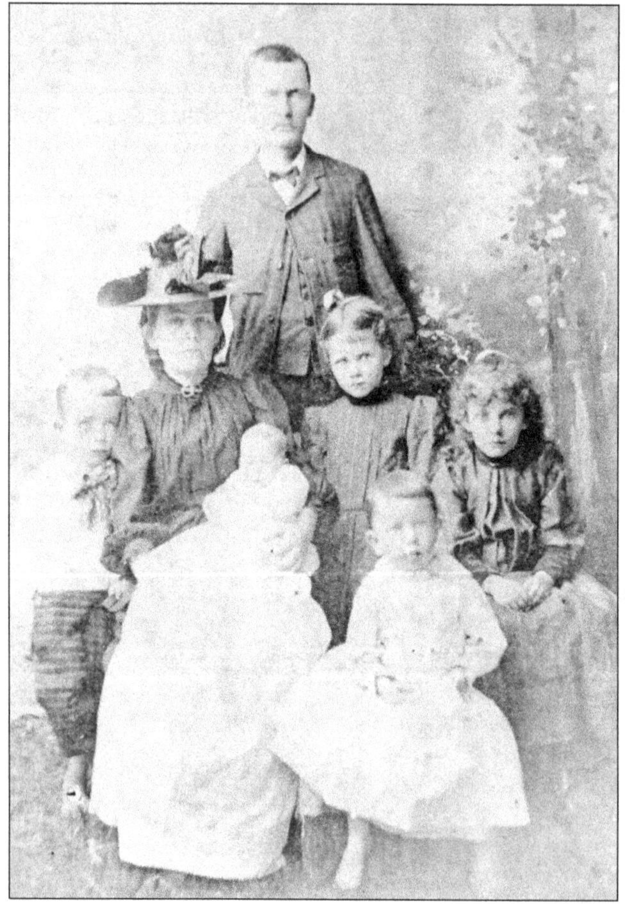

Pictured here is the Joseph Micajah Young family. Joseph is standing. From left to right are Henry, baby Bessie sitting on Lizzie's lap, Stella, and Mable. Robert is seated in front. Joseph was the first editor of the *Farmer's Alliance* newspaper. The *Choctaw Advocate* was sold to the *Alliance* in 1892, and the name reverted back to the *Choctaw Advocate* in 1901.

Annie Carlisle Mosley Boswell is pictured with her children from her marriage to Grover D. Mosley. The baby, Thomas Leon Mosley, was born on November 15, 1911. The girl is Vermelle Mosley. She was born on November 8, 1907. Annie was born on January 2, 1883. After her first husband died, she married Joseph H. Boswell. (Courtesy of Linda Pittman Mosley.)

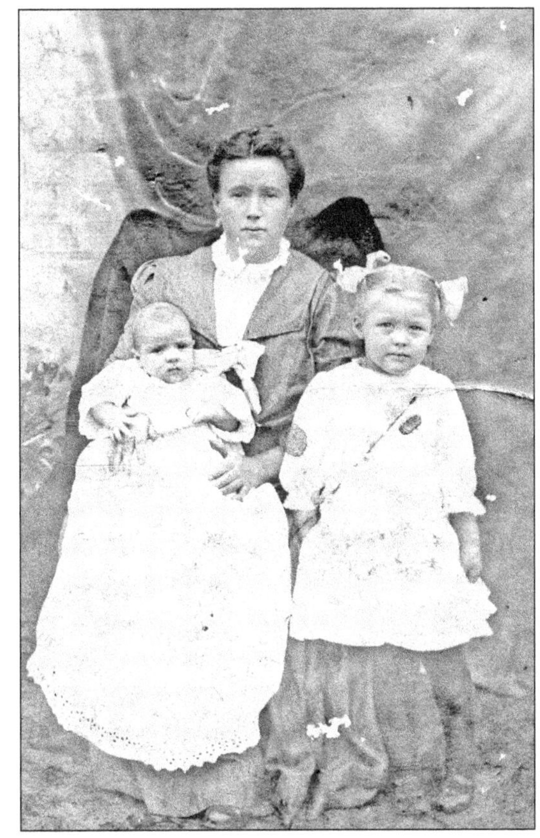

The James Alexander Bell family is shown in this undated photograph. Margaret Olivia is seated holding James Alford. Standing from left to right are James Alexander, Rozier, Frank, and Era. James Alexander was the son of Joseph Blythe Alston Bell and Martha Ann Lister. He married Margaret Olivia McInnis.

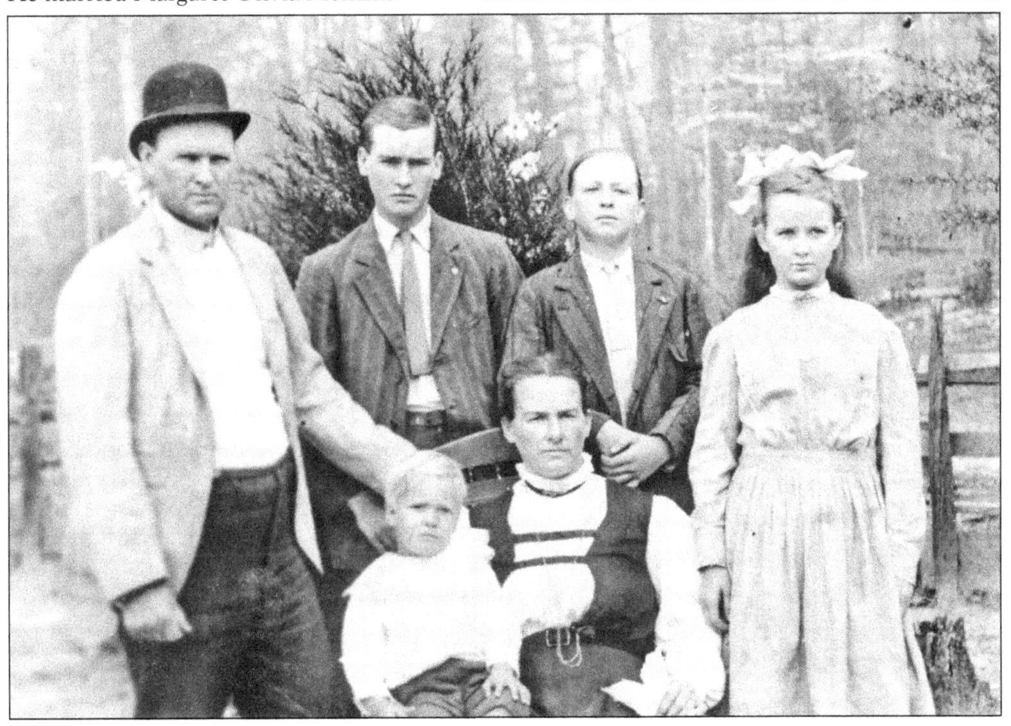

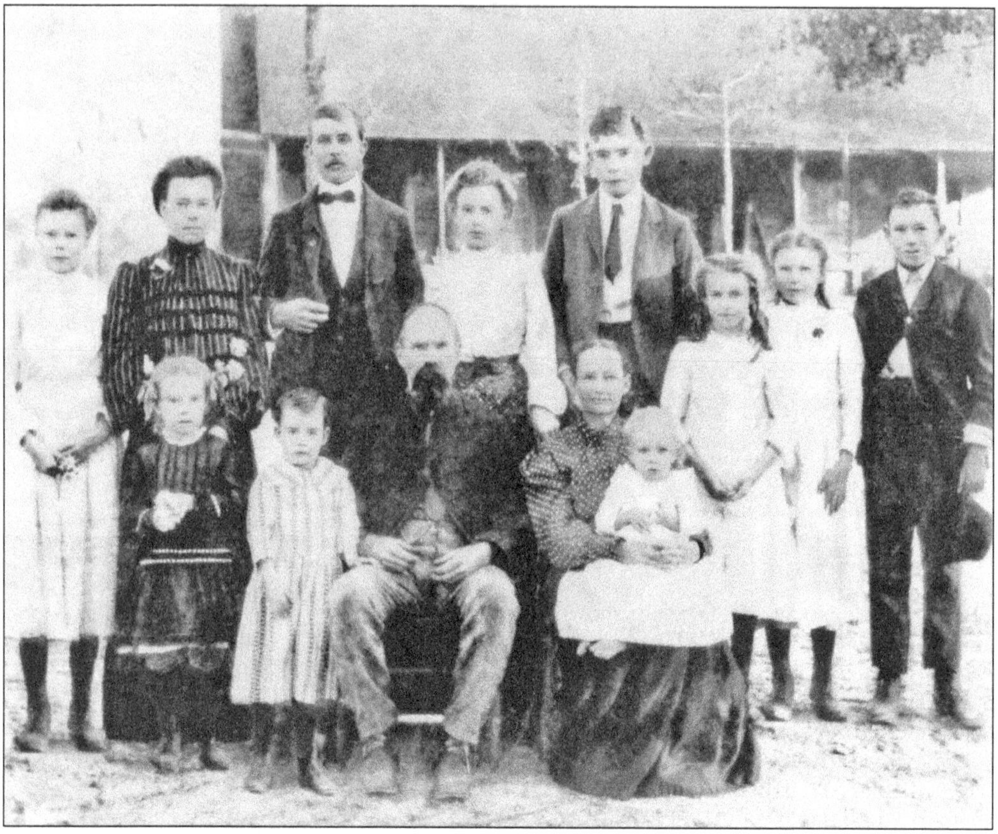

The Thomas Jefferson Campbell family gathered in front of their Womack Hill home around 1905 for a family photograph. From left to right are (first row) Mamie, Thomas Lenoir, Thomas Jefferson, and Clara holding Mike; (second row) Pearl, Jessie, Frank Odom (Jessie's husband), Lillian, Hubert, Vennie, Addie, and Ferrer. Clara Campbell was pregnant with Edna at the time.

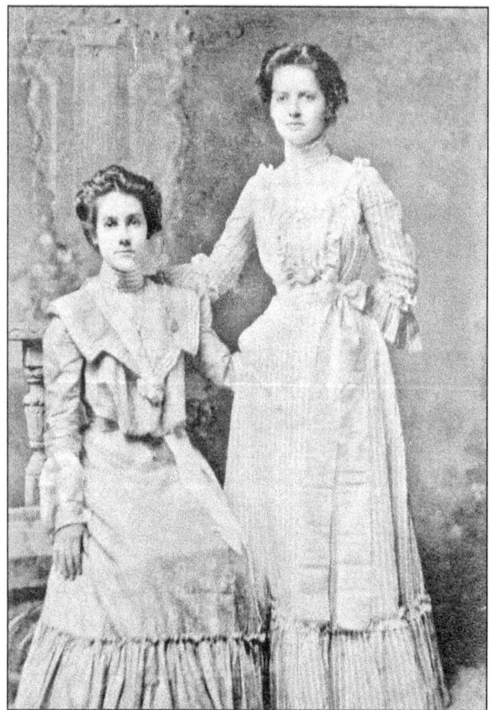

Sisters Bertie Minor Mills (seated) and Nias Nina Minor are pictured on Bertie's wedding day in January 1904. Nias Nina married William Tetsel Cook in Meridian, Mississippi, in 1906. Their children were Thracie Josephine, Horace Tetsel, Mildred Mason, Nina Tait, Henrie Blanche, and Melvin Haas. Bertie and Nias were the daughters of John Minor and Josephine Brashiers Minor. (Courtesy of Lanelle Turner.)

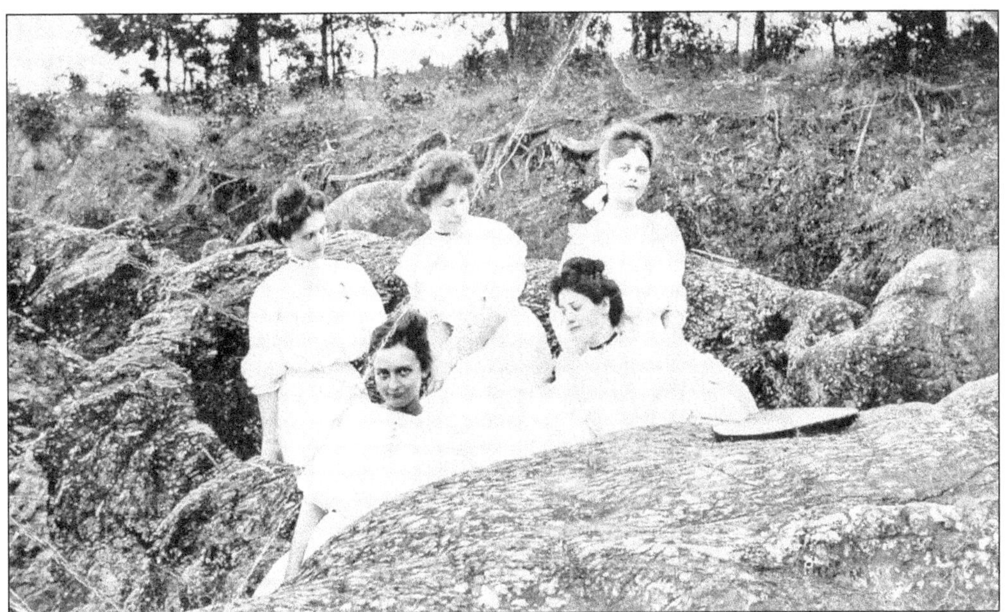

A group of young women pose in the rocks in July 1907. Entertainment was hard to come by in the early 1900s. The woman at center in the back row is Maude Patrick.

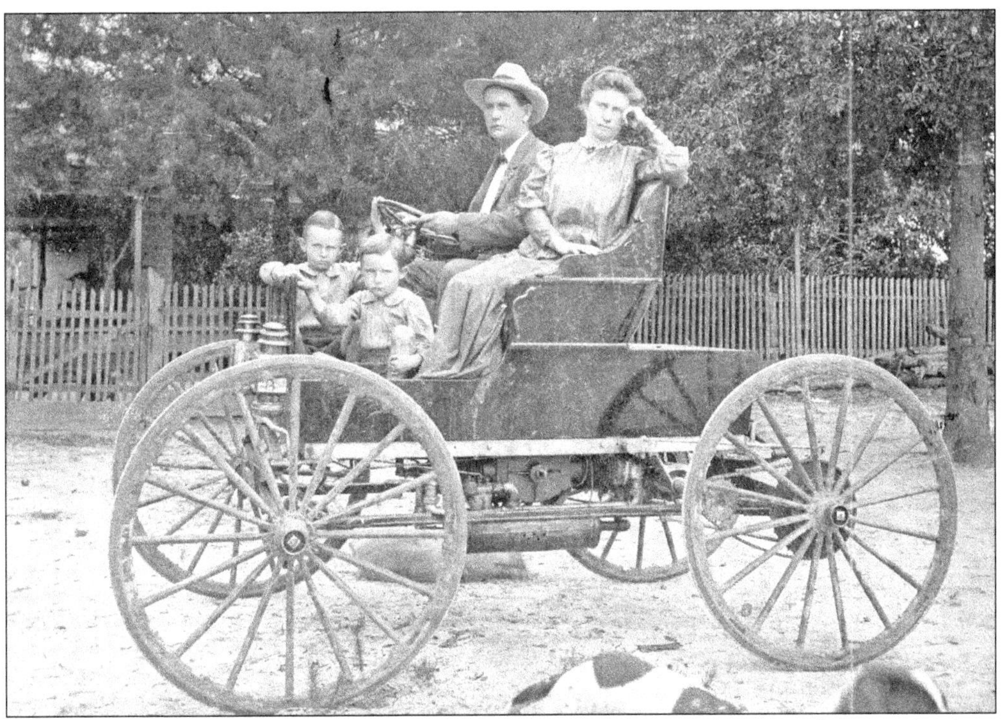

Dr. Sam Alman and his family are out for a drive around 1907. Dr. Alman was born on April 28, 1872, in Rankin County, Mississippi, and died on August 19, 1925. "Dr. Sam" was a medical doctor and surgeon practicing in Melvin and Gilbertown. He also owned the Choctaw Bottling Company in Gilbertown. From left to right are Rex, Sam Jr., Dr. Sam, and his wife, Alma Land Alman.

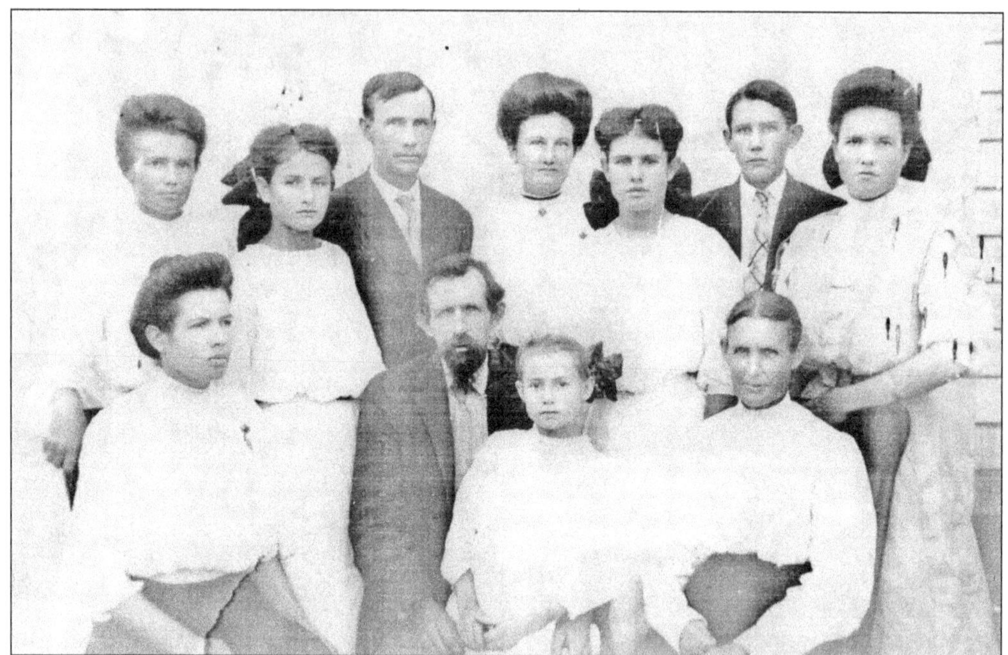

The patriarch of this family, Evander Jackson Campbell, was the son of John B. Campbell. Evander was born in Choctaw County and later moved his family to Clarke County, Mississippi. From left to right are (seated) Allie, Evander, Bertha, and Sarah Ann Burns Campbell (Evander's wife); (standing) Falbie, Cora, John Mason, Olive (John Mason's wife), Olivia, Washington, and Ada.

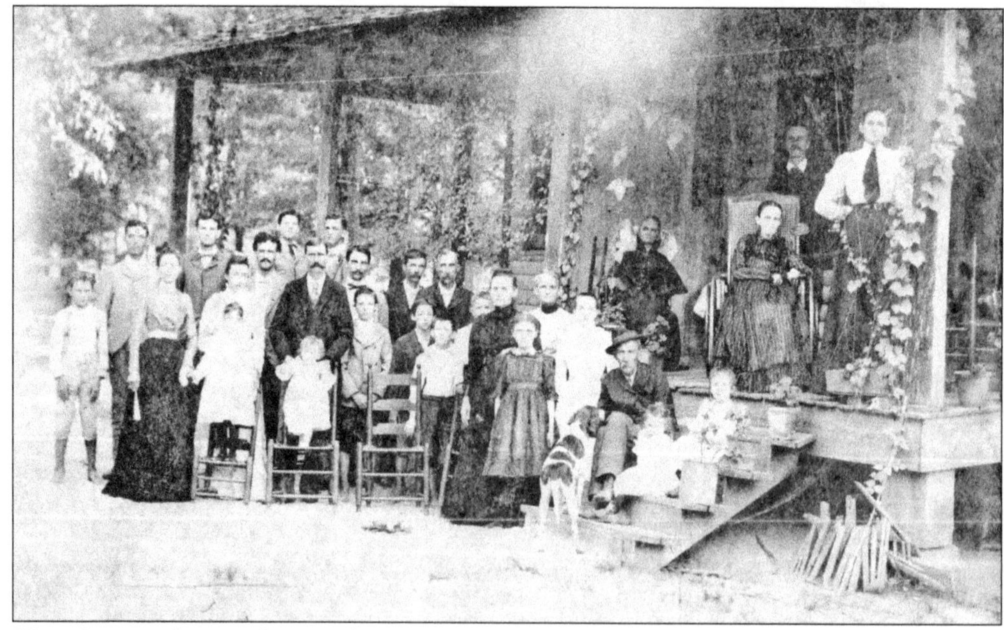

This photograph was taken on the steps of the old Carnathan place in Mount Sterling. From left to right are (seated on the steps) Joseph B. Turner, Mattie Anna Turner, and Josie Spinks Turner; (standing, first row) Daisy Rosenthal, Caroline Rosenthal, Inez Turner, Connie Turner Littlepage, Mary Fenley Turner, Gertrude Rosenthal, and Leslie Eugene Turner. (Courtesy of Lanelle Turner.)

Dr. John Massey was born in 1834 in Choctaw County. His career in education reached its peak when he became president of the college that was formerly named Huntingdon. The college relocated to Montgomery and was renamed Woman's College of Alabama at the end of his tenure. His book, *Massey's Reminiscences*, describes his early life in Choctaw County and his other achievements. He died on April 23, 1918.

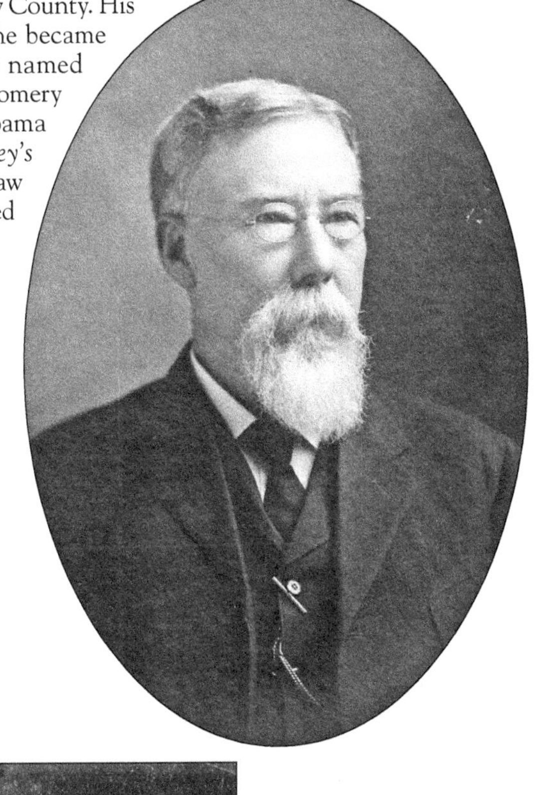

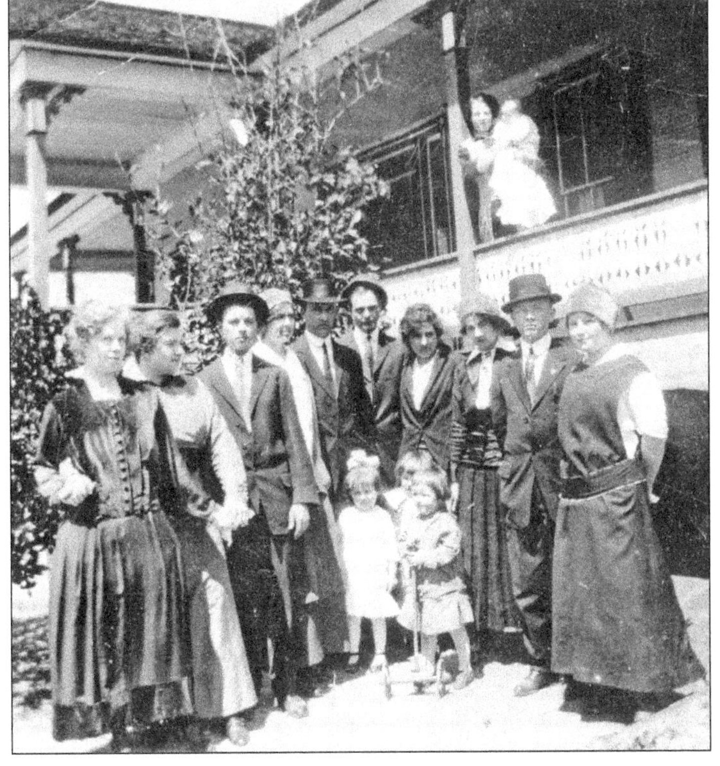

This photograph was taken at the W.R. Edwards home at Robjohn. The only people identified are Nellie Edwards (left), and the small children, Mary Ella, Marjorie, and William. On the front porch is Mrs. Edwards holding Margaret. W.R. Edwards also owned a store at Robjohn.

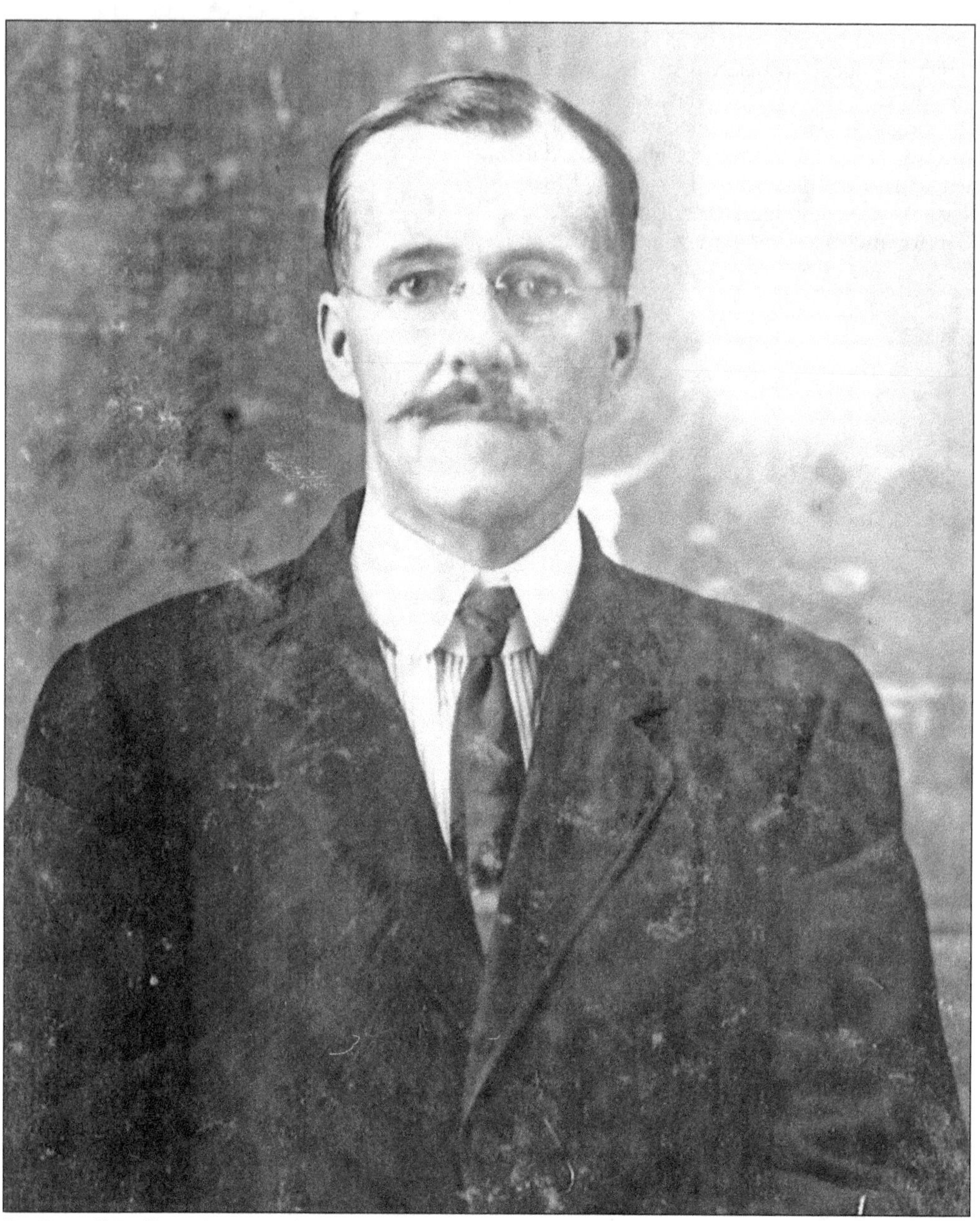

Dr. Rowell Wilbur Shaw was born on June 3, 1874, in Cuba, Alabama. He had to walk two miles each day to attend the Cuba School. He wanted to attend medical school, so he earned money by working for seven years as a mail clerk on trains. He attended medical school at the University of Tennessee at Memphis and did postgraduate study at the New York City Poly Clinic inside Belleview Hospital in 1907. He worked for the American Red Cross in England and France in World War I. After the war, he returned to the United States and purchased an old saloon that he turned into a drugstore across the street from the Mobile & Ohio Terminal Depot. He came up with a quick way to dispense bottled Coca Cola and presented his idea to Walter Bellingrath, the head of the Mobile Coca-Cola Company. Dr. Shaw was paid $5,250 for his dispenser. From 1924 to 1931, he worked in Service, Alabama, for the large Bladon Springs Lumber Company. After the death of Dr. Sam Alman in Gilbertown, Shaw filled his vacancy from 1931 to 1954.

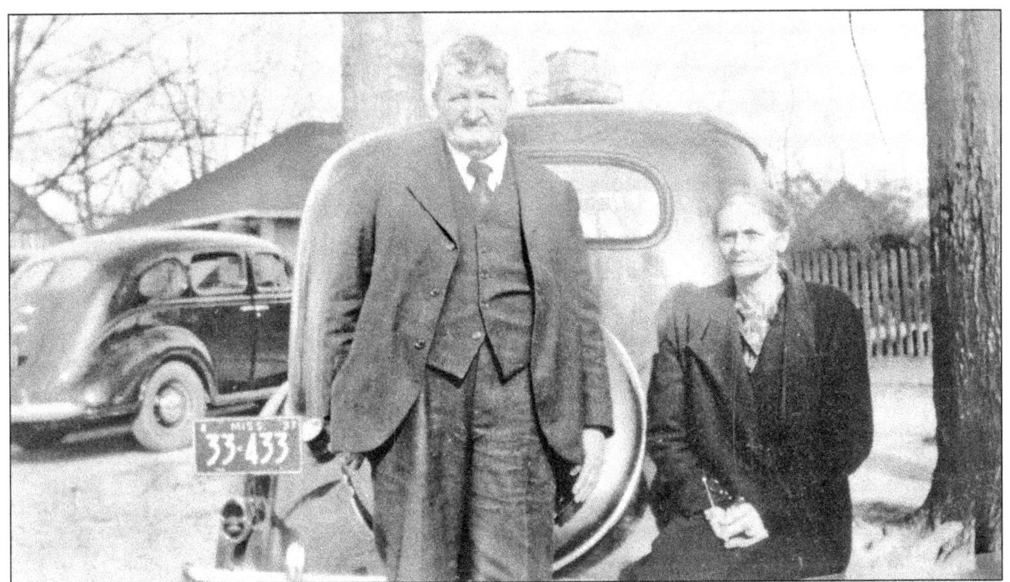

Moses and Lena Slay are pictured in this undated photograph. Moses Slay was born on February 6, 1860. He became very interested in public education in the county. After a school law was passed establishing county boards of education, he was elected as a member of the first Choctaw County Board of Education. He also served two terms on the Choctaw County Commission and was a member when the present courthouse was built in 1906. He died on September 7, 1949.

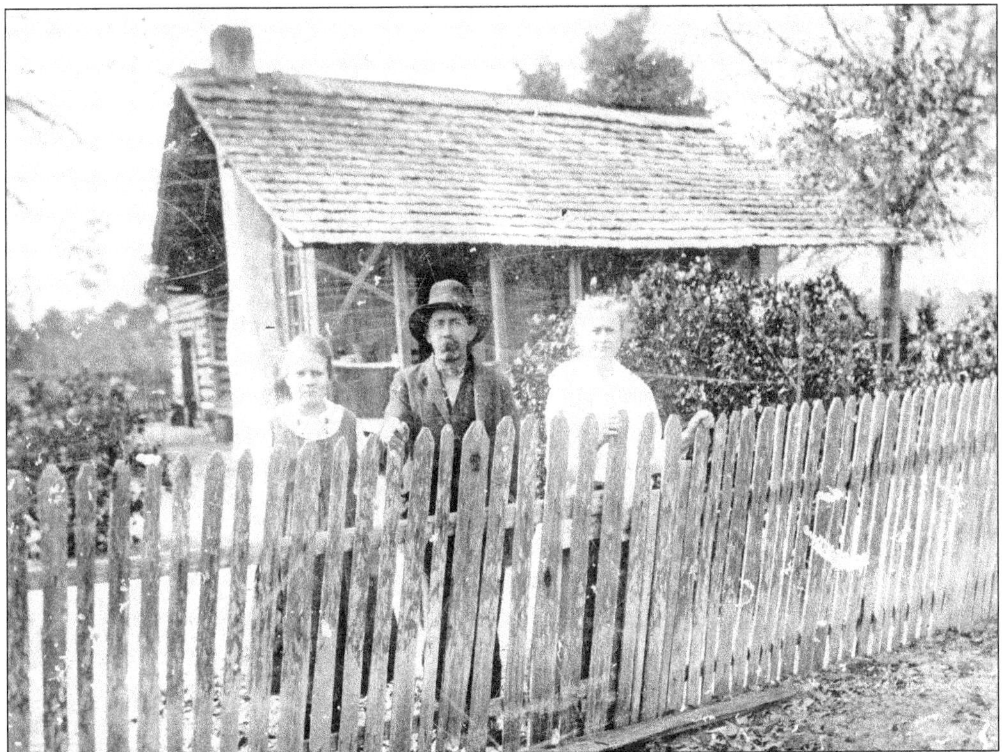

The people in this photograph are believed to be members of the Elbert Nordan family. The Nordan family lived in the Old Samuel community, near Gilbertown.

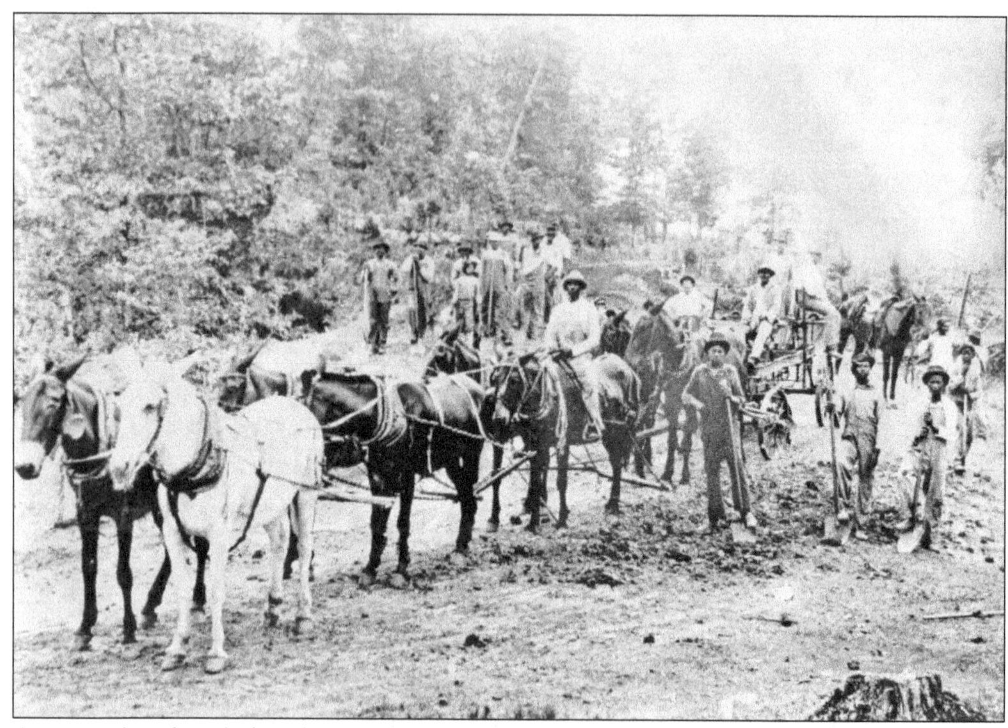

A group of unidentified workers gathers for a day of work at an unknown location.

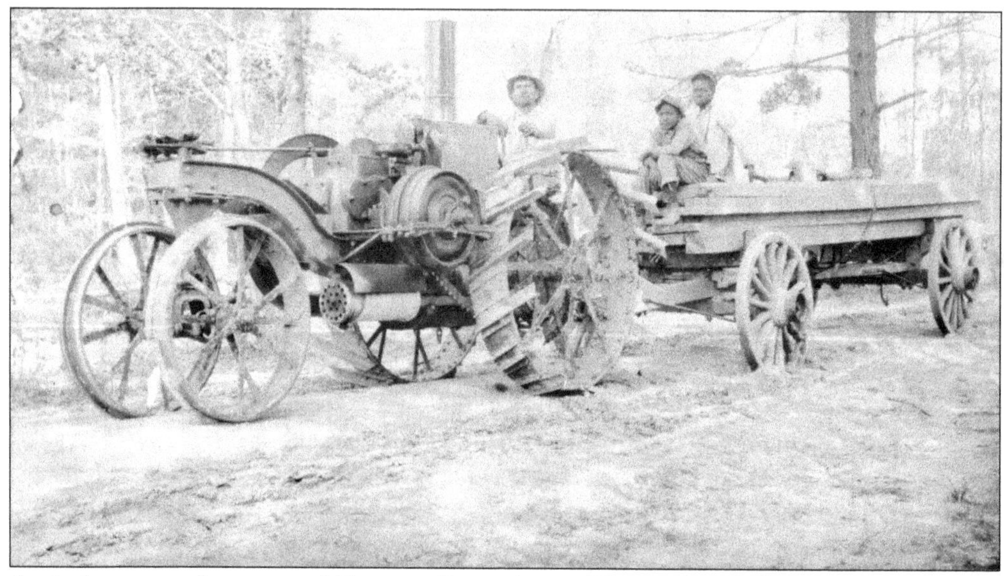

Agriculture was a large part of Choctaw County's past. The unidentified man on a tractor and two young boys in the wagon are most likely on their way to work in the fields. The photograph was taken in the mid-1920s.

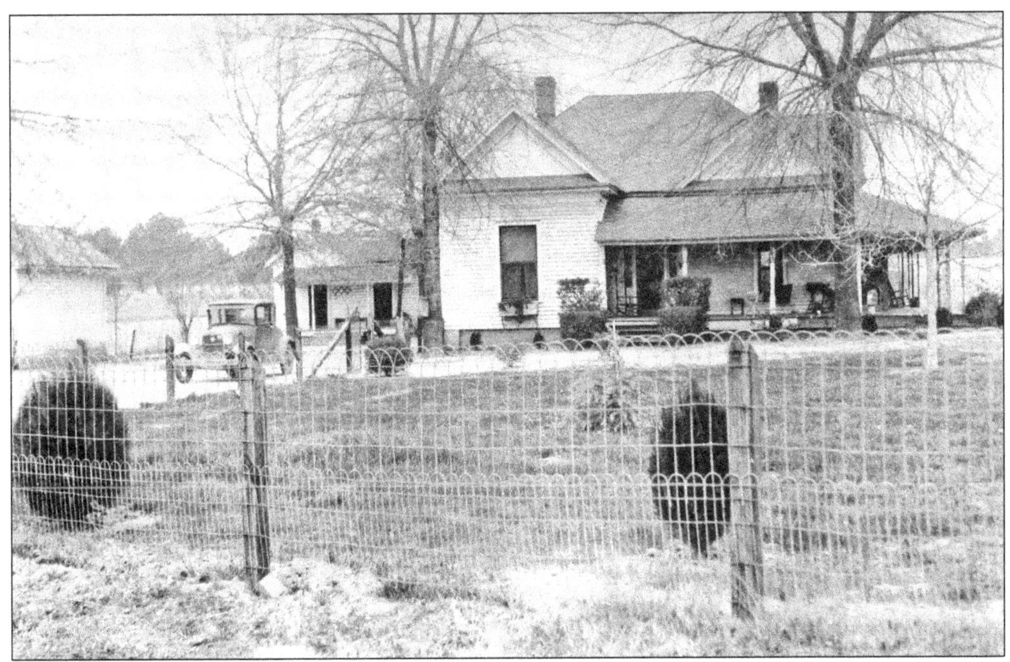

This c. 1920 photograph shows the home of Dr. Samuel Miller on Highway 10 West at Yantley. His office occupied two rooms of the home. The home is still standing and is now the residence of Eleana Matlock.

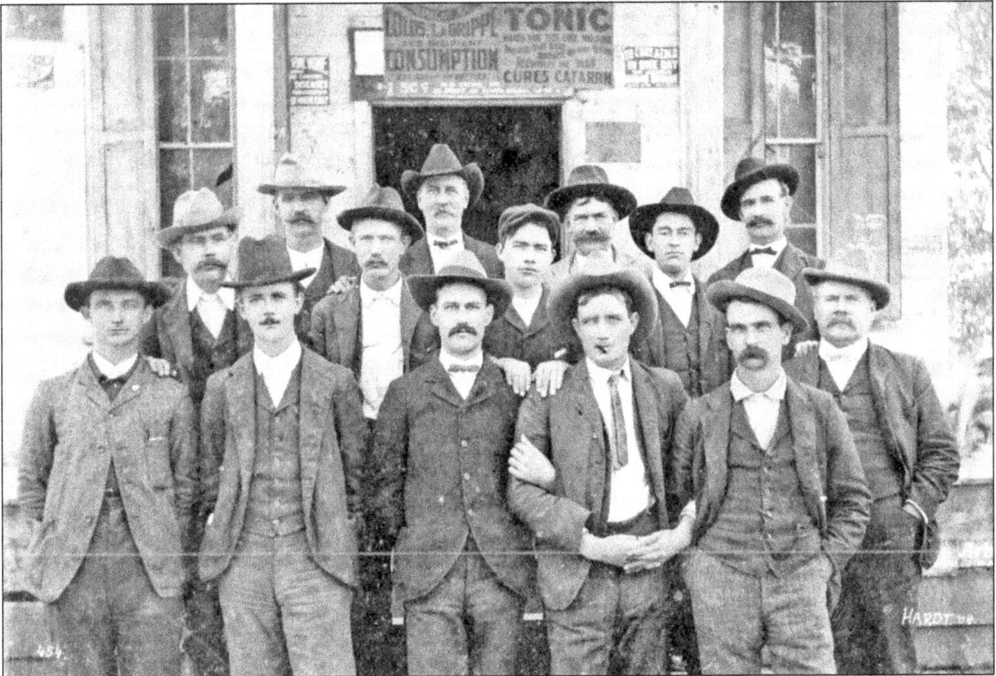

A group of Choctaw County citizens gathers at an unidentified store. From left to right are (first row) unidentified, Will Greton, Jessie Turner, unidentified, Will Mills, and unidentified; (second row) Jim Hurst, Charlie Will Dubose, Gross Turner, Bobby Hurst, Sam Jordan, Dr. Charles McElroy, Dr. McCall, and unidentified. (Courtesy of Lanelle Turner.)

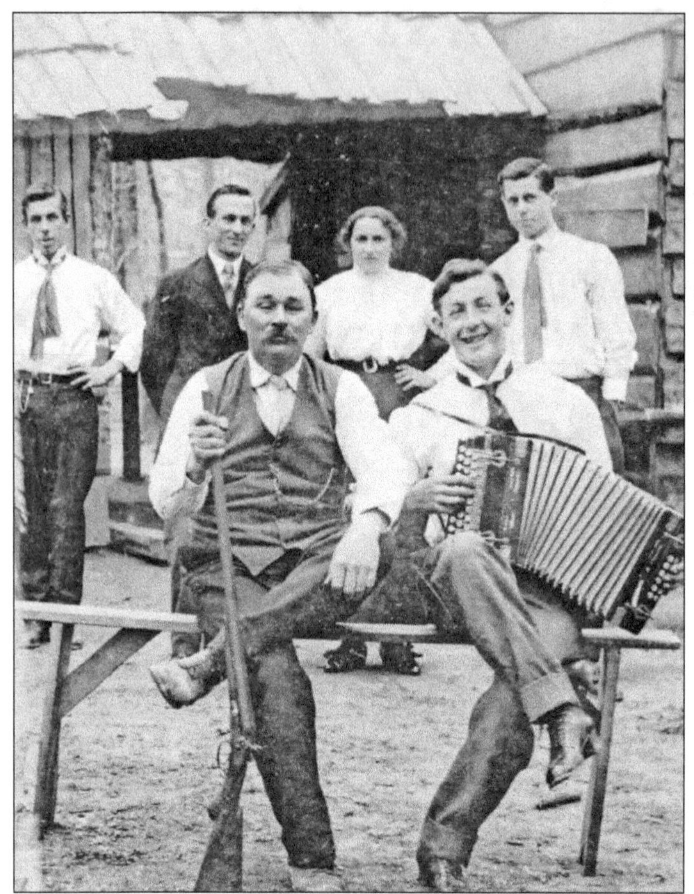

Recreation was important after working hard. The people in this photograph are members of Sam Rogers's sawmill crew. From left to right are (first row) Sam O. Rogers and John Stinich; (second row) Tony Kovac, Joe Kovac, Amelia Kovac, and Matt Lusk.

Oxen were an important part of life in the early 1900s. From left to right are Izzie Moore, Sallie Tyson, Mary Tyson, and Malachi Todd with Robert Simeon Tyson's oxen. The photograph was taken in the Cedar Springs area of Choctaw County. Sallie and Mary were two of Simeon and Sarah Elizabeth Bush Tyson's children. (Courtesy of Sandra Jenkins Little.)

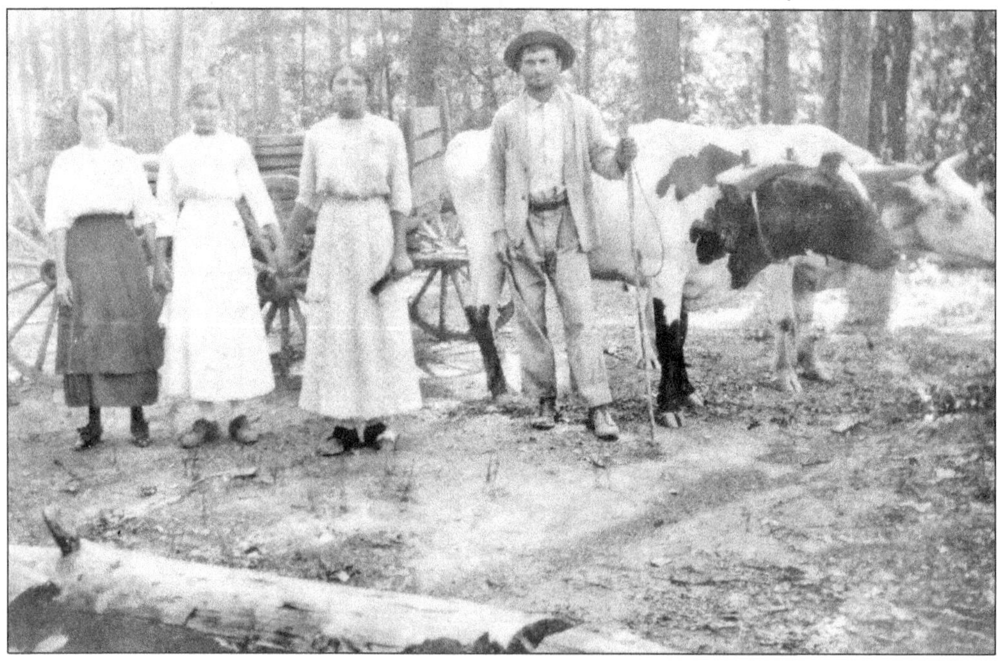

This photograph of Jessie Ona Campbell Odom was taken in 1923. She was the oldest daughter of Thomas Jefferson Campbell and Clarissa Ursula Wright Campbell. The family lived in the Womack Hill area of Choctaw County. She married Benjamin Franklin Odom and later moved to Meridian, Lauderdale County, Mississippi. The couple had 13 children. She and her husband are buried in the Pleasant Hill Cemetery along with the children who died in childhood.

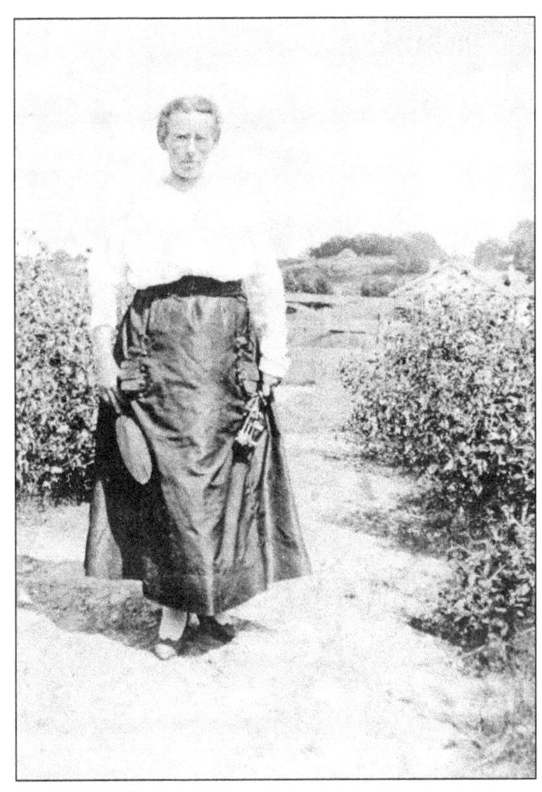

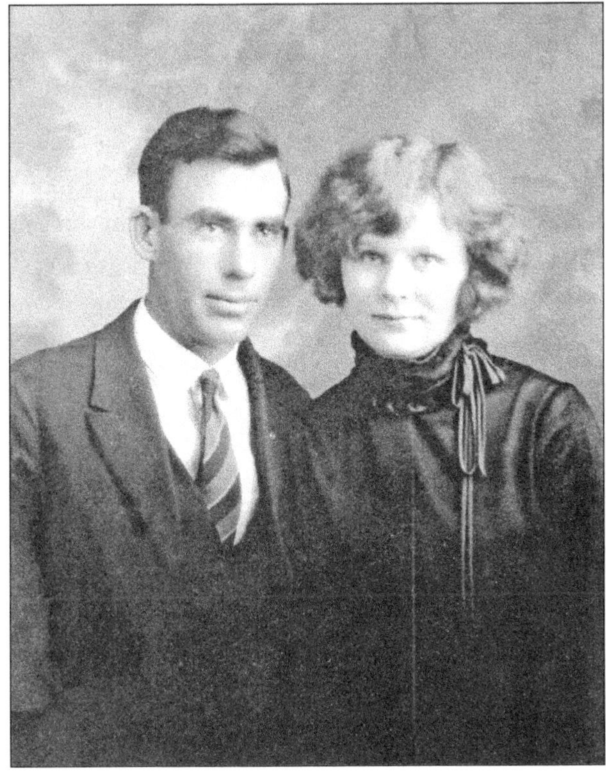

Thomas Lenoir Campbell and his wife, Lottie Henrietta Tyson Campbell, were photographed shortly after their wedding in April 1925. He was the son of Thomas Jefferson Campbell and Clarissa Ursula Wright, and she was the daughter of Robert Simeon Tyson and Sarah Elizabeth Bush Tyson. The couple had three children prior to his death in December 1932. Lottie would marry again in September 1933, to Thomas Grayson Sims.

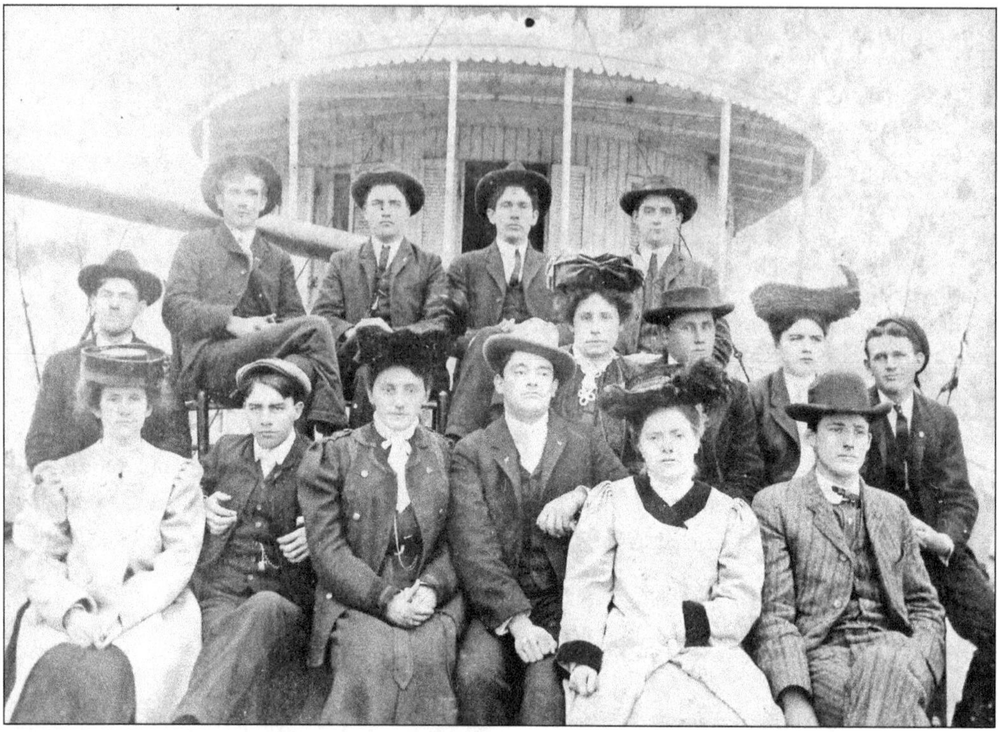

A group of people gather for a steamboat cruise on the Tombigbee River around 1926. From left to right are (first row) Johnnie Whitted, Bobby Hurst, Mattie Ezell, Dr. Charles McElroy, Vadie Hodges, and Henry Littlepage; (second row) Arthur McLeod, Maude Ezell, Taylor Ezell, Minnie Hurst, and Coleman Tillman; (third row) Leslie Wainwright, Lonnie Hurst, Howard Vaughn, and Sam Webb.

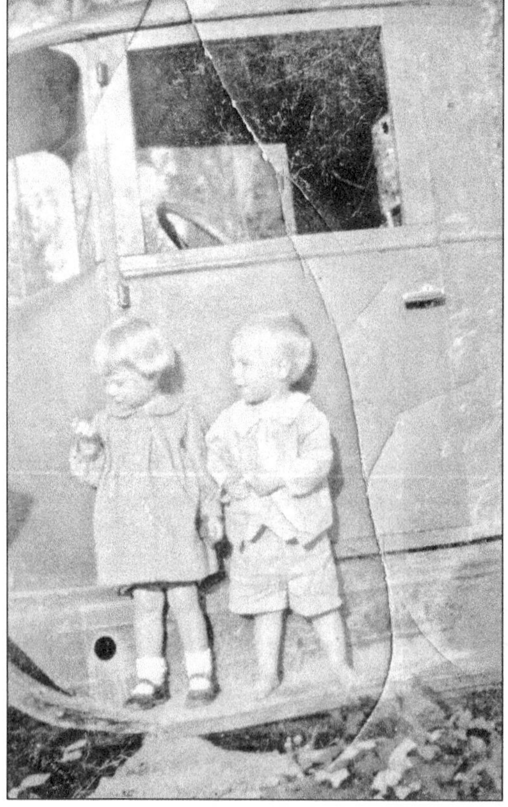

Hazel Campbell (left) and her brother, Thomas Jefferson (T.J.), were caught standing on the running board of an old Model T around 1929. There was only an 11-month age difference between the two. Hazel was born in January 1927 and T.J. was born in December 1927. They were the children of Thomas Lenoir Campbell and Lottie Henrietta Tyson Campbell. (Courtesy of Sandra Jenkins Little.)

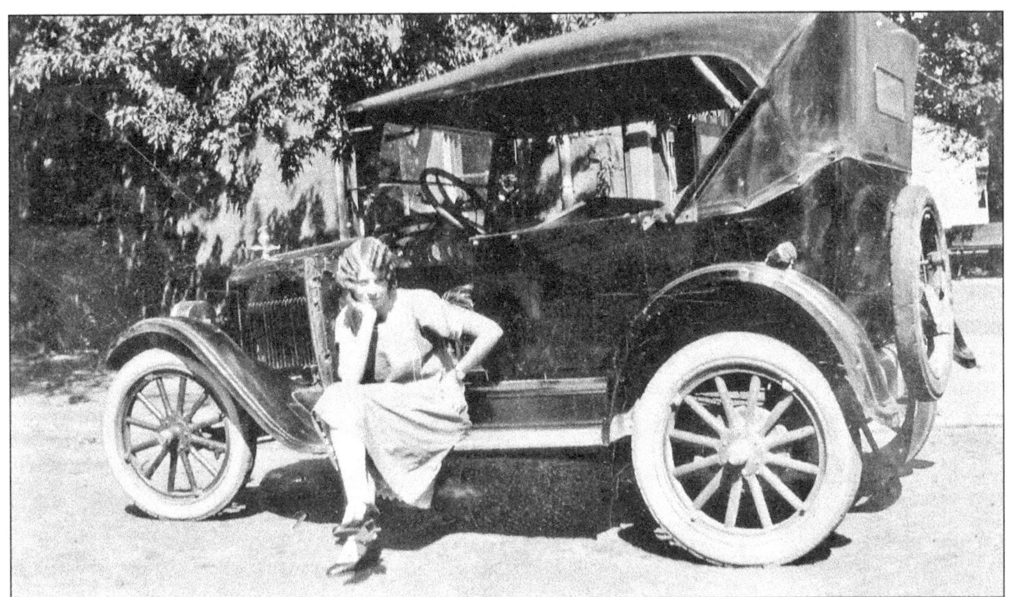

Ruth Anna Mixon was born on November 20, 1901. She was the daughter of George H. Mixon and Rebecca Stewart Mixon. Her first husband was Lula Floyd, with whom she had one son, Cecil. She later married Joe Wood Hutchinson. They had five children, Joseph Wood Jr., Andrew Jackson, Annie Ruth, Sarah Elizabeth, and Robert Leo. This photograph was taken around 1930. (Courtesy of Annie Ruth Hutchinson Schleth.)

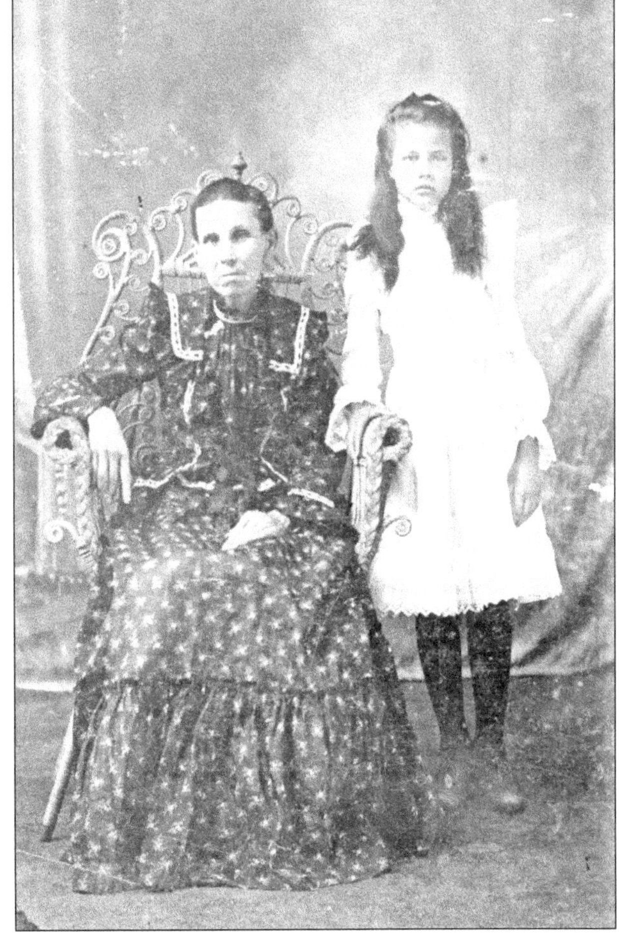

Sinthey Adeline Rogers Dubose, wife of Asia Malachi Dubose, is pictured with their daughter, Lillie Mae Dubose, in an undated photograph. Sinthey was born on January 15, 1851. Lillie Mae was born on February 19, 1894. (Courtesy of Shirley Mixon Perry.)

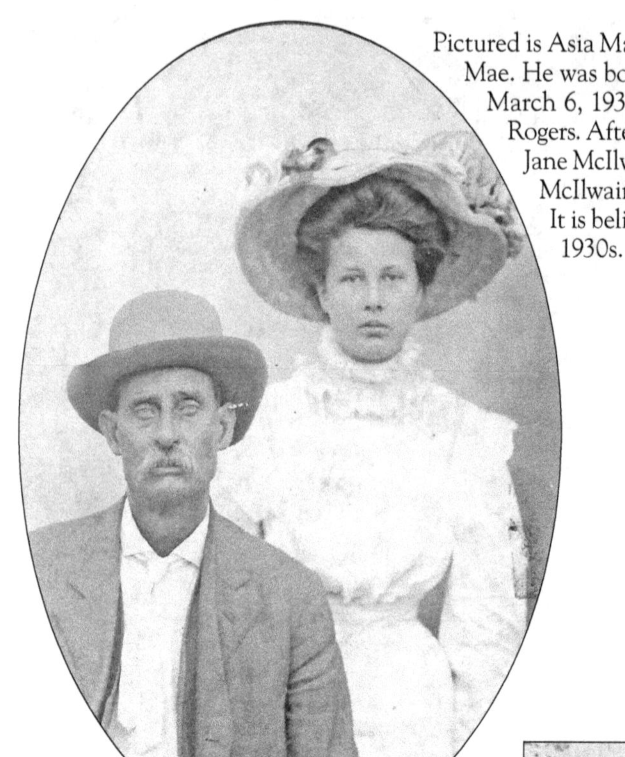

Pictured is Asia Malachi Dubose and his daughter, Lillie Mae. He was born on February 10, 1850, and died on March 6, 1937. His first wife was Sinthey Adeline Rogers. After Sinthey died, Asia married Mahalley Jane McIlwain. Lillie Mae married Mahalley Jane McIlwain's brother, Andrew Jackson McIlwain. It is believed that this photograph dates to the 1930s. (Courtesy of Shirley Mixon Perry.)

A small group of women enjoys the waters surrounding the Bladon Springs Hotel. The women in the postcard photograph have never been identified.

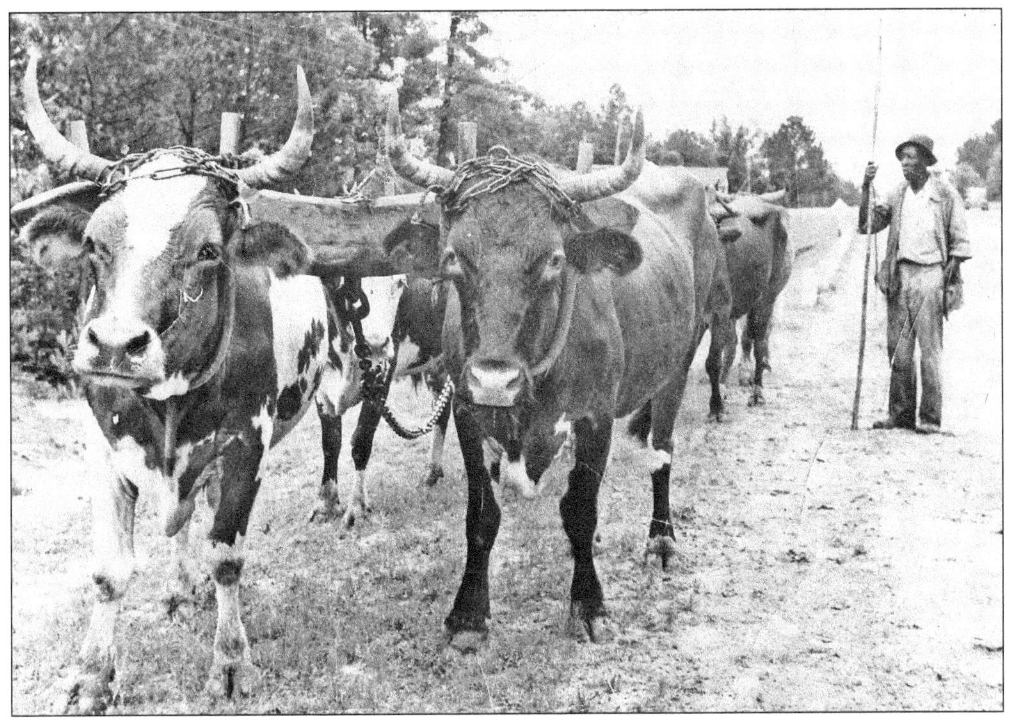

Oscar Sumerlin, who lived in Silas, is pictured with his oxen headed out for a long day of work.

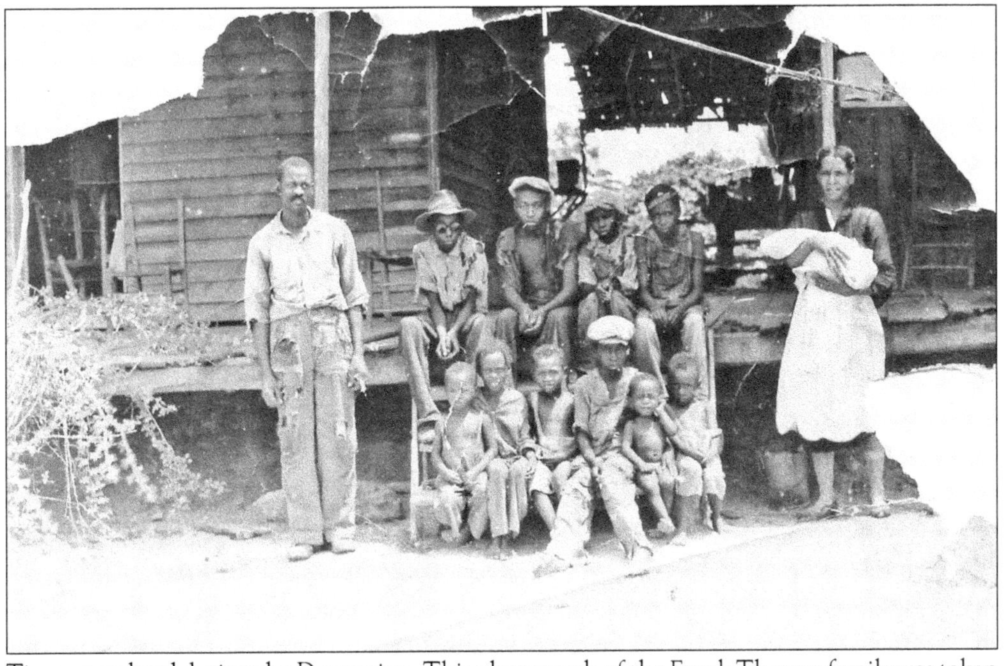

Times were hard during the Depression. This photograph of the Frank Thomas family was taken in 1932 by a county social worker. Frank and his family are believed to have lived on Bailey Road on a sharecropper farm. To make additional money, he also hand-crafted cotton baskets and sold them.

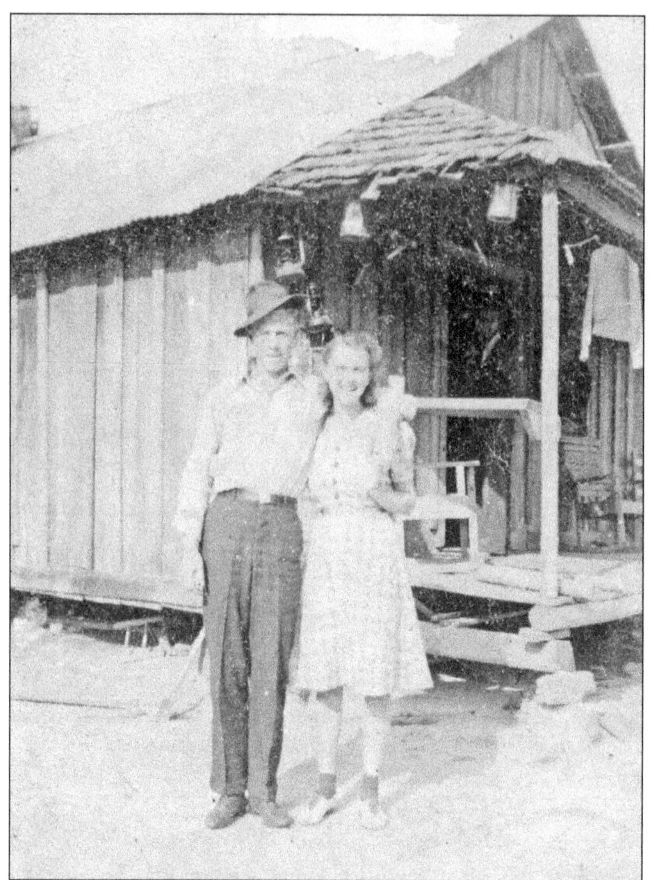

Edward and Dorothy James are shown outside their home in the Mosley Bridge community on December 14, 1941. Edward was the son of James Ferrell James and Hattie Virginia Abston. He died on November 11, 1996. (Courtesy of Sandra Jenkins Little.)

A group of friends gathers for a visit in September 1946. From left to right are Hazel Christine Campbell Jenkins, Annette Wade, Preston Jenkins, and Irene Norton. As of this writing, two of them have passed away, Hazel Christine Campbell Jenkins and Preston Jenkins. Preston Jenkins was a cousin to Hazel's husband.

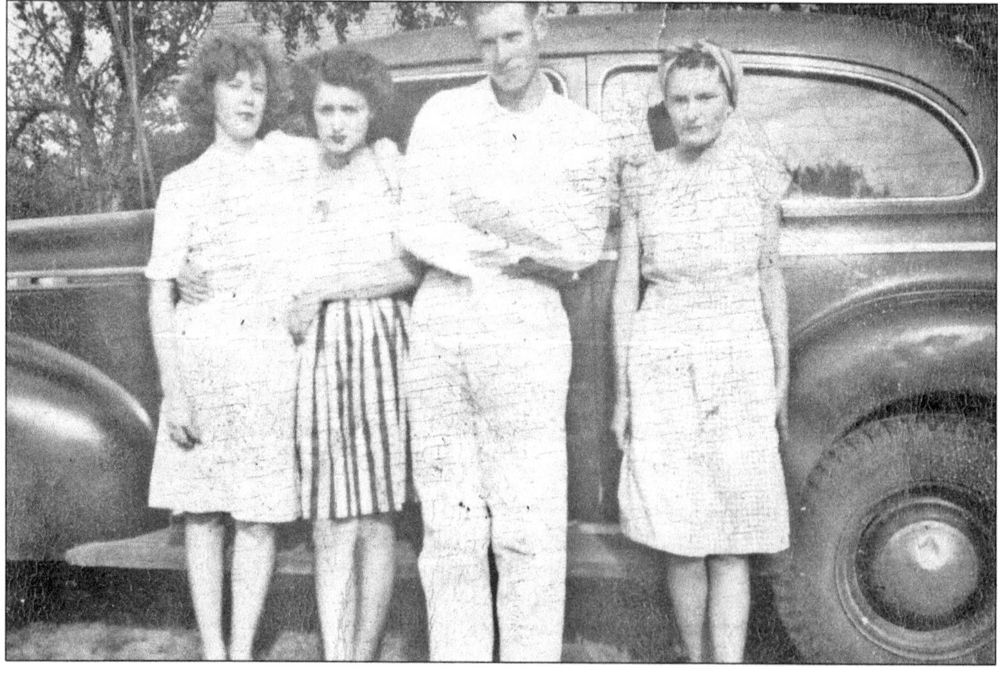

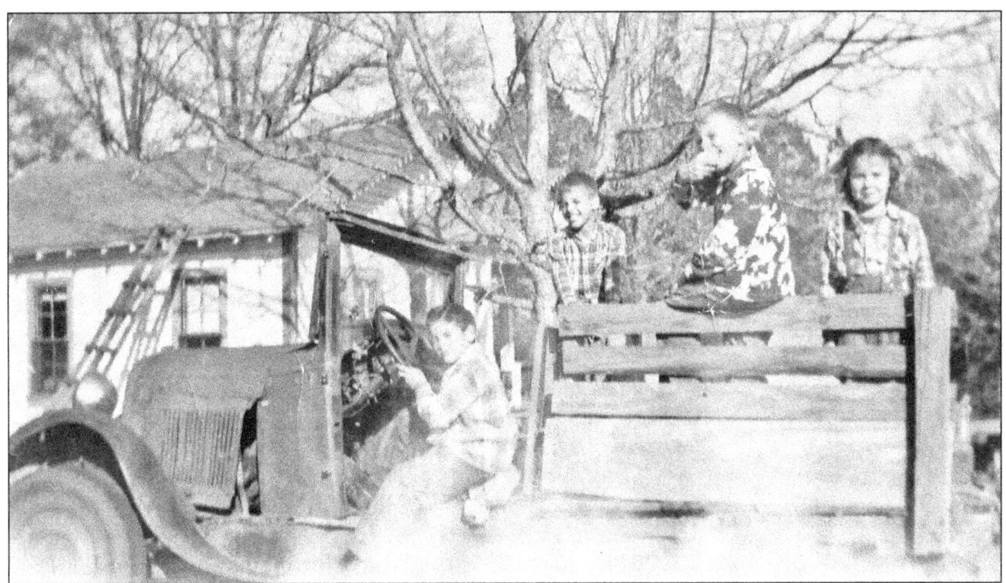

The Chadwick children are shown at their home in the early 1950s. From left to right are John Franklin Chadwick, James Benjamin Chadwick, Mattie Ann Chadwick, and William Jefferson Chadwick. (Courtesy of Sara Jane Welford.)

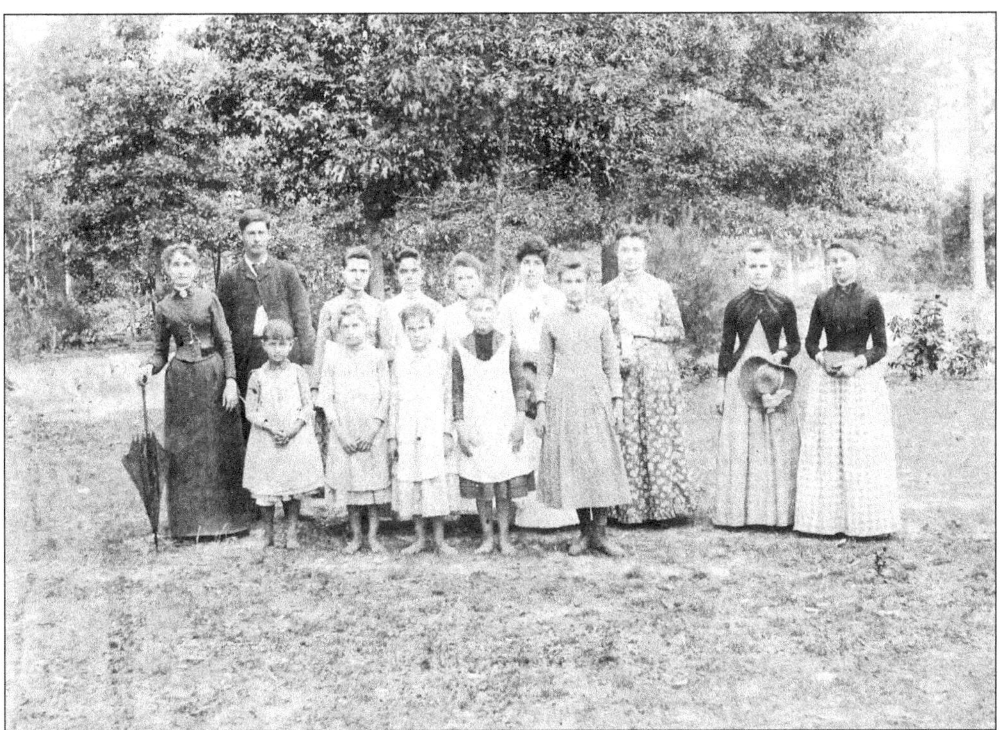

A group of people gathers for a photograph. It has not been determined if they were schoolchildren or just a local gathering. From left to right are (first row) Mary Smith, Maggie Phillips, May Phillips, Lizzie Brock, Cora Hearn, and ? Powell; (second row) Marvin Ward, Blanche McCall, Emma Boney, Bettie Phillips, Mattie Hearn, Katie Griffin, Sallie Brock, and C. Watkins.

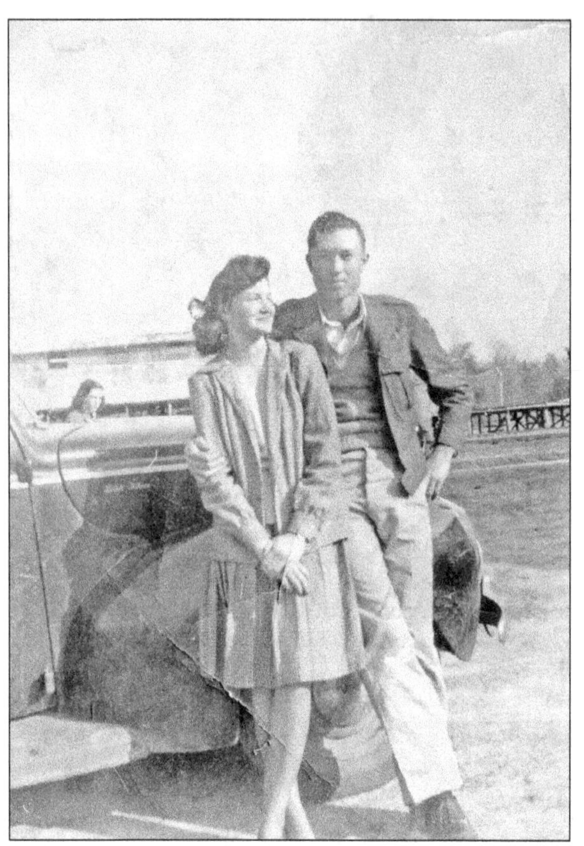

Florine and J.L. Pittman enjoy a movie night out at the Bolinger Theater. J.L. and Florine were married on August 9, 1947. They live in the Mosley Bridge community near the town of Gilbertown. (Courtesy of Linda Pittman Mosley.)

The Butler baseball club of 1947–1948 was the Black Belt League champion. From left to right are (first row) E.E. Stapp, Robert Hall, Clark T. Ezell, Charlie Gibson, Floyd McCary, Garfield Plowman, M.T. Ezell Jr., Robert Ezell, Johnnie W. Hannah, Hugh Sloan, and D.T. Hannah; (second row) Roy Garrison, Cliff Moore, Harry Moore, Frosty Lanier, Cecil Thrash, Buck McDonald, Cecil Tew, and Zack Rogers.

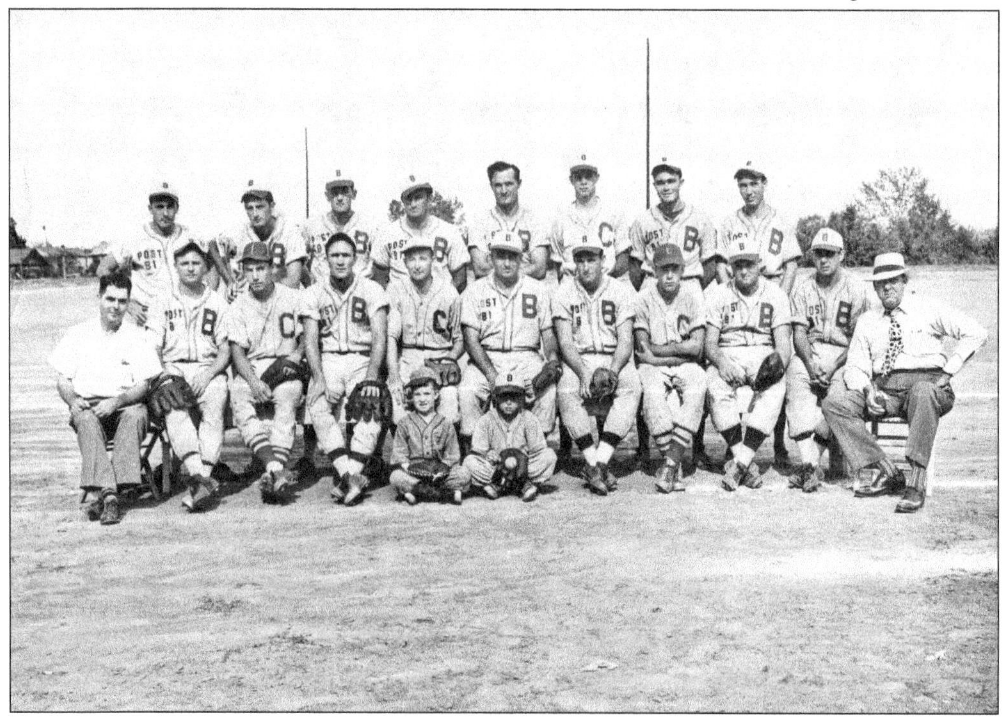

Grady Norton, a native of Womack Hill, was in charge of the Hurricane Forecast Center in Jacksonville, Florida, when it was organized in 1935. He was the US Weather Bureau's chief hurricane forecaster from 1935 to 1954. He reportedly became a legend for his ability to predict the paths of hurricanes.

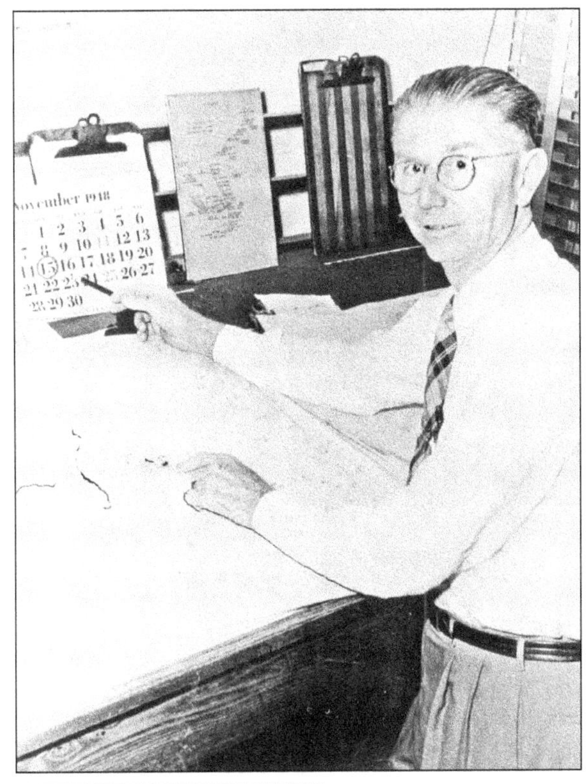

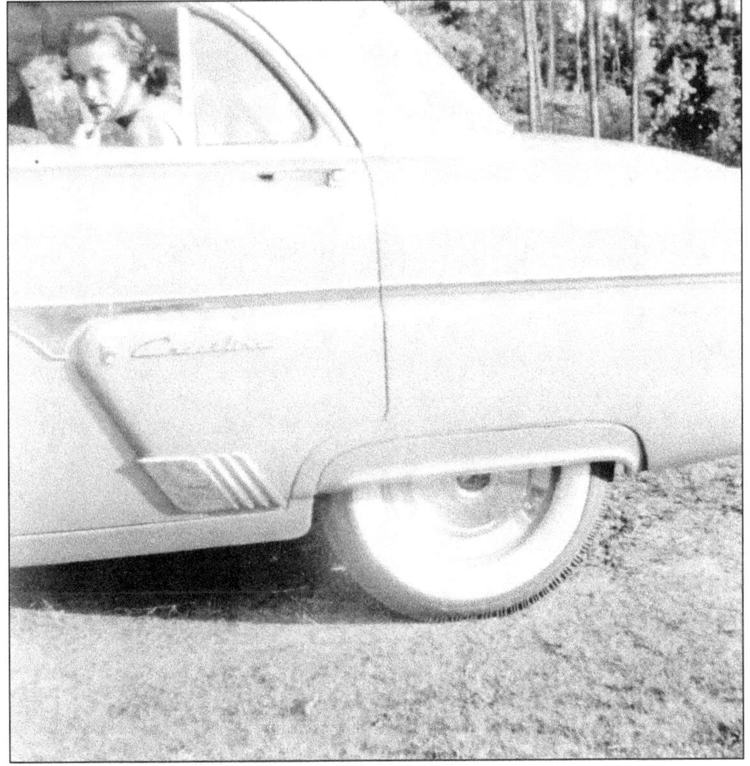

Elsie Thomas Etheredge is captured looking out the window of an old automobile, getting ready for a road trip. She was born on June 6, 1928, and died on August 16, 2013. She was married to Eugene Whacker Etheredge. (Courtesy of Lora Jane McIlwain.)

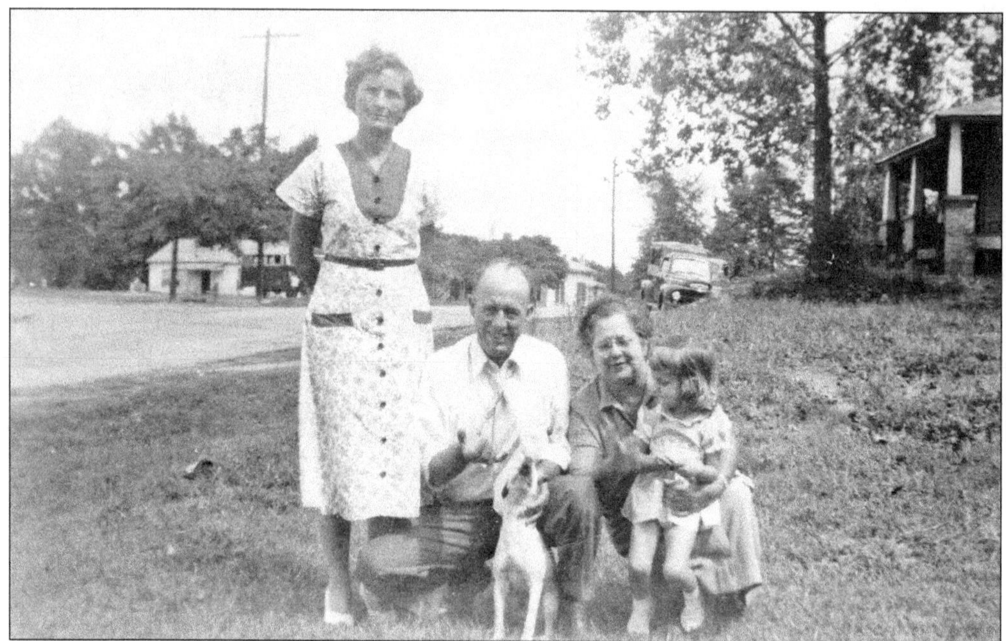

Pictured in 1951 are, from left to right, Eula Singley McDowell; her husband, William McDowell; and Mary Jane McDowell Dahlberg (William's sister) holding great niece Sandra Thomas. The McDowells lived on Smith Street directly behind the old Choctaw County High School that is no longer standing. Black Warrior EMC now occupies that space. (Courtesy of Lora Jane McIlwain.)

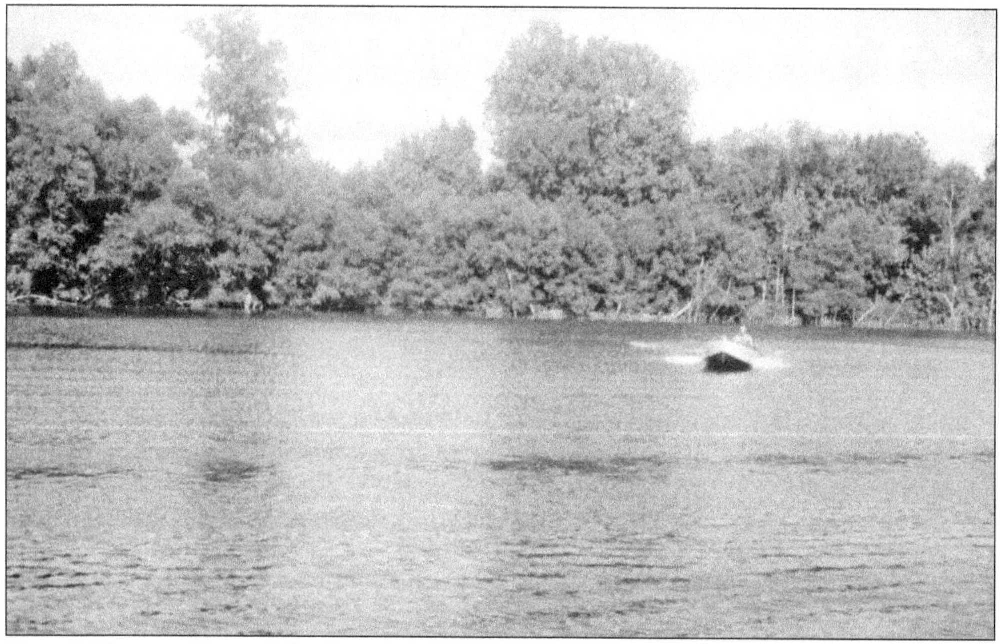

One of Choctaw County's borders is the historic Tombigbee River. In addition to the barges carrying cargo, many residents spend their weekends on their boats cruising up and down the river. There are several boat landings on the river that serve Choctaw County. (Courtesy of Lora Jane McIlwain.)

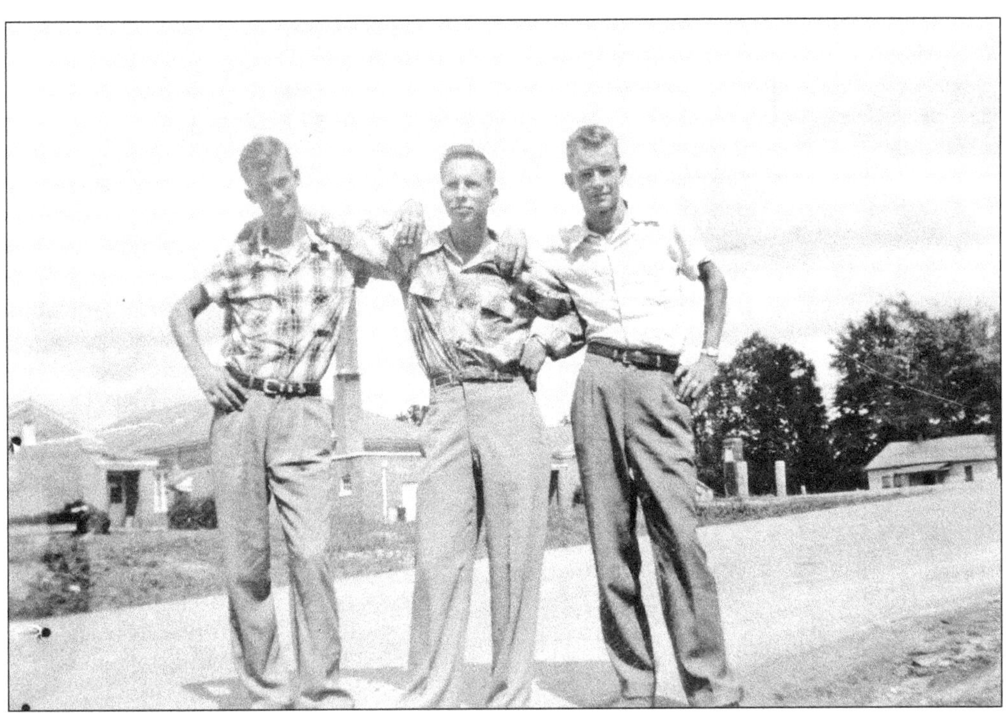

Shown in 1951 are, from left to right, Bobby Dahlberg, Billy Joe McDowell, and Richard McDowell. They are standing on Smith Street directly behind the old Choctaw County High School. They were visiting their uncle, William McDowell. (Courtesy of Lora Jane McIlwain.)

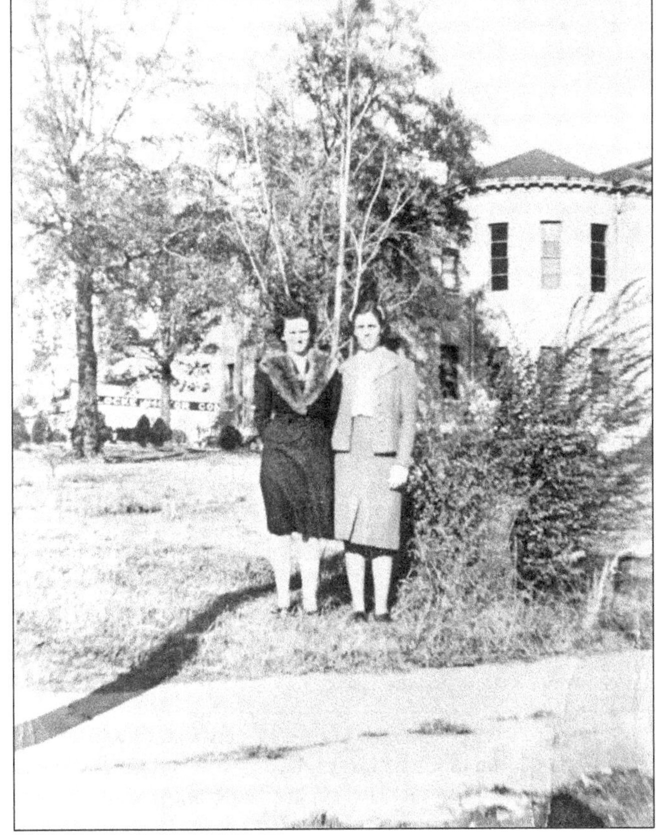

Irene Sanderson (left) and Maggie LeNoir Haguewood stand on the Smith Street side of the Choctaw County Courthouse. Irene was the wife of Claude Sanderson. Maggie was born in 1908. She was the daughter of Robbie Mills LeNoir and Margaret Cornelia Hadaway.

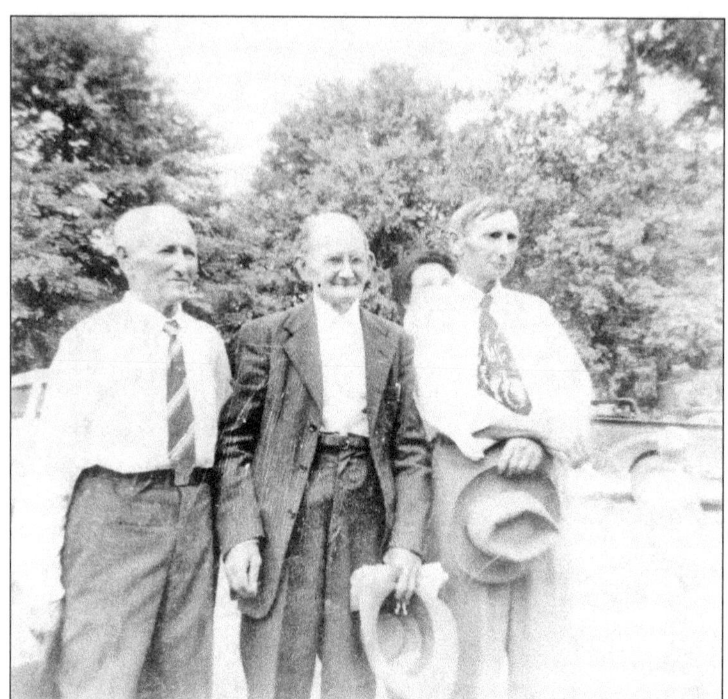

Shown from left to right are Wyatt Carlisle, Obadiah Carlisle, and John Carlisle. Standing behind John is Beulah Carlisle. Wyatt and John were half-brothers to Obadiah. Their father was Jasper Collin Carlisle. Obadiah was the son from Jasper's first wife, Mary Howell. Wyatt and John were Jasper's sons from his third wife, Mary J. Roberts. Beulah was Obadiah's daughter. This photograph was taken during a family gathering in 1950. (Courtesy of Sandra Jenkins Little.)

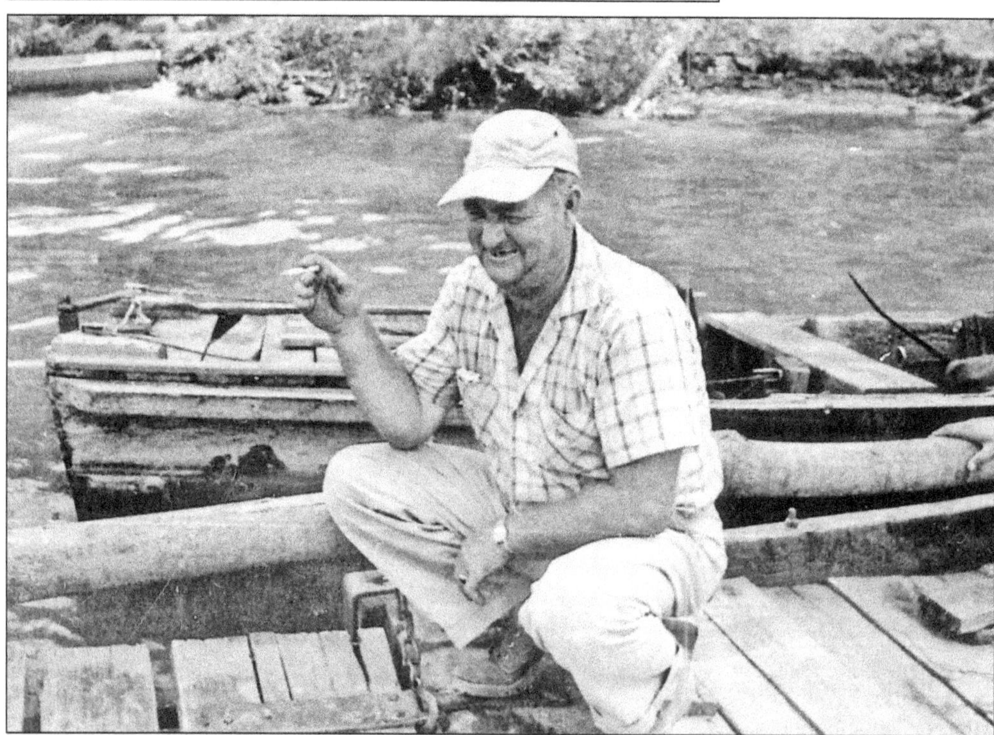

Earl Grey Etheredge is shown on the old ferry that crossed over the Tombigbee River from Choctaw County to Clarke County. Grey was a businessman who owned and operated a barbershop near Bladon Springs. He was born on September 14, 1906, and died on November 28, 1982. He is buried in the Bladon Springs Cemetery. (Courtesy of Lora Jane McIlwain.)

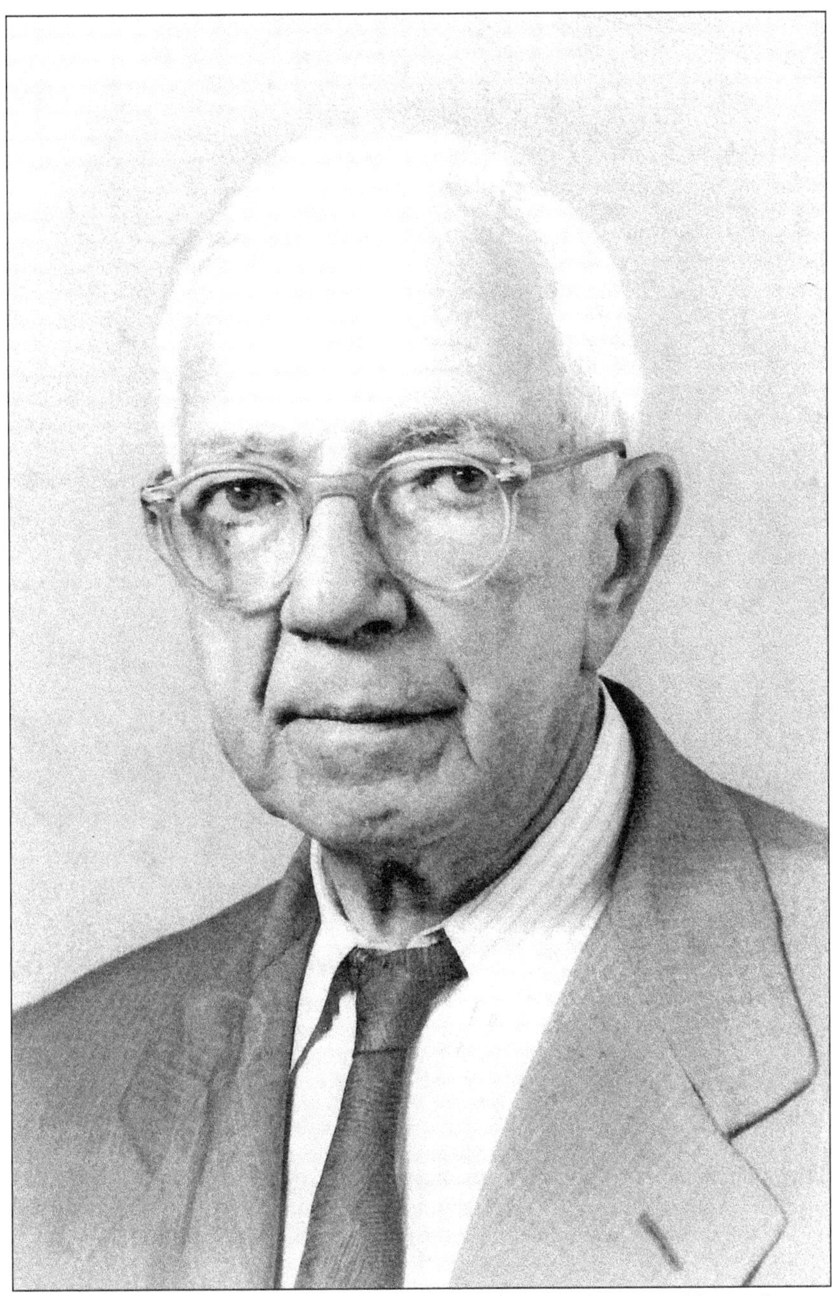

Zack Rogers Sr. was a well-known leader in Choctaw County education. He was born on a farm six miles west of Bladon Springs at Rescueville (now Cullomburg) on September 13, 1884. After public school in Choctaw County, he attended the First District Agricultural School at Jackson for one year and then attended three years at Troy State Normal School, where he graduated in 1907. After college, he had a couple of other jobs in education prior to returning to Choctaw County as assistant principal and math teacher at Choctaw County High School. He became principal in 1913 and served in that capacity until he was appointed superintendent of education in February 1918. He filled that role until 1931. During his tenure, he administered 55 schools, 100 teachers, and about 2,500 pupils. He died in Butler in 1962.

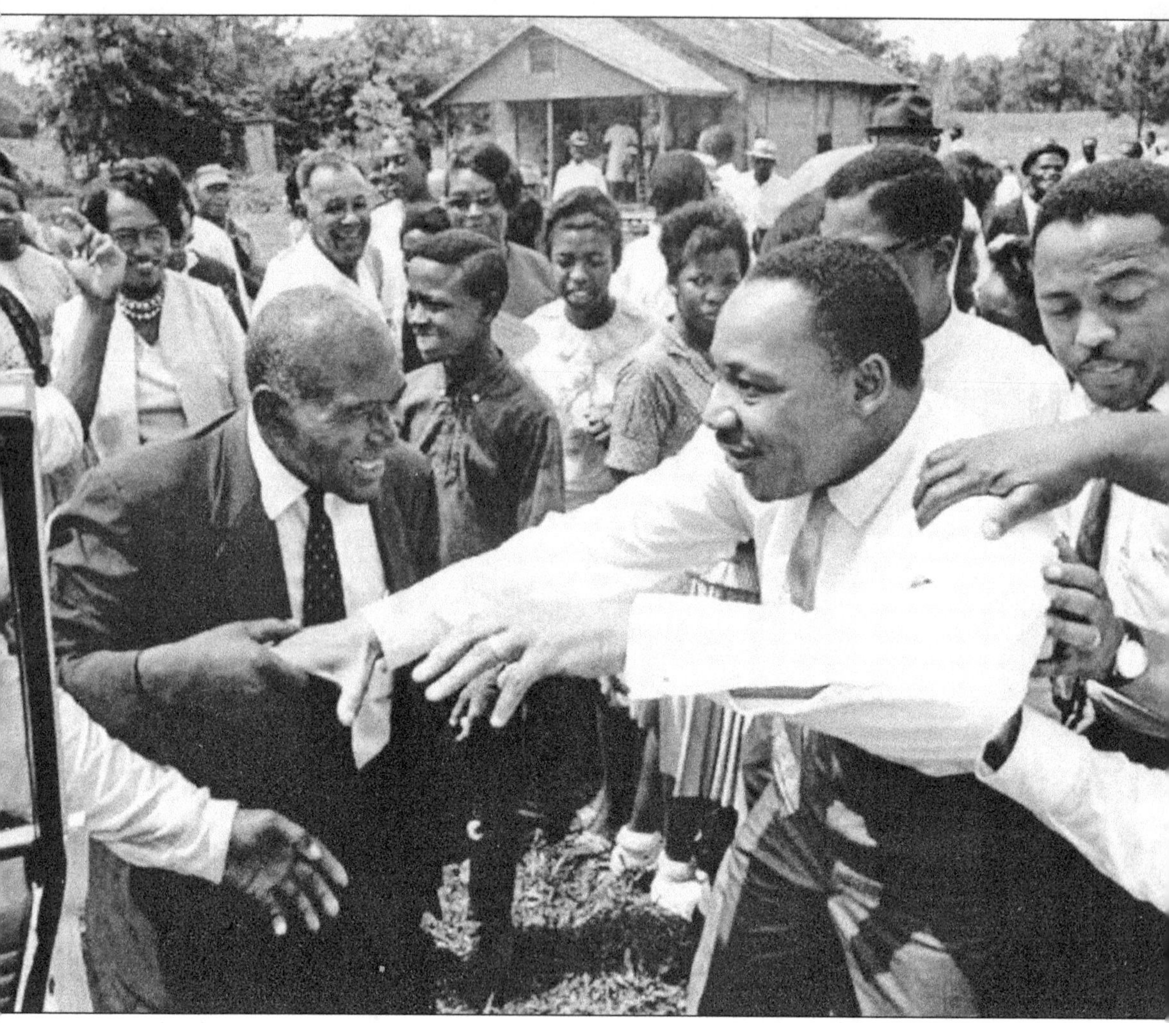

Civil rights were a large issue in Choctaw County during the 1960s. There were many rallies held in regard to the desegregation of the school districts. It was an issue that carried over into the 1970s. Here, Dr. Martin Luther King Jr. is preparing to enter the Greater First Baptist Church in Lisman for a rally on April 30, 1966. He is shaking hands with Rev. L.W. Kinniebrew. Lisman was one of nine stops in Alabama's Black Belt region that Dr. King was making in an effort to unify the African American community for the primary election that year. It has been said that groups of young children were tugging at Dr. King's arms to pull him into the church. This photograph was donated to the museum by Associated Press photographer Jack Thornell.

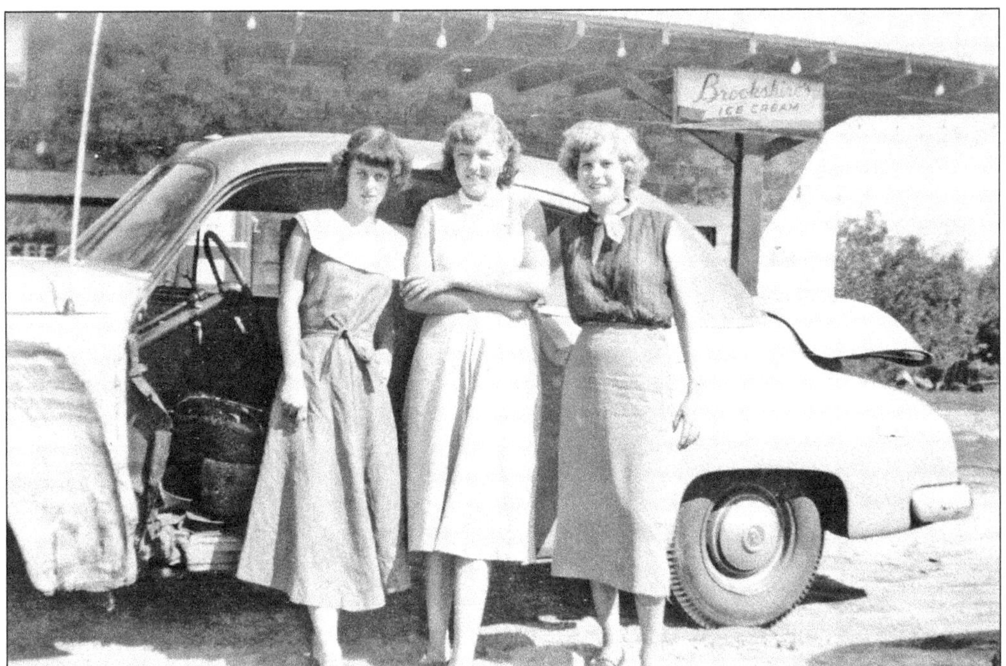

Pictured are, from left to right, Mary Dahlberg Robertson McPhearson, Elsie Taylor, and Malda Covington. They were out for a wild drive in 1951. Elsie Taylor Kayda lived in Silas just behind the main street through town. Her mother, Alvie Taylor, was a teacher at Southern Choctaw Elementary School. (Courtesy of Lora Jane McIlwain.)

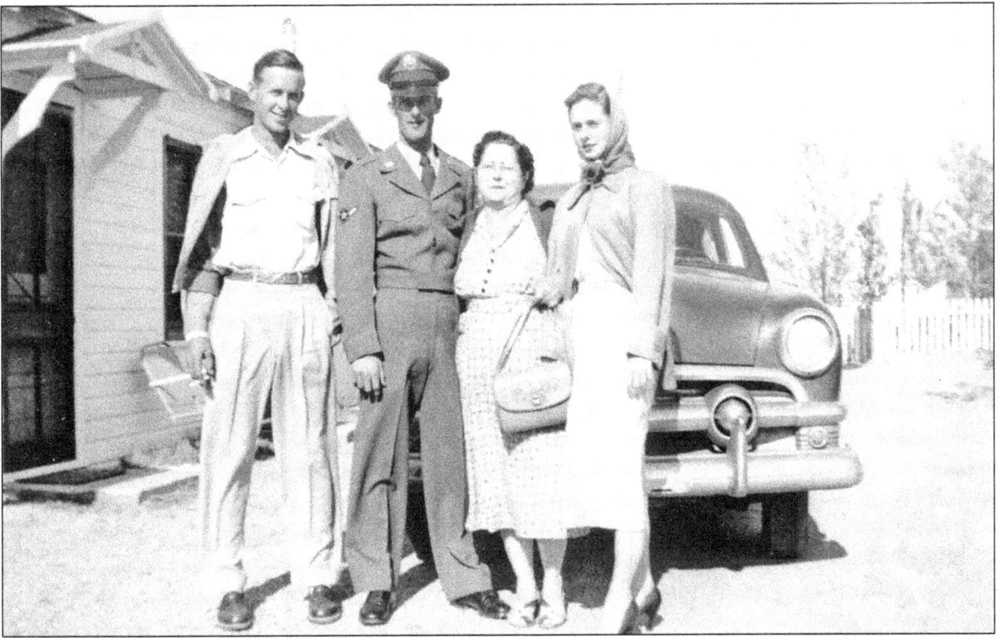

Pictured here is a family gathering in 1951. From left to right are Gaines Knight, Bobby E. Dahlberg, Mary Jane McDowell Dahlberg, and Mary Dahlberg Robertson McPhearson. Bobby is Mary Jane's son, and Mary is her daughter. Gaines, Mary Jane's son-in-law, is married to her daughter Sally. (Courtesy of Lora Jane McIlwain.)

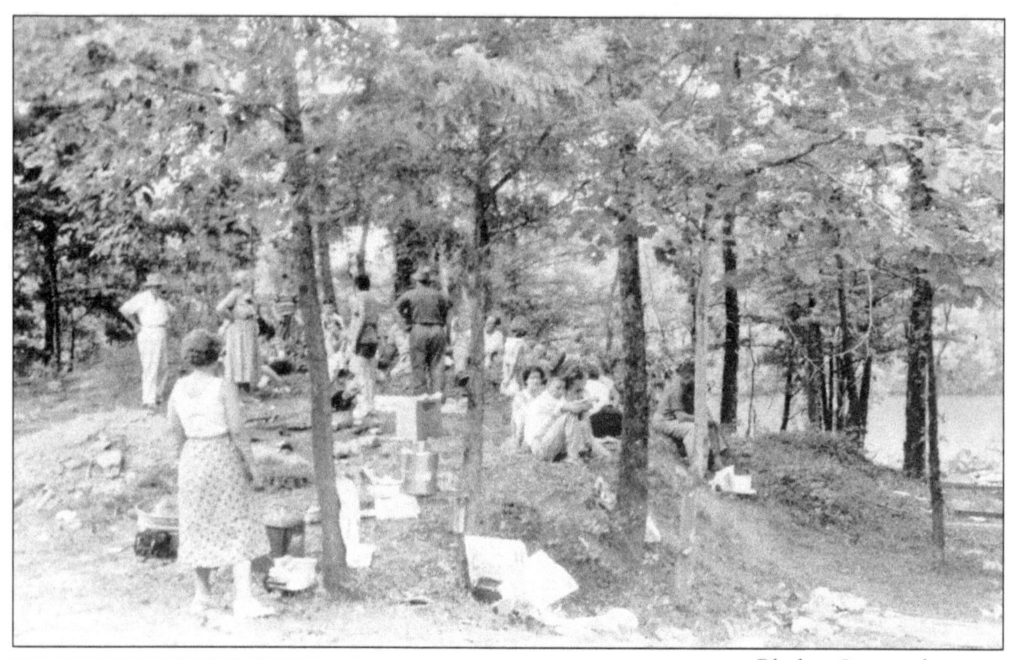

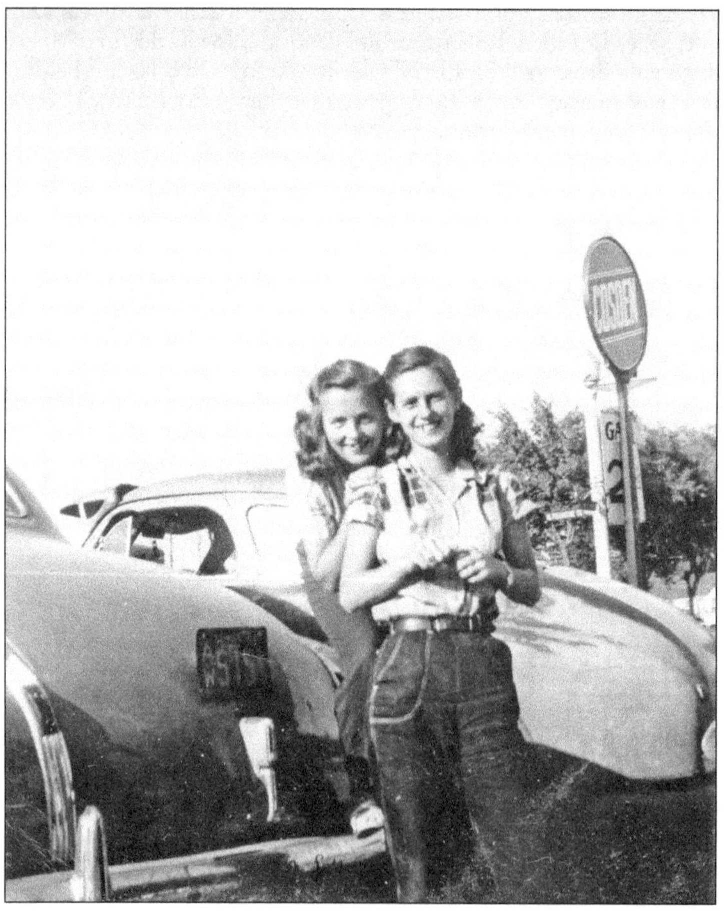

Bladon Springs has always been renowned for its recreational activities. This photograph shows a group of residents gathering for a picnic at Bladon Landing on the Tombigbee River in 1951. (Courtesy of Lora Jane McIlwain.)

Pictured are Sally Augusta Caroline Dahlberg Knight (left) and Mary Dahlberg McPhearson. When this photograph was taken in 1952, Sally was 18 years old and Mary was 17. (Courtesy of Lora Jane McIlwain.)

Dr. John McCormack owned and operated a mixed veterinary practice in Butler during the 1960s. He left Choctaw County in the 1970s and taught at veterinary schools at Auburn University, University of California-Davis, Louisiana State University, and the University of Georgia. His specialty was farm animal practice. He also authored several books of tales from his veterinary practice.

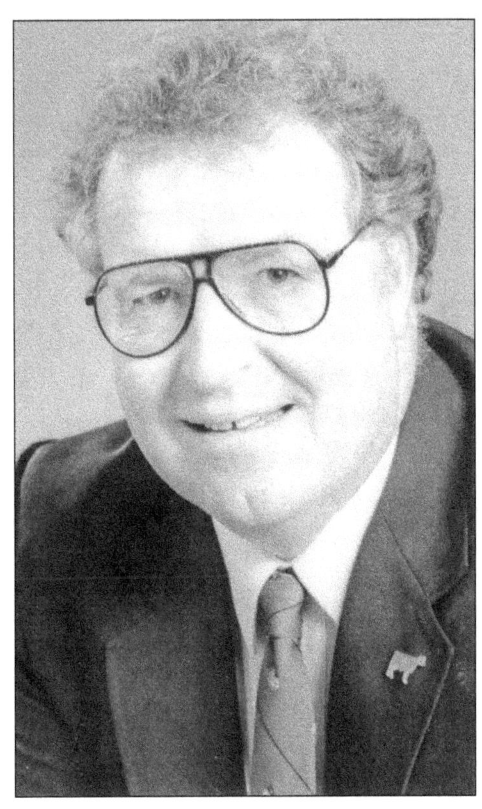

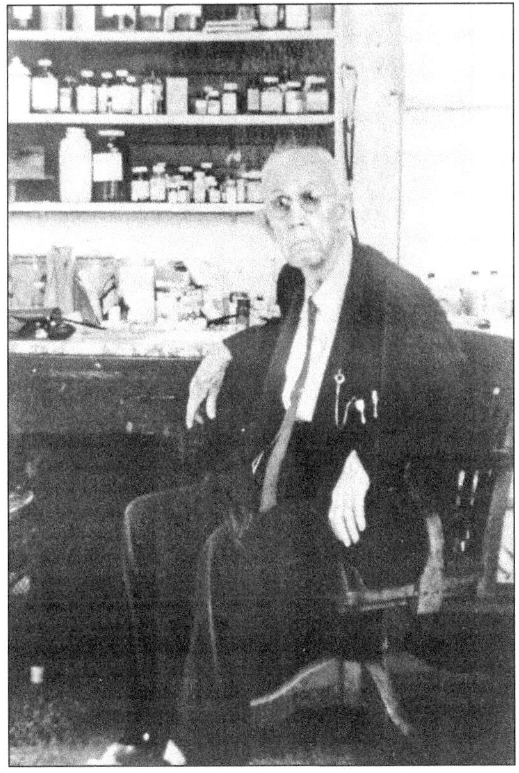

Dr. Samuel T. Miller was born in 1877 at what is now known as Halsell. He attended medical school at the University of Alabama in Mobile and graduated in 1901. Dr. Miller's office was located to the side of his and his wife's residence in Yantley. It contained two large rooms. The second room was furnished with a bed for people who needed to lie down during examinations.

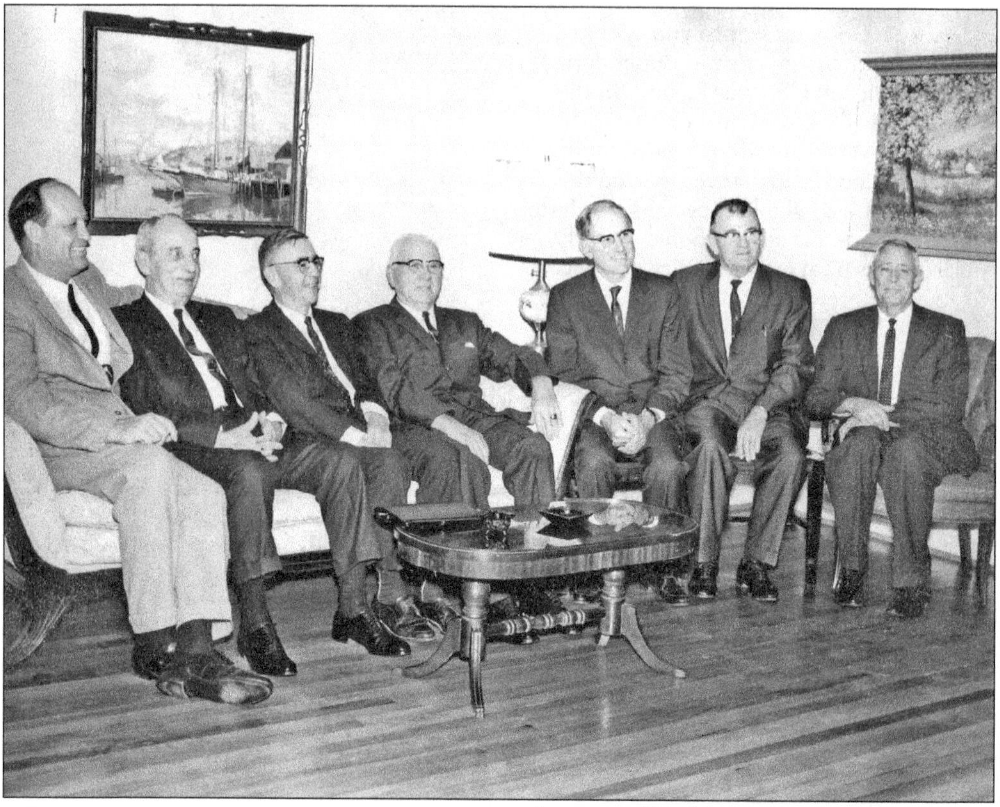

A group of local businessmen gathers for a meeting in the 1950s. From left to right are James Hutchinson, Gerald A. Rentz, Raymond F. Lee, Charlie Ford, Theodore Pearson, Hunter Phillips, and Connie Taylor. Hunter Phillips was the probate judge. (Courtesy of Debbie Rentz.)

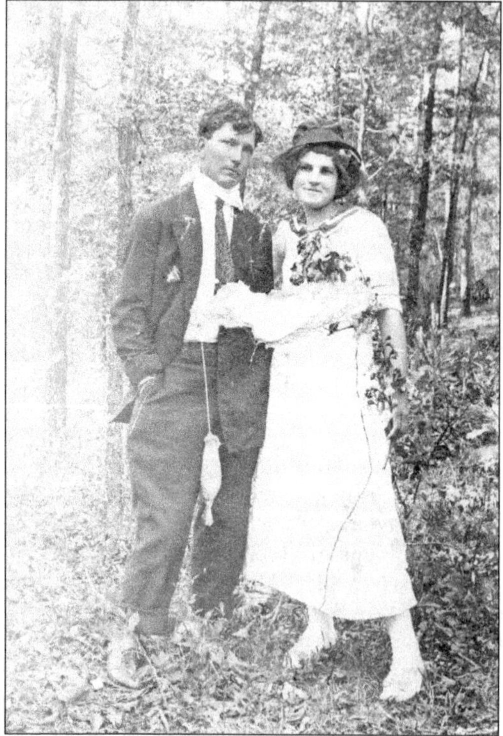

John Franklin Young was born on September 10, 1895, and died on June 12, 1970. He is pictured with his wife, Alice Elizabeth Jacobs Young, who was born on March 5, 1889, and died on September 7, 1985. The couple lived in Toxey on Alabama Highway 17. Frank was a rural mail carrier for many years. (Courtesy of Ruth Jacobs Corley.)

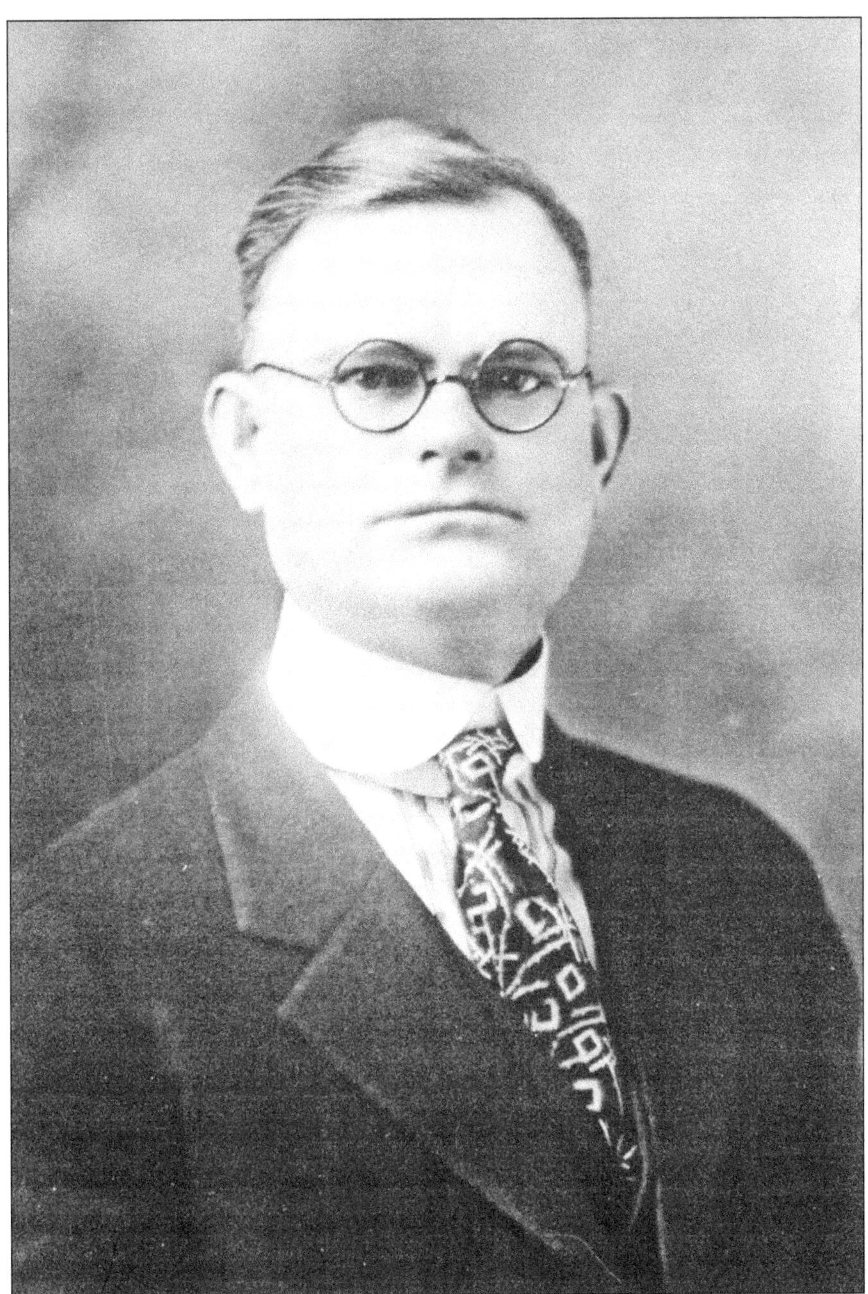

William Jefferson Dansby was born on December 28, 1880, to James Madison and Lucy Ann Virginia Wright. He attended the public Pine Grove School. Upon graduation, he attended Troy State Normal School (now Troy University) and graduated with a bachelor's degree in the class of 1902. After graduation, one of his positions was as a professor at the West Alabama Male and Female Institute in Yantley. He continued his education by taking up law and graduated from the University of Alabama in 1913 with a law degree. In January 1915, he was elected president of the Choctaw Bank in Butler, and later served as a director until his death in 1941. He was the cofounder of the Dansby and Evans Insurance Group, which is still in business today. He married Marcita Moseley on December 31, 1914.

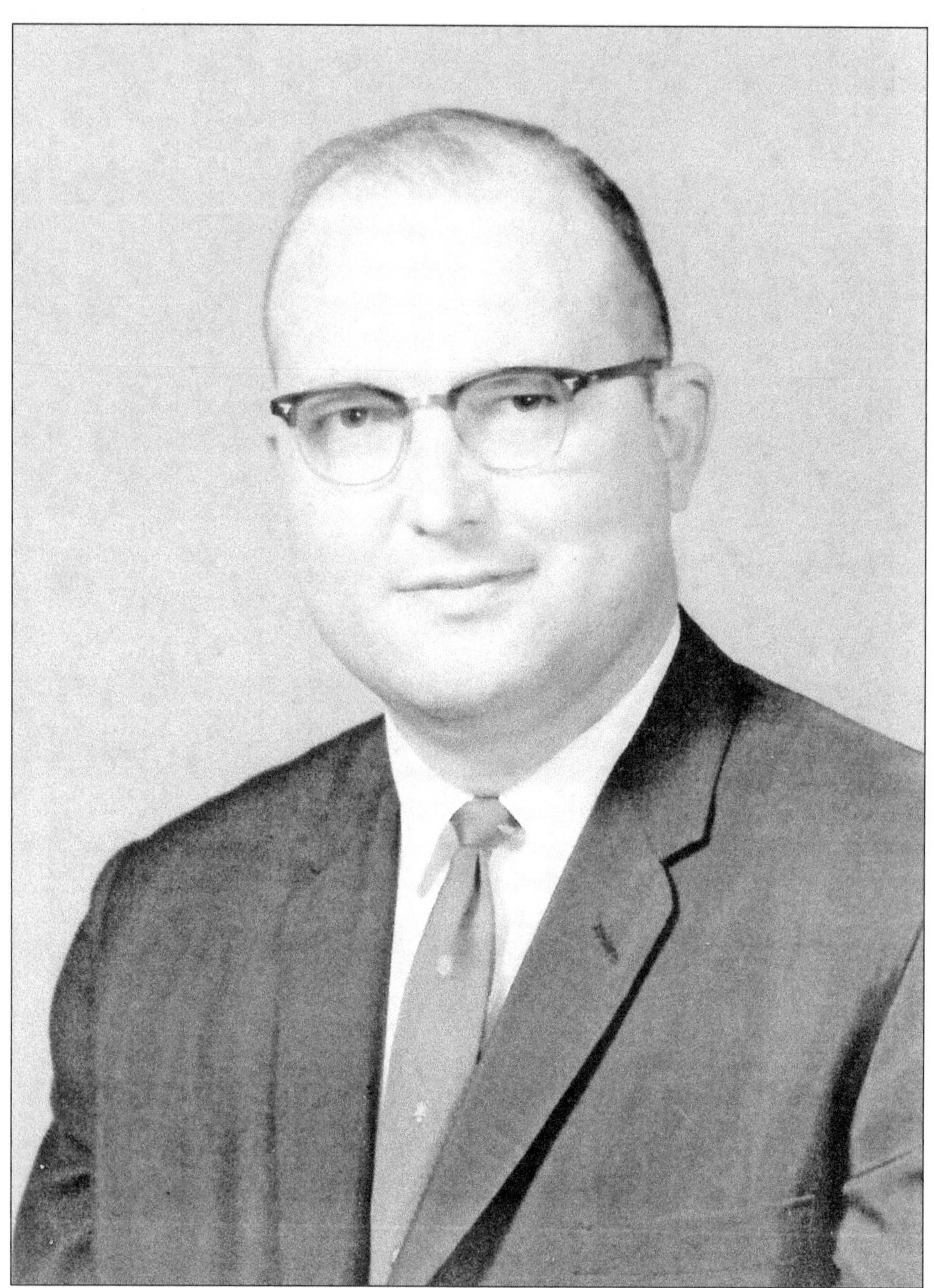

Richard Edwin McPhearson was the son of John Lorenzo and Rosa Batson McPhearson. Richard attended Silas Elementary School and Gulf Coast Military Academy. At the age of 16, he entered the University of Alabama, where he earned both his undergraduate and law degrees. In college he met his wife, Nancy Lee Tatum. They were married in 1950. He had a law office in the Knowles Building in Butler (now the law office of Jeff Utsey and dental office of Julie Utsey). He bought the old Chevrolet dealership in Butler from Bob Locke but continued to practice law until he ran for the office of probate judge. He was elected at the age of 29 in 1958. At the time, he was the youngest person elected to that office in the state of Alabama. He was reelected two more times but did not live to serve out his third term. He died at the age of 40 on April 11, 1969.

Joseph Benjamin Jenkins was born on November 25, 1861, and died on February 13, 1940. He was the son of Tom Jenkins (an assumed name), who was a Choctaw Indian, and Emma Doggette. He married Alice Lavenia Taylor. She was the daughter of Robert Anderson Taylor and Harriett Virginia Bonner. They had seven children. According to family members, he was a deputy sheriff when Bob Sims was hung in 1891. (Courtesy of Barry Roberts.)

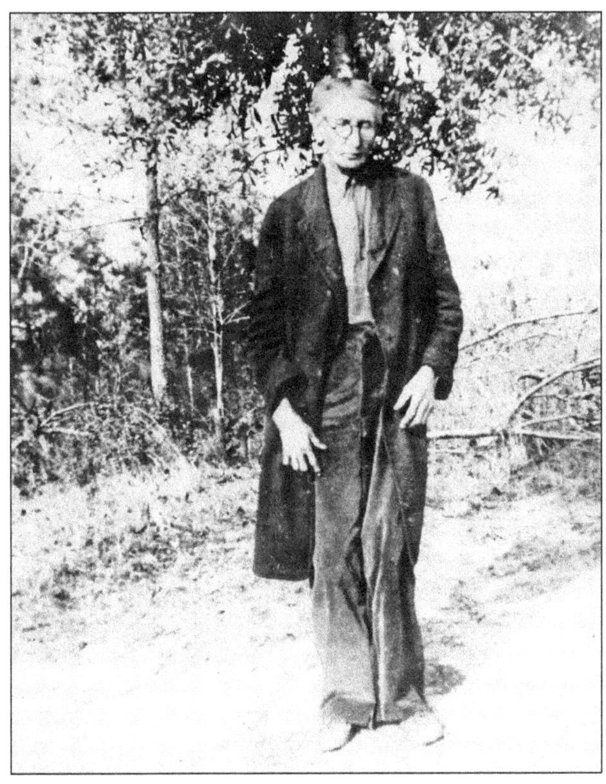

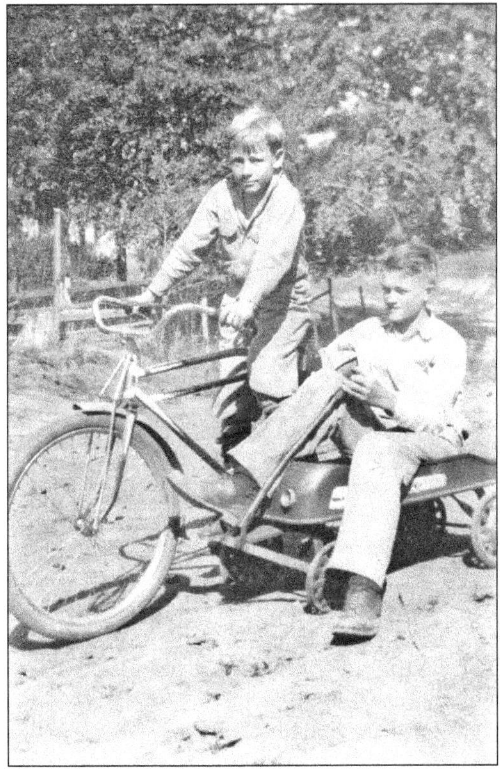

Shown here are friends James Christopher (left) and Cliff Dansby. James was 12 years of age, and Cliff was 15. James was born on May 12, 1926. He worked in education. In 1957, he opened the State Farm Insurance office in Butler. Cliff was the son of William Jefferson Dansby. He was a self-employed land and timber owner.

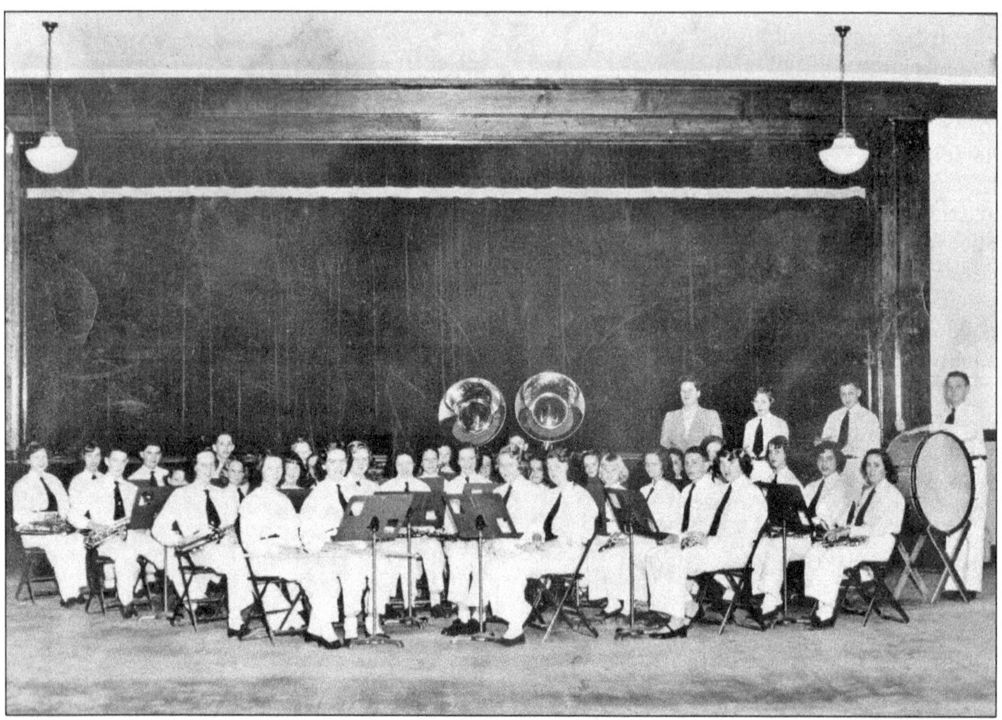

Members of the first Choctaw County High School band are pictured in 1951. Initially, the band wore white pants, white shirts, and black ties. The uniforms did not arrive until 1952. The band director was Blanche Simmons. (Courtesy of Joan Thompson Kelley.)

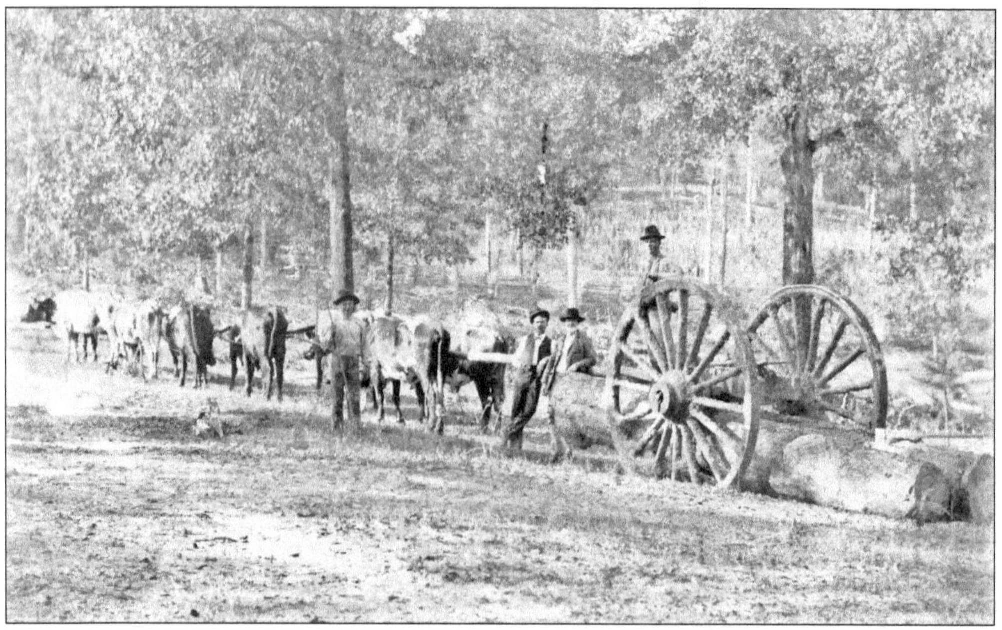

Logging was very important in all areas of Choctaw County in the early years. Some members of the LeNoir family and possibly a couple of neighbors are taking this log to a nearby sawmill. The LeNoir family lived in the Womack Hill community. Note the large five-yoke oxen team. (Courtesy of Joan Thompson Kelley.)

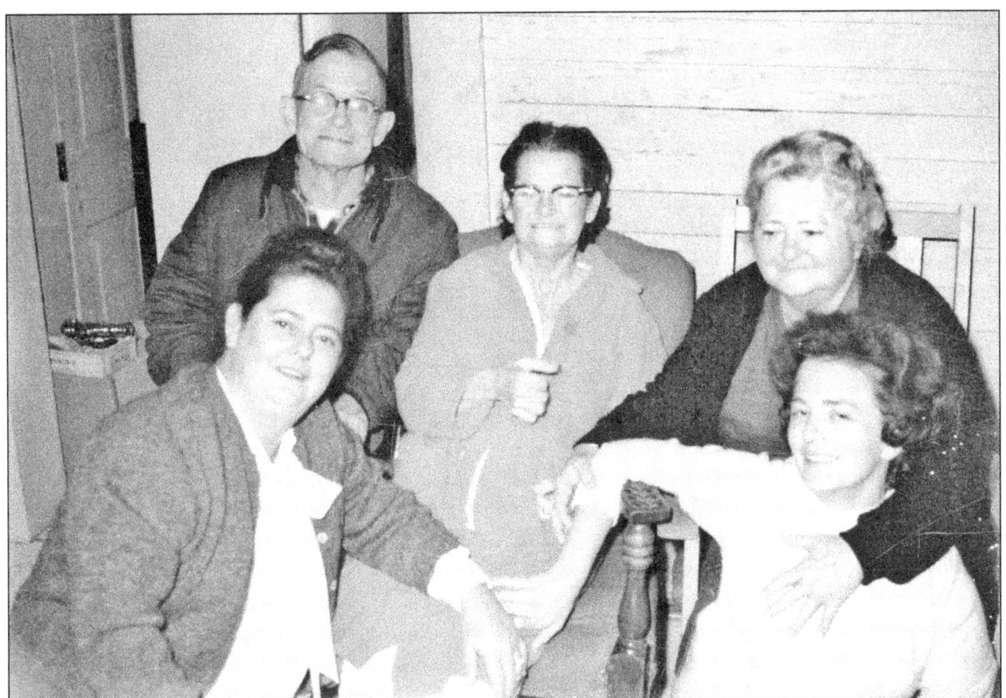

Several members of the McDowell and Dahlberg family gather for a photograph. From left to right are (first row) Mary Dahlberg Robertson McPhearson and Sally Dahlberg Knight; (second row) Ray Bolden McDowell, Laura McDowell Thomas Beard, and Mary Jane McDowell Dahlberg. (Courtesy of Lora Jane McIlwain.)

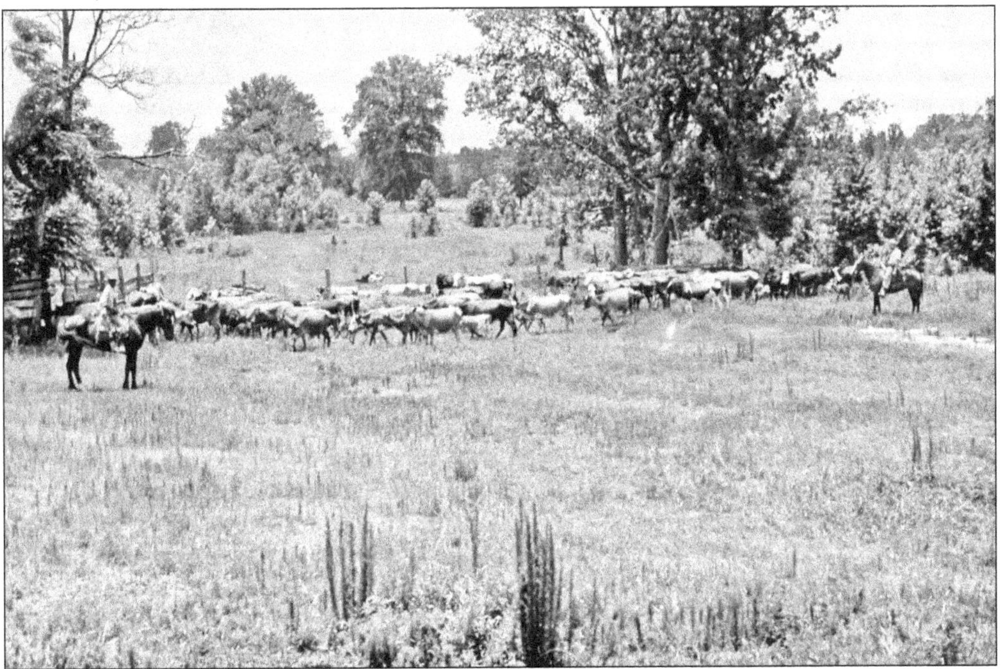

A couple of men are pictured moving cattle on the LeNoir farm in the Womack Hill community. (Courtesy of Joan Thompson Kelley.)

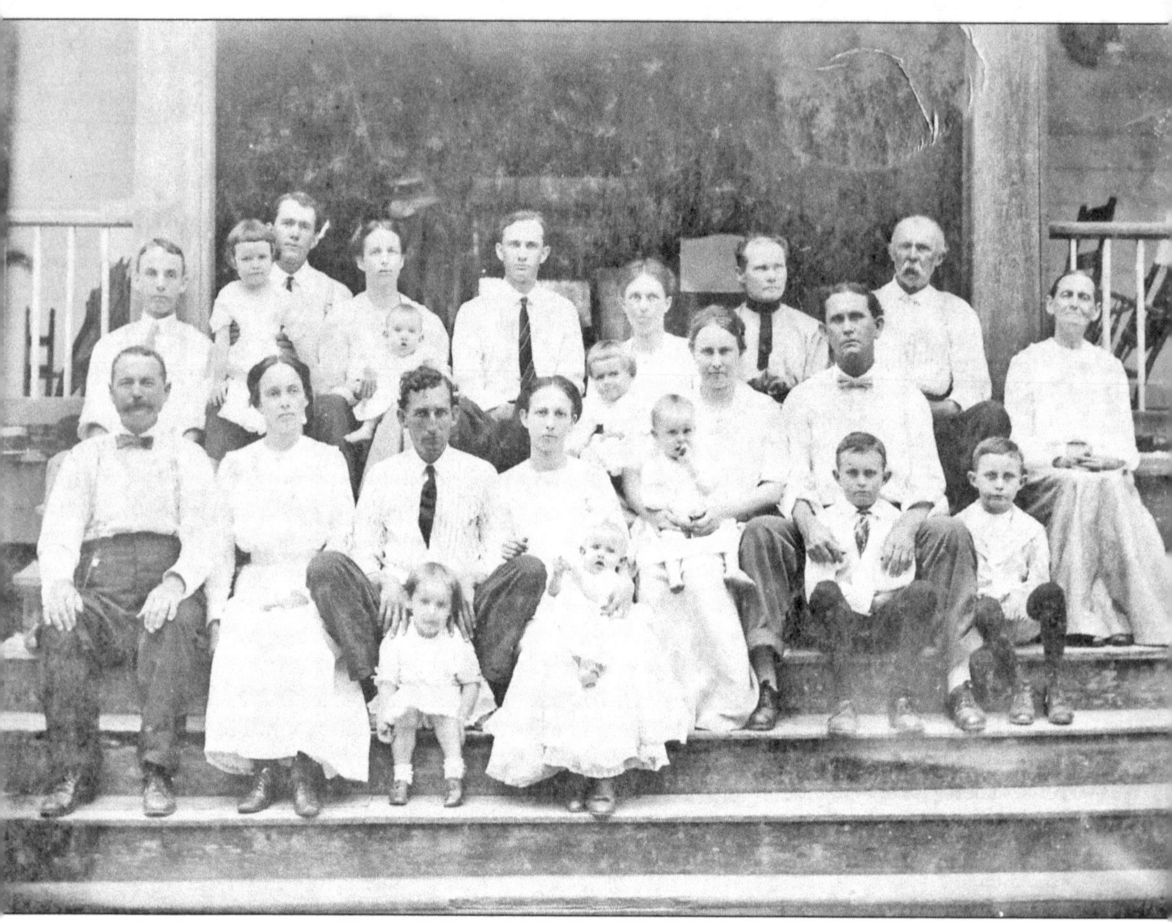

This family photograph was taken on the front porch of the John Robert and Mary Angeline Boney Land home in Melvin in 1911. From left to right are (first row) Eugene A. Rentz, Ella Land Rentz, Dr. John W. Rudder holding Katherine, Lula Land Rudder holding John W. Rudder Jr., Alma Land Alman holding Robert Land Alman, Dr. Sam Alman holding Rex Alman, and Sam Alman Jr; (second row) Gerald A. Rentz, John E. Chatham holding Louise Chatman, Mary Angeline Land Chatham holding Frank Chatham, Robert Land, Alva McGowan Land holding Margaret, Karah Land, John Robert Land, and Mary Angeline Boney Land. (Courtesy of Debbie Rentz.)

Seven

Military

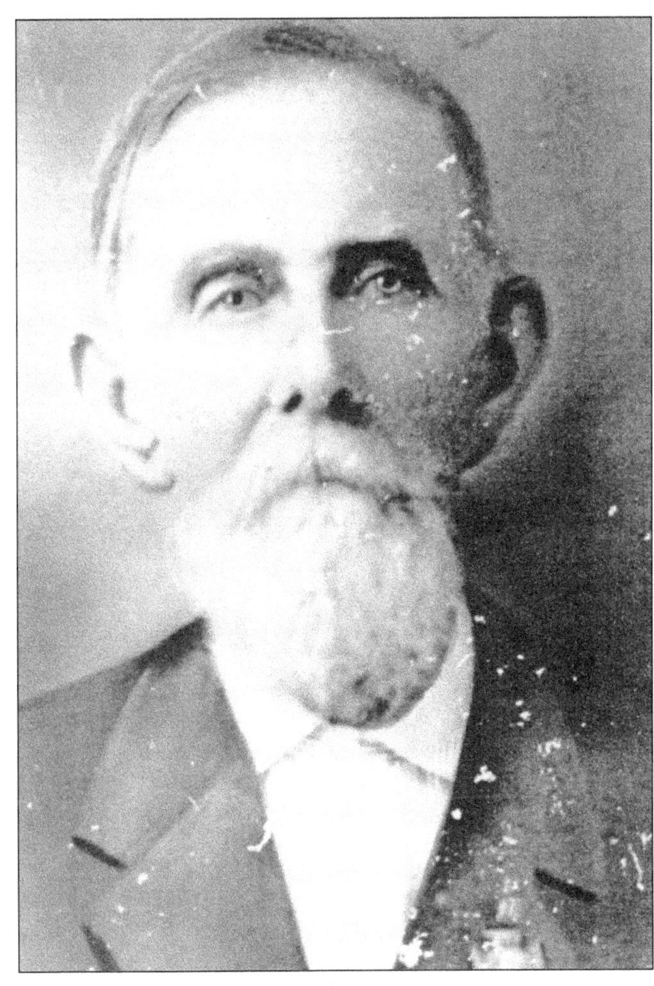

James Alonzo Campbell was born on May 8, 1846, in Bennettsville, South Carolina. He later moved to Choctaw County and served in Company C of the 8th Regiment Alabama Cavalry from 1864 to 1865. He died on July 26, 1933, and is buried on the old Campbell home site off US Highway 84 on the Branch Road.

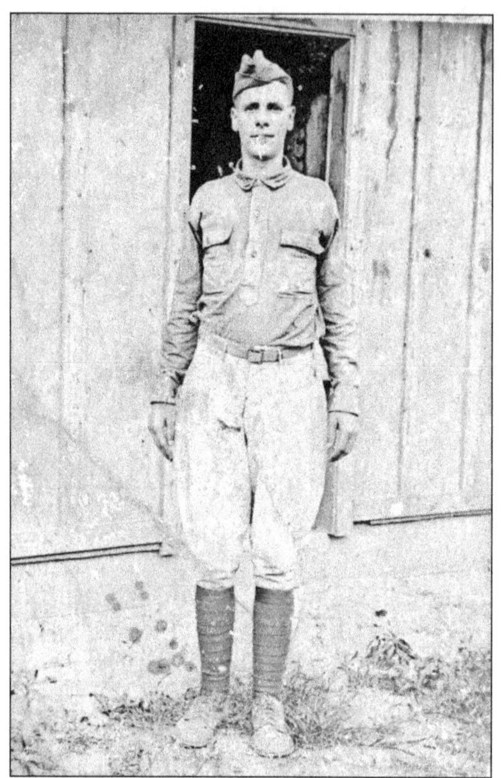

Pvt. Joe Granberry Ford is shown in his World War I uniform. This photograph was taken shortly after he arrived in Europe in 1918. He registered for the draft on June 5, 1917, when he was 22 years of age. He and his family lived in the Cromwell community. He spent his entire tour of duty in France. He was born on September 28, 1895, and died on October 29, 1987.

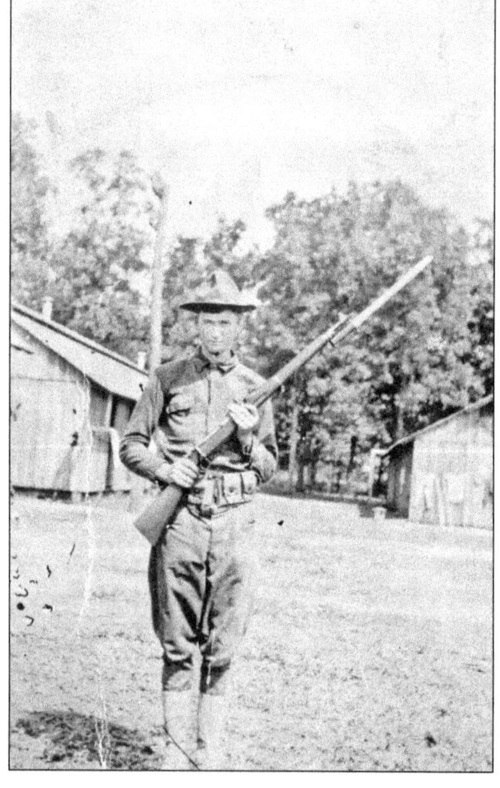

Robert Houston Champion registered for the draft on June 5, 1917. When he registered, he was a stave maker working in the Land community. His job in the US Army was a wagoner. He was born in Melvin on September 1, 1892, and died on June 1, 1973. Champion was married to Allie Jane Todd. He is buried in Valhalla Memorial Gardens in Semmes, Alabama.

Virginal Kennedy McMillan registered for the World I draft in Wayne County, Mississippi, in 1917. He was born on December 22, 1895, in Melvin, Alabama, and died on September 22, 1981. He was the son of Emanuel C. and Alice McMillan. He is buried in the Mount Zion Cemetery, just across the Choctaw County line in Wayne County, Mississippi. This photograph was found in an old McMillan family Bible the museum holds in its collection.

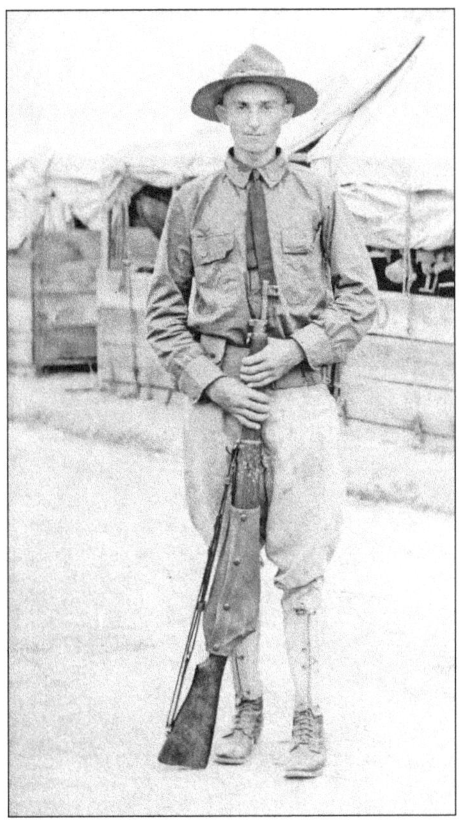

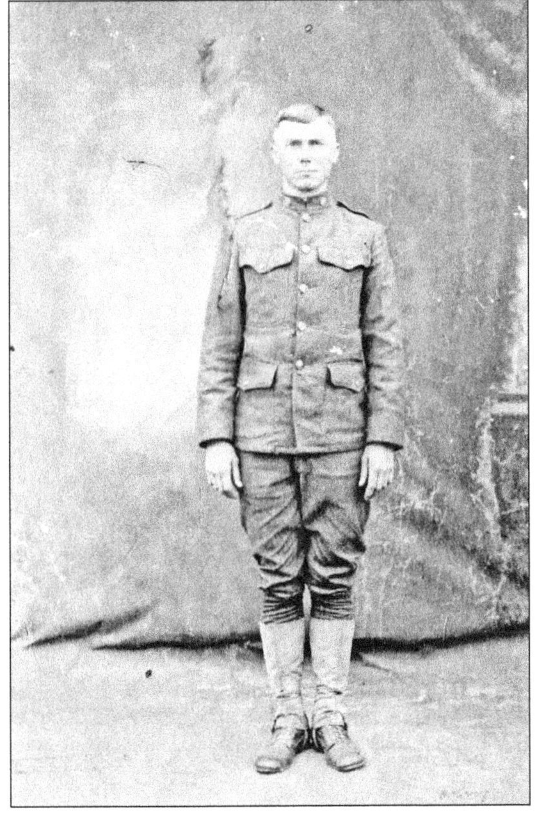

Willoughby Wesley Gibson registered for the World War I draft on September 19, 1917. He was 30 years of age at the time and a farmer. He was born on August 26, 1887, and died on August 31, 1970. He is buried in the Pleasant Hill Cemetery.

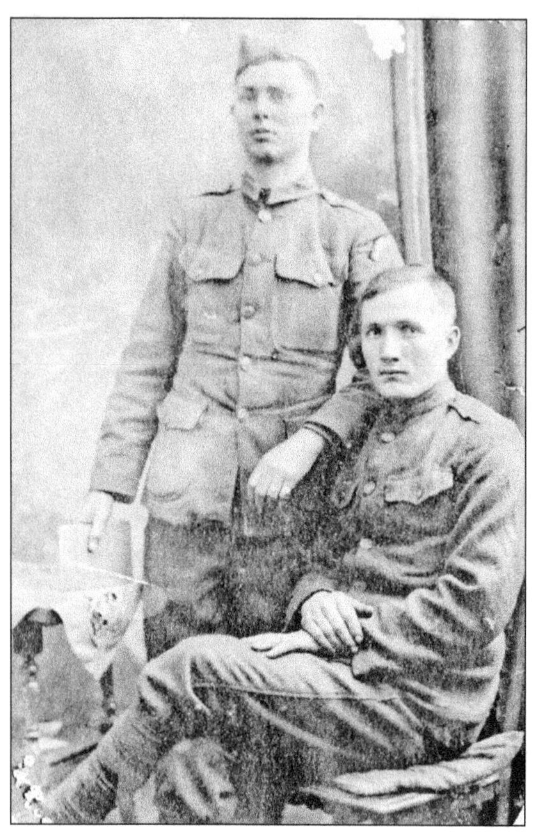

Shown in this photograph are Robert Whittington (standing) and an unidentified buddy. Robert was inducted into the US Army on May 24, 1918, in Butler. He was born on August 2, 1895, in Bergamot. When he registered for the draft, he was 21 years old and working at a sawmill in Toxey. He is buried in the Brightwater Cemetery.

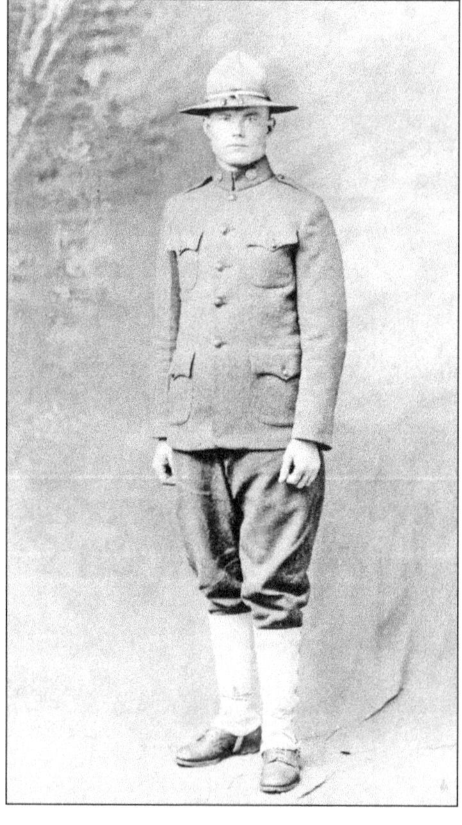

Thomas Diamond is pictured in his World War I uniform. He was 29 years of age when he registered for the draft on June 5, 1917. He was born on October 4, 1887, and died on November 16, 1964. He was married to Bonnie Ivey from Clarke County, Mississippi. He and his wife had four children: John Thomas, Irma Dee, Etta Vee Ruth, and an unnamed infant who died in May 1925.

Jesse Frank Porter enlisted in the US Army for World War II on October 16, 1940, at Fort McPherson, Georgia. He was born on September 27, 1919, and died on February 21, 1949. He was the son of Jesse Frank Porter Sr. and Erin Stafford. He is buried in the Pleasant Hill Cemetery.

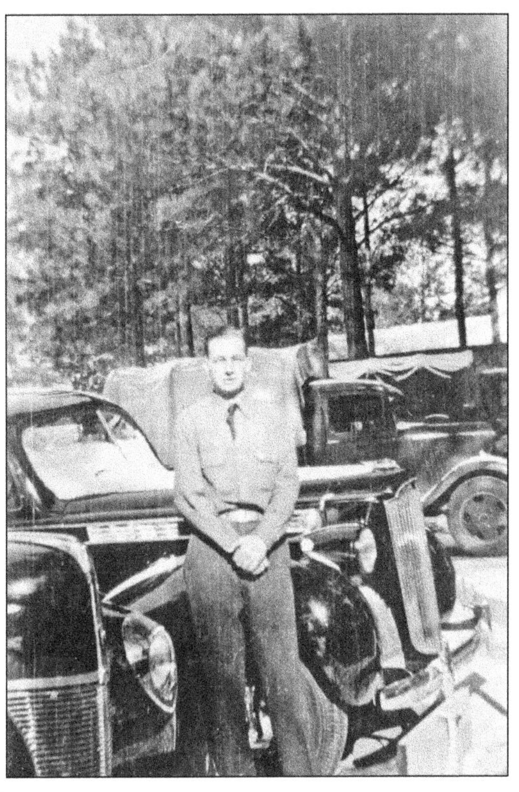

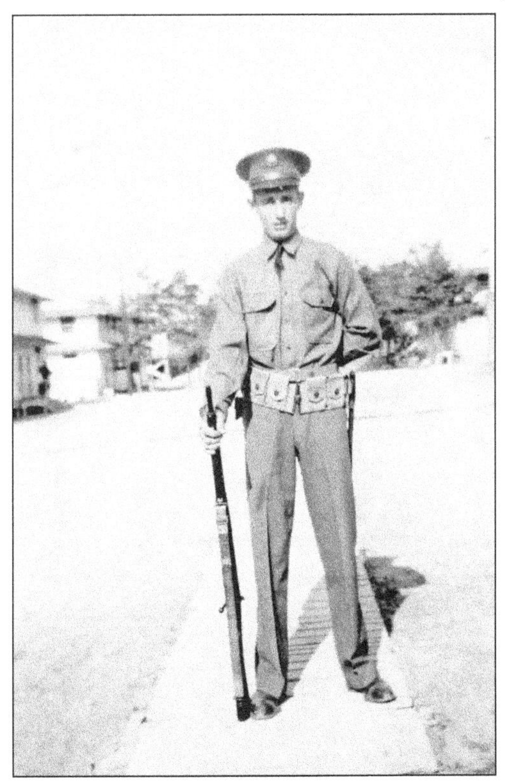

James Rexton Singley served in World War II from March 13, 1941, until September 26, 1945. He also served in the Korean War. He retired as a staff sergeant on January 8, 1962. He was born on September 25, 1916, and died on June 20, 1999. He is buried at Rest Haven Memorial Gardens.

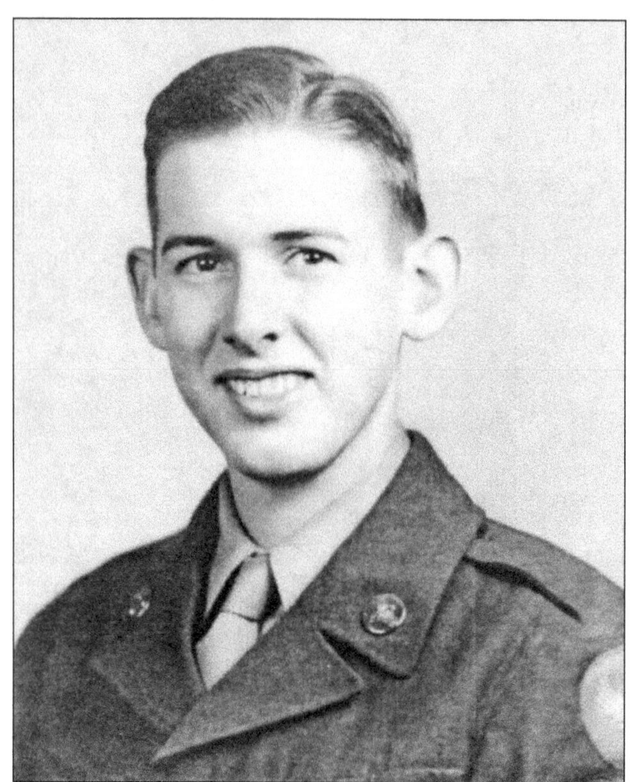

This photograph of Paul Lauglin Gay was taken in 1946 at San Antonio, Texas, during basic training. He enlisted in the US Army Air Corps at Meridian, Mississippi. After basic training, he went to Chanute Air Force Base in Illinois for atmospheric sounding technician training. After training, he was made an instructor. He worked on Operation Sandstone in the Marshall Islands and was discharged in September 1949 as a second lieutenant.

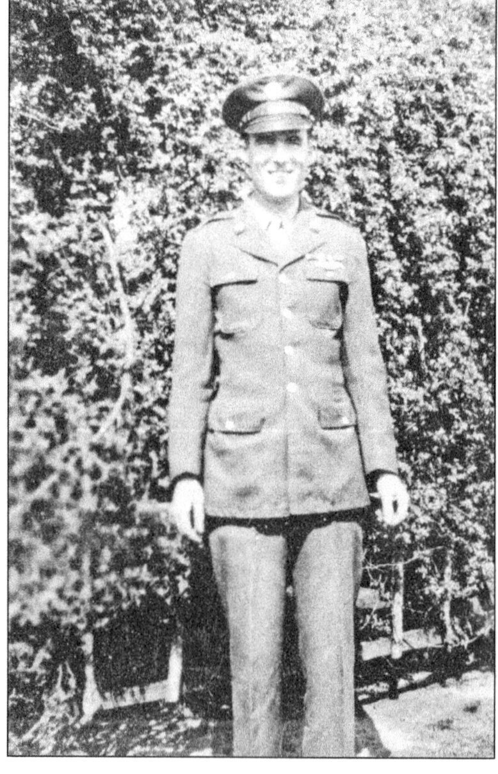

Howard Erastus Norton enlisted for World War II on January 17, 1944, at Fort McClellan, Alabama. He served in the 320th Infantry. He received a Purple Heart, an Oak Leaf Cluster for a second wound, and a Bronze Star. He was born on July 4, 1916, and died on April 2, 2007. He is buried in Morgan Chapel Cemetery.

Henry Juarez "Tobe" Lassiter enlisted for World War II service on February 13, 1942, at Ft. McPherson, Georgia. He served in the US Army Air Corps. He left the service in 1945 as a master sergeant. He was born on October 18, 1919, and died on April 13, 1997, and is buried at the Cullomburg Cemetery.

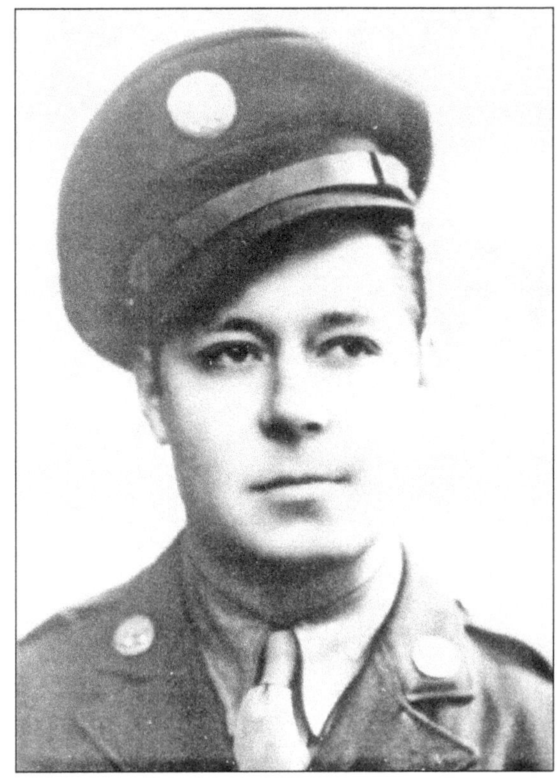

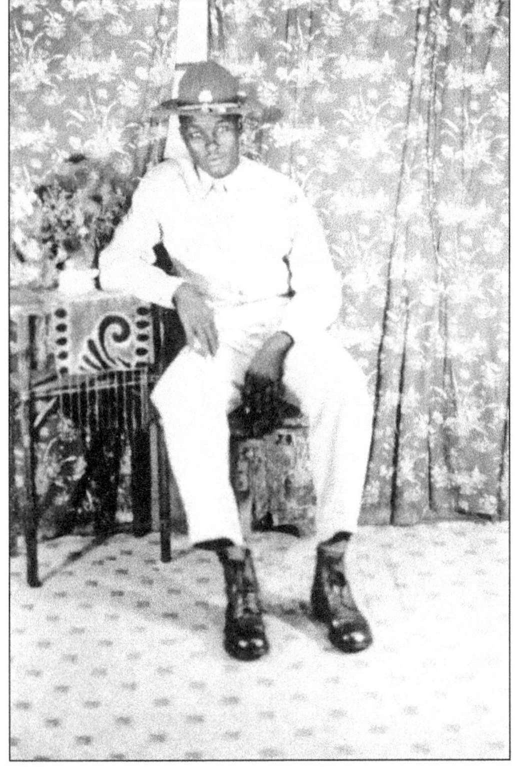

Charles Leonard Figures served in 1941 with a black infantry that had been originally formed during the Civil War. He also served three years during World War II in the 13th Air Force. He spent three years fighting in the jungles of the Pacific and was awarded the Victory and Good Conduct Ribbons. He was born on April 3, 1919, in Womack Hill to Abraham and Luvenia Parker Figures.

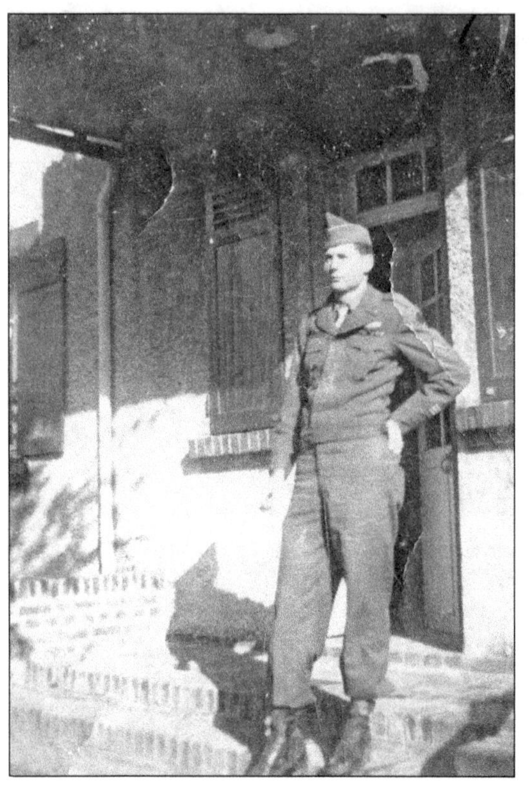

Jesse Willard Kelley was born on April 5, 1925, in Cyril, Alabama, to John Norris and Mary Olevia Josephine Turner. He was married to Clara Dona Broadhead. Jesse is a decorated veteran of World War II. He received a Purple Heart, a Bronze Star, and three major battle ribbons. He worked in the logging business until 1969, when he started working at American Can. He retired in 1990.

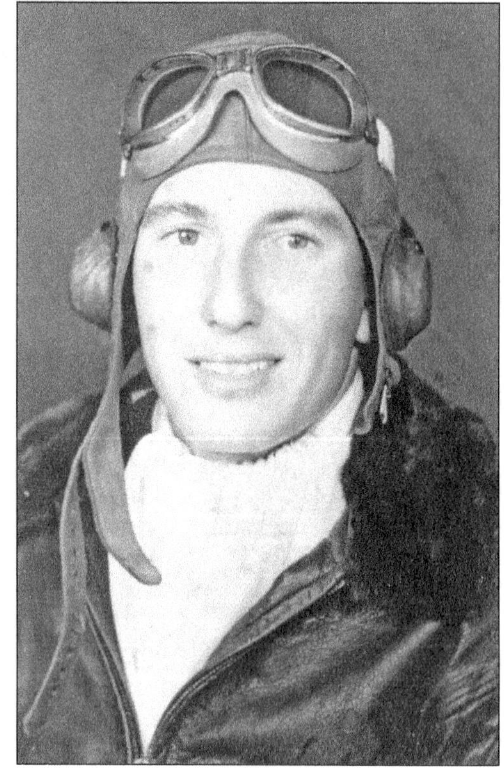

Prentice Powe Pruitt graduated from Southern Choctaw High School in 1935 and enlisted on August 7, 1940. He was a pilot at Pearl Harbor when it was bombed. He was released from service on February 25, 1943. He was the son of Albert P. Pruitt and Artie M. McIlwain and is buried in Roselawn Cemetery in Tallahassee, Florida.

Jimmie Rayford Mixon served in the US Navy from September 18, 1943, through August 15, 1945. He served aboard the USS *Belleau Wood*. He wore one Bronze Star for the Philippines Liberation Campaign. He was the son of George Hilliard and Betty Stewart Mixon. He worked with the US Army Corps of Engineers for 27 years. He was born on May 29, 1909, and died on November 9, 1987. (Courtesy of Shirley Mixon Perry.)

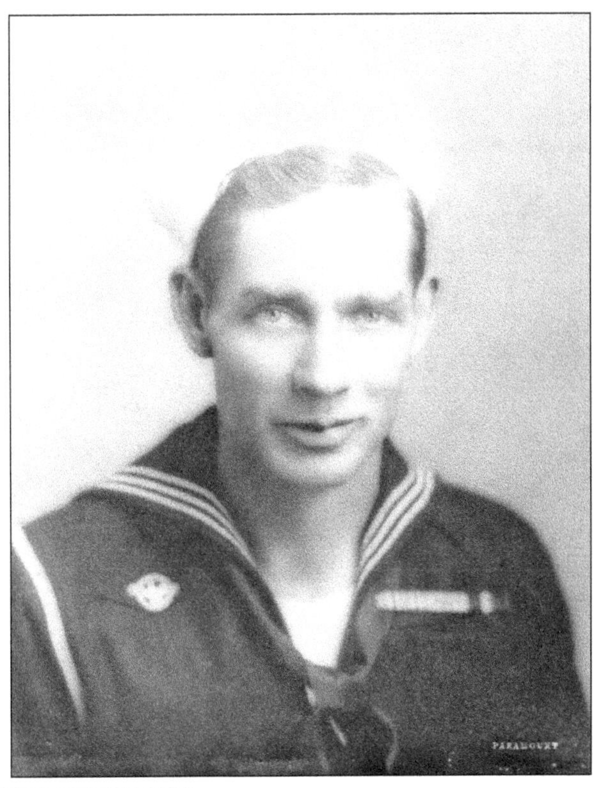

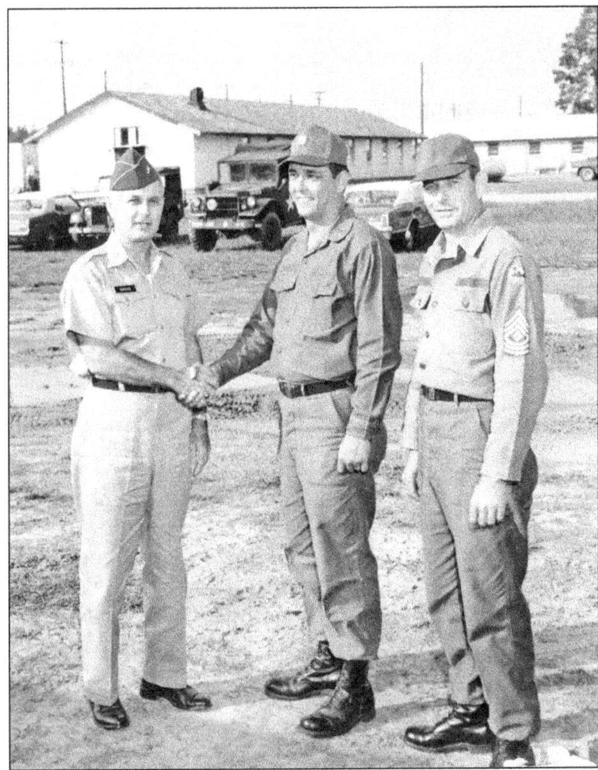

This August 1967 photograph shows Wallace Patrick Lindsey III (center) with two unidentified men. Pat graduated from the University of Alabama School of Law in 1963 and served two years of active duty as a second lieutenant in the US Army. He served as counsel for both the Choctaw County Commission and the Town of Butler starting in 1965. He also served several terms in the Alabama state senate.

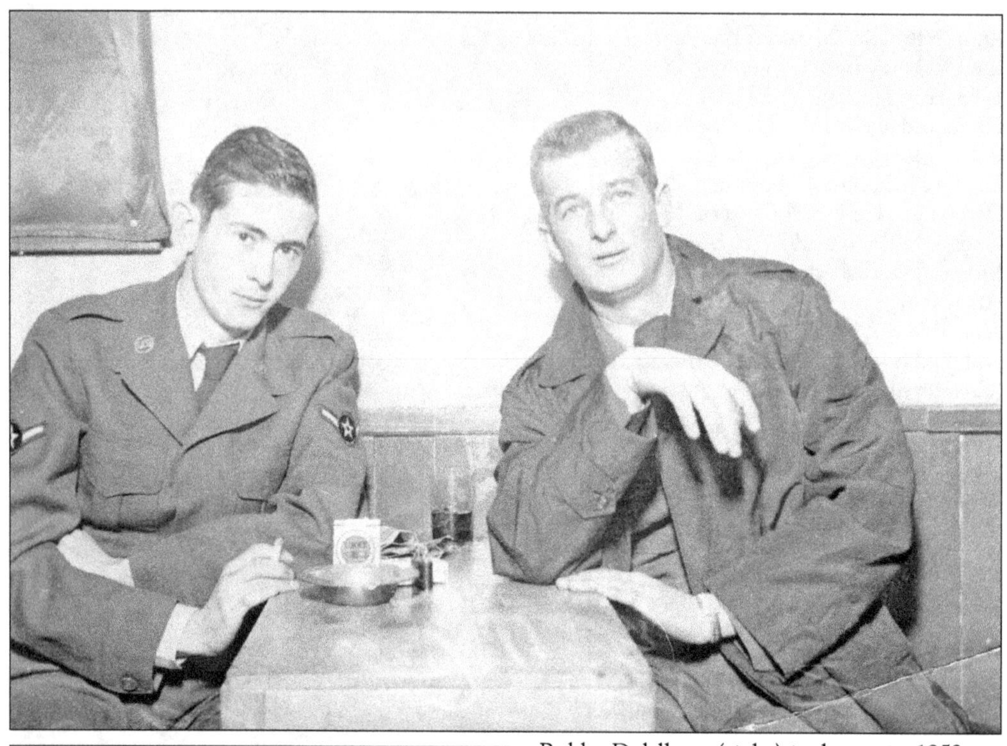

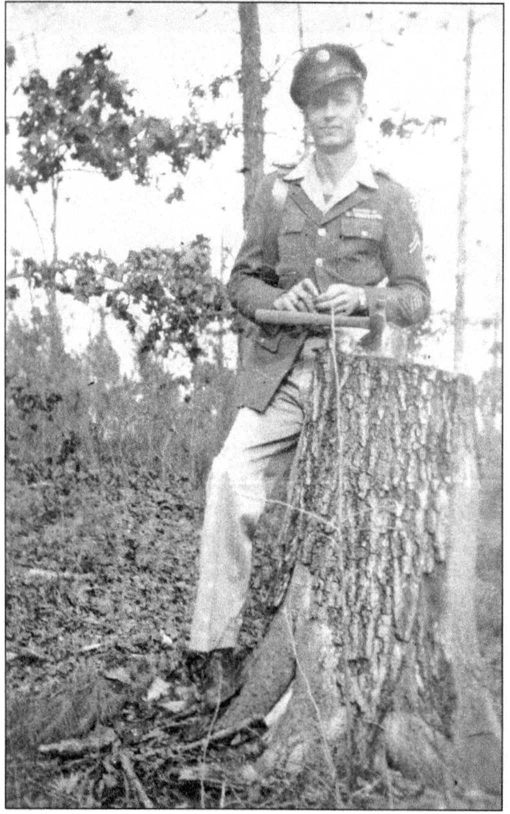

Bobby Dahlberg (right) is shown in 1953 with an unidentified Air Force buddy from Arkansas. This photograph is part of a collection he sent to his sister, Sally Knight. Bobby Dahlberg later owned and operated Bobby's Fish Camp on the banks of the Tombigbee River near Bladon Springs. This restaurant is currently operated by his daughter. (Courtesy of Lora Jane McIlwain.)

This photograph of Heyward Edward Jenkins was taken in 1946. Heyward served during World War II in Company B of the 612th Tanker Battalion. He went ashore at Omaha Beach on June 7, 1944, and participated in campaigns in Normandy, the Ardennes (Battle of the Bulge), the Rhineland, Northern France, and Central Europe. He later married Hazel Christine Campbell. He was born on May 9, 1923, near Gilbertown and died on September 11, 2014, at the age of 91.

Shown here are Lewis Charlie Slay with two children. Slay enlisted in the US Army on July 16, 1942, at Fort Benning, Georgia. He was single without dependents at that time. He was born on September 5, 1915, and died on May 21, 2002. He is buried at the Shiloh Cemetery in Lisman. (Courtesy of Ann Harwell Gay.)

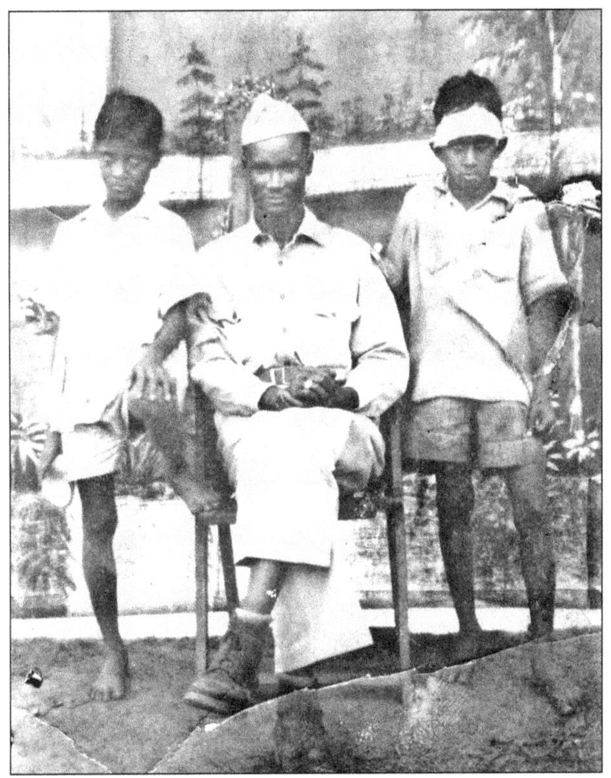

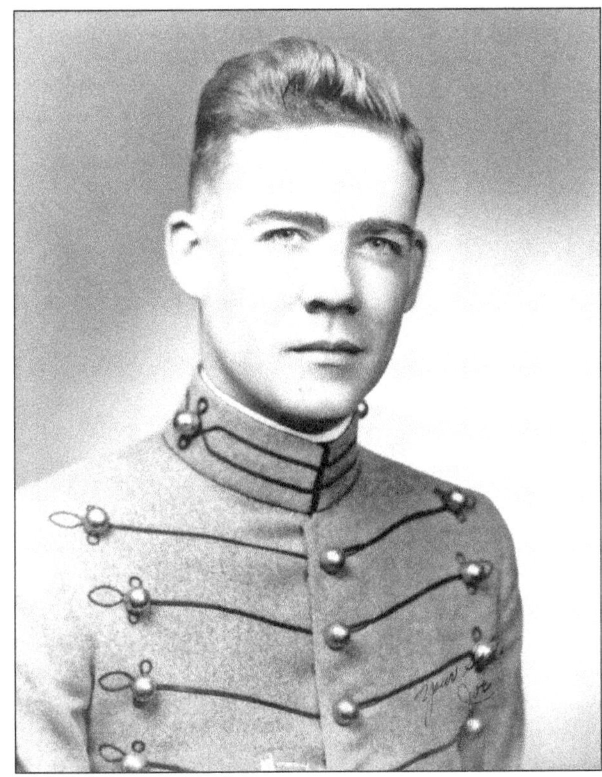

Joseph Wood Hutchinson Jr. is pictured at West Point in 1949. He attended from 1949 to 1951 and graduated on June 5, 1951. He was a second lieutenant in the infantry. He was born on February 11, 1928, to Joe Wood and Ruth Anna Mixon Hutchinson. He was the first person to be admitted to West Point from Choctaw County. (Courtesy of Annie Ruth Hutchinson Schleth.)

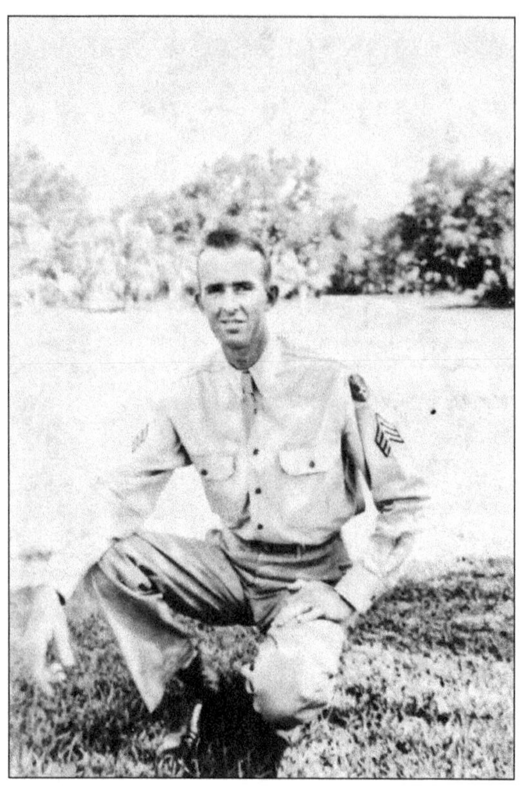

Edwin Griffin Britton was born on August 14, 1916, in Robjohn. He enlisted in the Army on November 16, 1942, at Camp Blanding, Florida, when he was 26 years old. He had moved to Dade County, Florida, from Choctaw County. He died on September 13, 1966, at the age of 50. He is buried in Arlington National Cemetery. He was the brother of Robert Edwards Britton.

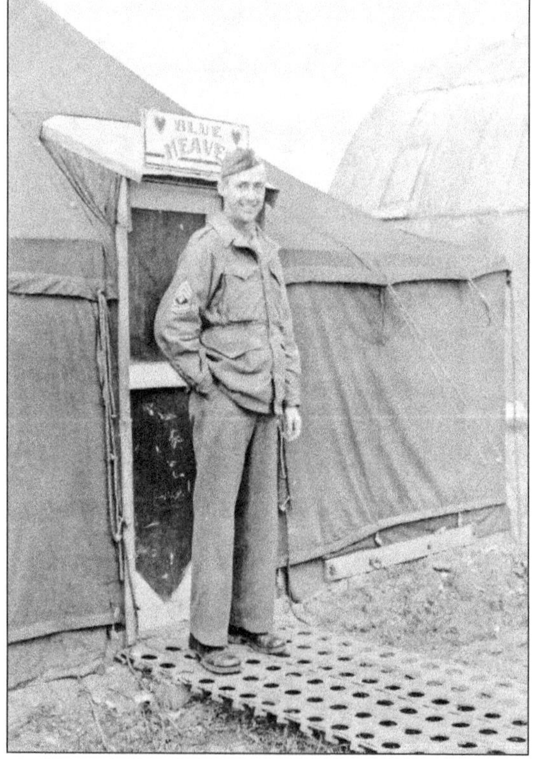

Robert Edwards Britton was born on April 14, 1919, in Robjohn. He had a twin sister, Fannie Marie, and a brother, Edwin Griffin. He was married to Pearl Boney in March 1946. He later became a minister and lived in Birmingham. He died on August 9, 2006, and is buried in Jefferson Memorial Gardens East in Trussville, Alabama. This photograph was taken in Italy in December 1944.

James Young LeNoir served in World War II as a first lieutenant in the US Army. He was born on April 6, 1915, and died on January 17, 1993. He spent most of his adult life in Tennessee. He is buried in the Union Cemetery in Bolivar, Tennessee. He was the brother to Robert William LeNoir. (Courtesy of Joan Thompson Kelley.)

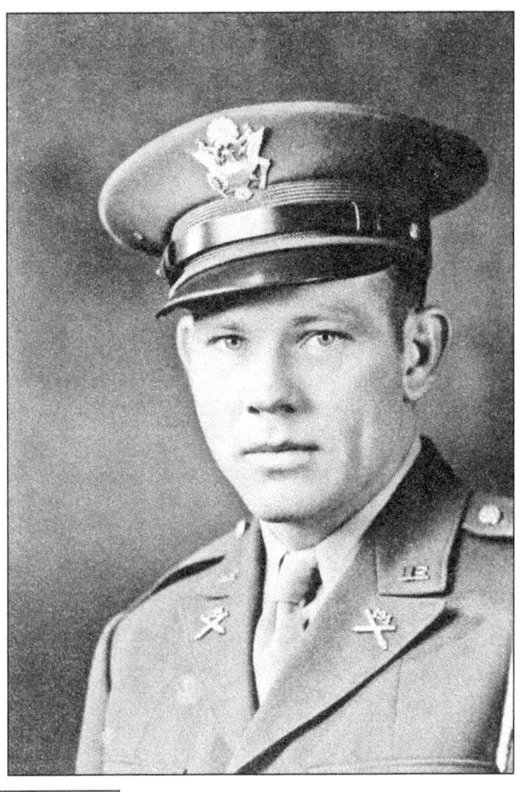

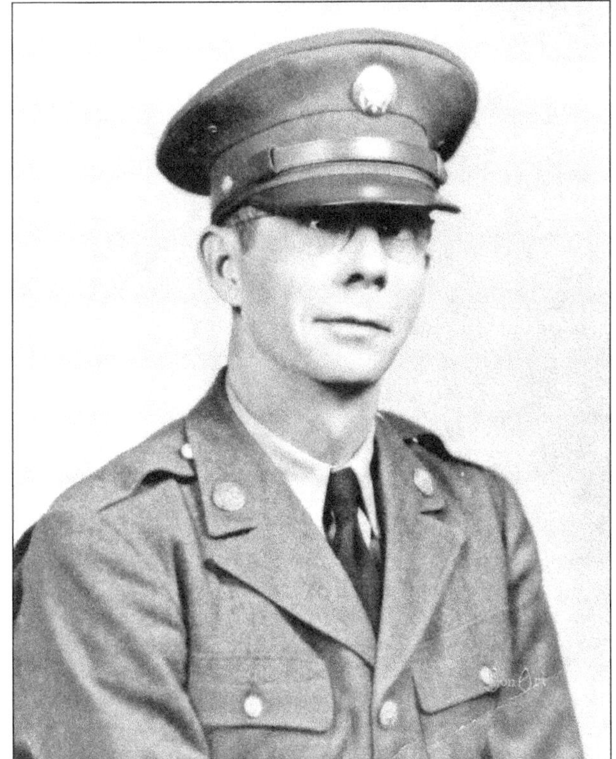

Robert William LeNoir enlisted in the US Army to serve in World War II on August 14, 1942. He was released on April 13, 1943. He was the son of Robbie Mills LeNoir and Maggie C. LeNoir. He is buried in the Butler City Cemetery. He was the brother to James Young LeNoir. (Courtesy of Joan Thompson Kelley.)

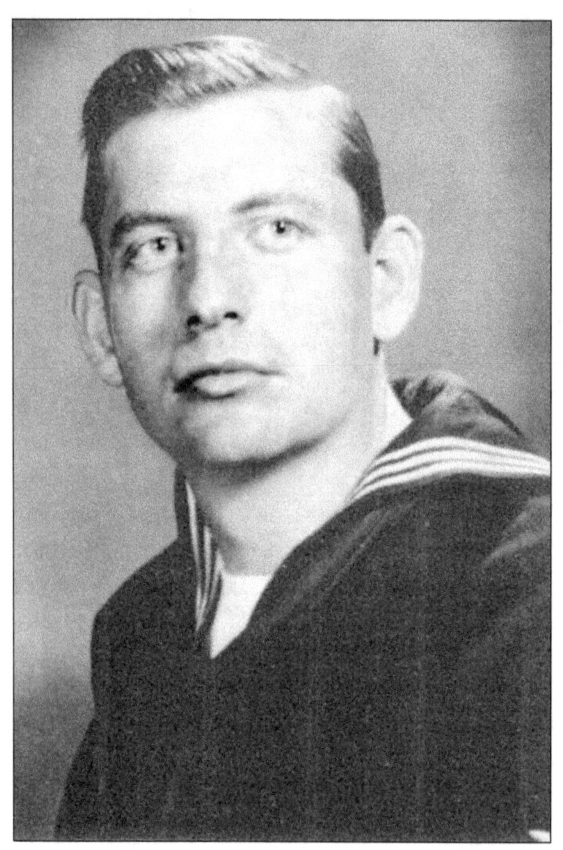

Charles Bonner Beard served in the US Navy from October 1, 1958, until September 28, 1962. He served in the reserves until September 30, 1964. He was born on June 8, 1937, in Souwilpa to Simon S. Beard and Laura B. Beard. He died on October 27, 1994, and is buried in the Advent Cemetery near Silas. Charles Beard owned and operated Beard's Florist in Butler.

Sgt. Thomas E. Dailey is shown building a bunker in Long Binh, South Vietnam, in 1968. He served in Vietnam from November 1967 to October 1968 as part of the 199th Light Infantry Brigade. Dailey served his country again during Operation Desert Storm from October 6, 1990, until July 24, 1991.

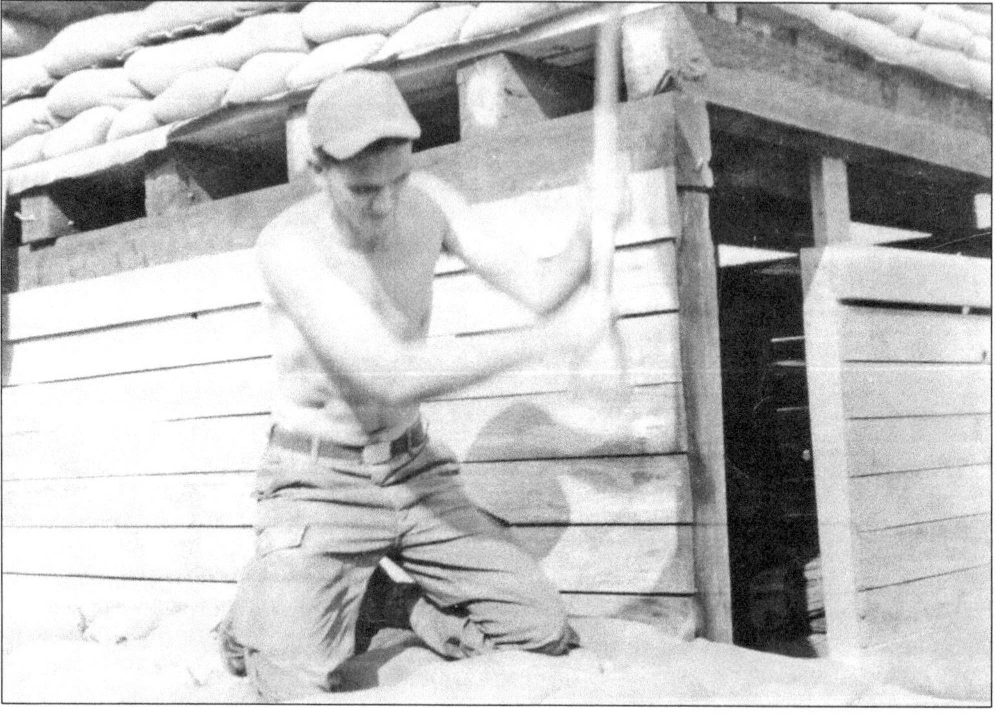

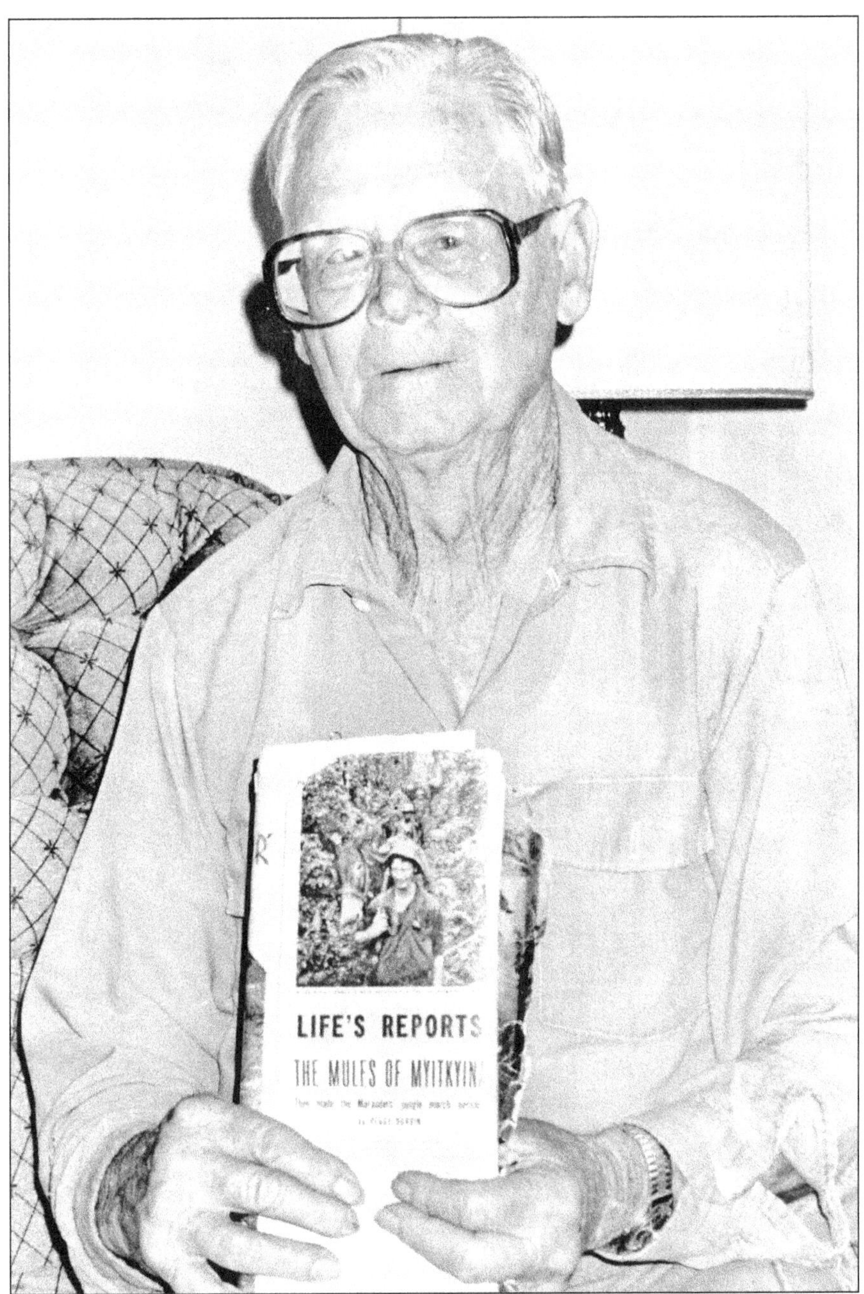

Spurgeon Sellion Taylor Jr. was a private first class in the US Army during World War II. He served in the 5307th Composite Unit (Provisional) during the Northern Burma Campaign in 1944. The recruitment for this unit began on September 1, 1943, and the unit was disbanded on August 10, 1944. This unit, known as "Merrill's Marauders," was the first US ground combat force to meet the enemy in World War II on the continent of Asia. At that time, Burma was held by the Japanese. The unit entered the war with 2,997 men, of which only 1,310 survived. After the unit seized the airfield at Myitkyina and finally seized the town, they were sent home. In this photograph, Taylor is holding up an article that was written about his Army unit. He died on August 26, 2005, and is buried in the Ebenezer Baptist Church Cemetery.

www.ingramcontent.com/pod-product-compliance
Lightning Source LLC
LaVergne TN
LVHW081533100826
845153LV00004B/263
9781540226716